PAST PRAISE FOR 1

—— ⟨⟩ ——

For *A MARRIAGE IN FOUR SEASONS*

"An often beautifully written work that lays its characters low with grief and lifts them high with the bliss of travel."
—*Kirkus Reviews*

"The drama, serene Spain setting, and complicated family relations make *A Marriage in Four Seasons* a must-read."
—Bookbub

—— ⟨⟩ ——

For *FIELDS OF FIG AND OLIVE*

"It is difficult to heap enough praise on this author for her astonishingly vivid depictions of landscape and her ability to evoke spirit of place."
—*Seattle Times*

"The skillful and realistic presentation of characters...along with other narrative techniques, contributes to making her collection one of the most successful of its kind."
—World Literature Today

"She has been blessed with the ability to make foreignness familiar."
—*Chicago Sun Times*

"Her politics are feminist, her theme is human ethics, and her writing is finely honed."
—Ms. Magazine

"She challenges Western ways of thinking about the nature and behavior of Arab women and men."
—The Trenton Times

For *TOWER OF DREAMS*

"She shines in her ability to penetrate the psyche of young Arab women."
—*Seattle Times*

For *GHOST SONGS*

"A tranquil and beautiful novel."
—Philadelphia City Paper

"She presents Arab culture in narratives of exquisite technique, deep insights, and beautiful English. It bids fair to establish her as an Arab-American fiction writer worthy of wide recognition."
—World Literature Today

Dancing

into

the

Light

Dancing
into
the
Light

An Arab American Girlhood
in the Middle East

by
Kathryn K. Abdul-Baki

SHE WRITES PRESS

Published 2023
Printed in the United States of America
Print ISBN: 978-1-64742-537-1
E-ISBN: 978-1-64742-538-8
Library of Congress Control Number: 2023906792

For information, address:
She Writes Press
1569 Solano Ave #546
Berkeley, CA 94707

Interior design by Stacey Aaronson

She Writes Press is a division of SparkPoint Studio, LLC.

For my mother, Jean, whose light went out too soon; for my father, Khalil, who kept my world bright;

and for Ahmad, who learned to dance.

prologue

AS I DODGE THE DANCING BODIES THAT RICOCHET ACROSS the dimly lit room thick with smoke and rhythm, I nearly collide with the tall figure materializing before me.

"Hello, darling." His voice encircles me in a rich African croon.

I recognize him in the haze as we hug like old friends. A name comes to mind. Abraham. From Mali. Although I am happy to run into him here, we aren't quite friends, merely sporadic dance acquaintances. But Abraham is a charmer with a honeyed baritone. I've chatted with him about Mali. He told me he comes from a town not far from Timbuktu.

The fabled Timbuktu. As a child, whenever I asked my father where he was going, he'd often wink and say, "To Timbuktu." The sound of the word itself was aromatic, carrying mysterious scents and textures and such a heady sense of festive adventure, I suspected my father had made it up. Until I met Abraham, I wondered whether Timbuktu truly existed.

"Where's your man tonight, darling?" Abraham asks casually.

I'm not sure whether he is referring to my husband, who he frequently sees me with, or any of the other male dancers in our small dance group.

"Busy," I say, leaving out the part about the frustration

simmering under my skin. How I haven't been able to dance all night in the way I yearn to. With an early love of rhythmic music, particularly Latin music and Latin dance, my lifelong instinct to move to drums has both haunted me and brought me great joy.

On this Saturday night at Pimiento, a popular Latin dance club in Washington, DC, my husband and I are with friends in a less congested room off the main dance floor. I've danced for an hour with the men in our group, spurred on by the beat of the clave, timbales, conga, and trumpets. During the past several dances, though, I've been battling my instincts.

We usually take each other's good-natured missteps with humor. But tonight, I'm irritated by the men's insistence on fancy footwork that feels more like complex, geometric patterns than a pleasurable dance. The stiffness stifles me.

Needing a break, I excuse myself and head toward the restrooms across another dance floor in another room. I'm searching for something but not sure what. Then, seemingly out of nowhere, Abraham appears.

"Where are you going?" Abraham asks, his lilting African accent resonating like a song.

Before I can explain why I am alone and where I am going, the music changes. A deep drumroll leads to a lyrical calypso beat not often heard these days in trendy Latin dance clubs. It is Harry Belafonte's "Banana Boat Song" from the 1950s.

"Day-o . . . da-a-a-o . . . "

The urge to sway to the seductive tune I know well from my childhood grabs me as I'm flooded with memories of my mother and father dancing to it in our living room in Tehran. This music always possesses me, makes me want to dance the way I used to dance with my father. I'm no longer upset with anyone, only desperate to fill the deep well of sorrow my father's recent passing has dug into me.

The entire space within the walls of the dance club suddenly overflows with memories of my happiest childhood times with my parents—my Arab father and American mother—sharing their youthful moment in a land and time far away. The music conjures up those early years when the grown-up world was filled with exuberant parties: crystal glasses holding bitter drinks topped with a sweet cherry; the lulling scent of tobacco smoke; the hypnotic, rhythmic calypso beat.

I catch my breath, then offer Abraham my hand. "Shall we dance this?"

He smiles, perhaps sensing the urgency in my voice. "Of course, darling."

I lean toward him, spellbound, knowing he will lead me in the natural way I long to dance.

"Day-o . . . da-a-a-o . . ."

Abraham embraces me with his right arm, my right hand placed high in his left palm. From previous dances with him, I know we feel the music in the same visceral way. As Harry Belafonte's voice and words echo inside me, I cease to care about anything but dancing to this island song in this simple, timeless style. The Caribbean rhythm pounds in my chest. I sense it with my heart. Swaying in step with him, I play with the music and fly high with the drums and the intoxicating sensuality that explodes from the earthy beat. It's as though the rhythm flowed through my veins in my mother's womb. I've been delivered to where I want to be.

We barely move from our spot as Abraham leads me to take short "street dancer" steps, rather than intricate choreography or perfected ballroom strides. It's the way my father danced.

Although I've been training in Latin ballroom dance technique for several years, something is missing in those elegant, stylized steps. Something inside me remains submerged, an agitation in my muscles that yearns to be expressed. As I sink into the Caribbean melody now, a primal urge bubbles to the surface, intuitive and raw. I dance from my soul rather than my head, moving from a place of complete bliss.

I smile, wondering what Abraham would say if I told him my joy in dancing with him has more to do with a soothing, ancient memory than anything else. Neither of my parents had any connection to Latin America or the Caribbean, yet the unexpected Harry Belafonte song brings back my suave, dark-haired father and my flame-haired mother as they danced to the Afro-Cuban and calypso rhythms they loved so much.

I envision the young couple. My father holds my mother in a casual embrace, his left arm held high, nearly above his head, where he cradles her palm in his. Latin style. They sway their hips sensuously to the music. She gazes up at him. He pulls her closer.

Harry Belafonte's music—the calypso songs of the Caribbean islands that ignited the 1950s international dance scene—is what my parents always played and danced to. It never failed to awaken my father's indomitable passion for dance, one that he would instill in me. Harry, the "King of Calypso," would rescue and buoy us in the best and worst of times.

I inch closer to Abraham. I feel a vital, embarrassing need to connect to him and through him to *them*. This is home.

I've run into my mother's embrace in the dark, the way I often do in dreams that end abruptly as she melts away, just when I am about to reach her.

And yet the exquisite dance moment holds more than recollections of my mother. At the core of this mysterious force is my father, and the way it used to be for the three of us when they were both alive.

one

Young Love

THE DANCING WOULD COME LATER. FIRST, A NINETEEN-YEAR-OLD Southern belle from Tennessee and a twenty-two-year-old Muslim Palestinian from Jerusalem had to meet and marry in 1951.

I imagine a muggy Washington evening in late summer. My mother and her girlfriend walk into the Middle Eastern deli where they often pick up groceries and cigarettes. My father stands behind the counter, glancing up at the two women. The pretty redhead catches his eye. Although he is dazzled, he doesn't flirt with her. It isn't his way. My affable and inquisitive mother, though, isn't shy. Instinctively drawn to the handsome dark-haired man glancing her way, she watches him light a cigarette, his lips pursed, his fingers confidently cupping the lighter. She flashes him a smile.

Over the coming weeks, as my mother learns the exotic young foreigner at the deli is an Arab from Jerusalem, she knows she's found her match—a man with an eye to the wider world she's been yearning to explore.

"That's for me!" she tells her girlfriend, sealing her fate.

My mother, Jean Ashburn Pedigo, grew up in Old Hickory, outside of Nashville. At seventeen, she enrolled at Vanderbilt University, her parents' alma mater, with dreams of becoming a writer. Two years later, restless and eager to explore beyond her native southern town, she transferred to Northwestern University in Chicago to pursue a degree in journalism. By the end of the school year, however, my mother's wanderlust got the better of her. Disillusioned by the Midwest—and despite her parents' vehement objections—she paused her studies and headed to the cosmopolitan city of Washington, DC, in search of a more exciting life.

My father would travel a rockier road to cross paths with her. In 1946, at the age of seventeen, Khalil Mohammad Karjawally arrived in the United States by ship from the port of Haifa, Palestine, prepared to study economics at Michigan State University. He had left his hometown of Jerusalem, against his father's wishes, with a promise to obtain his degree in America and return.

Not long after he left for America, however, fate changed his course when war broke out in his homeland. In 1947, the news reports reached my father in Michigan. The recent, ongoing violence between the Arab and Jewish communities in British-controlled Palestine had escalated. Fighting had erupted between the neighboring Arab countries' armies and the local Jewish forces over a United Nations resolution that the territory of Palestine be partitioned into Arab and Jewish states.

By 1948, a decades-old British Mandate over the territory of Palestine had ended, and a new state of Israel had been created. Hundreds of thousands of Palestinians had fled or been displaced from their cities, towns, and villages of origin.

Borders were reconfigured. Western Palestine, with its coastal cities and towns on the Mediterranean, along with the western portion of Jerusalem, were to be incorporated into the nascent Jewish state. My father's home of East Jerusalem, with the inland towns of Eastern Palestine, were to be absorbed by the neighboring Hashemite Kingdom of Jordan across the Jordan River.

Unlike the Palestinians displaced from their homes in what became Israel, my father's family remained in what was now Jordanian-controlled East Jerusalem. Yet my father's old passport, a British-issued Palestinian one, was no longer valid. Cut off and alone in America—technically a refugee—my father was conflicted. Should he try to return home to help his family? Should he stay in the United States and complete his studies? Could he even travel now without valid citizenship?

Realizing that returning to Jerusalem now would serve no useful purpose, my father decided to stay. Aware of Jerusalem's war-torn economy, and not wanting to burden his family with the expense of his studies in Michigan, he moved to more affordable New Mexico, where he enrolled in a smaller university. To support himself, he found work on a ranch, exchanging the frigid snows of the Midwest for a cowboy hat and the vast Southwestern desert and tabletop mesas.

A fan of film Westerns, he enjoyed the idea of becoming a cowboy and learning to ride and take care of the horses and barn; he even shortened his name from the hard-to-pronounce Arab "Khalil" to "Kal." The camaraderie with the Anglo ranch hands, who took my father's foreignness with good-natured acceptance, reminded him of the warm relationships with Arabs back home. In a photograph of him wearing a Stetson, he leans against the fence of a corral, grinning and talking to another ranch hand—a young man pleased with the new world that had taken him in.

After graduating, he heard of good job opportunities in Washington, DC. Once there, he got a job as an accountant in a department store while studying for a master's degree in economics at George Washington University. In the evenings, he was a cashier in the Middle Eastern deli my mother frequented.

IT WASN'T LONG before my parents, along with my father's Arab roommate and my mother's girlfriend, began to go on double dates together. After going out a few times, my father got up the courage one night—it was his birthday—to invite the redhead from Tennessee out alone.

At the restaurant, they happened to sit near a young couple who were cuddling affectionately. My father commented to his new acquaintance that it must be nice to have someone special in one's life. To be engaged. Or married.

Intrigued, my mother responded, "Do you have someone special in your life, Kal?"

"No, I don't," he replied.

Not one to be coy, she promptly asked, "What's wrong with the girl sitting across from you right now?"

Her American directness caught him off guard. Steeped in the conservative mores of his Arab upbringing, which mandated important matters be done with the blessing of one's family, my father didn't know how they were going to get engaged, much less marry. Although he'd had a crush on the redhead from the start, he hadn't thought about how he would tell his family back in Jerusalem that he'd fallen in love with an American girl. An *Amercaniya* nobody knew anything about. His father was likely already looking for a young woman from a fine Jerusalem family for him to wed when he got home.

Over the next few weeks, my mother, too, assessed her situation with the young man she'd fallen in love with. She knew her own family, though worldly by Nashville standards, wasn't likely to condone her marrying a penniless foreigner they knew nothing about. Her parents had deep roots in Middle Tennessee. Her father, James Monroe Pedigo, was an established Old Hickory dentist; her mother, Helen Hopkins, was the daughter of lawyer Raleigh Hopkins who had run for governor of the state several years earlier.

Since my mother had various boyfriends throughout high school and college, her parents hadn't paid much attention when she'd recently talked of having met a "fine-looking Arab from Jerusalem." My mother probably knew her Protestant parents' open-minded toleration of her fickle attachments of the past might not extend to her marrying a Muslim from the Middle East, especially considering the racism of that time. "A skinny, half-starved refugee," was how she playfully described her new beau in a note to a cousin.

She explained to my father that the best thing for them would be to have a civil marriage locally and *then* inform their families. My father, although not wanting to offend her family before he'd even met them, went along with her idea. Unbeknownst to my mother, my father had not mentioned her in his correspondence with his family in Jerusalem.

They were married in 1951 in a civil ceremony in Chevy Chase, Maryland. She was nineteen; he was twenty-two. My father's roommate and my mother's girlfriend were witnesses. My mother then sent a jubilant telegram to her parents and younger brother in Tennessee announcing the happy news.

"Dear Mama and Daddy. Just married Khalil Mohammad Karjawally from Jerusalem."

IN OLD HICKORY, my grandmother had barely recovered from her daughter dropping out of a prestigious university to work in Washington as a typist. My grandmother had a master's degree in English from Vanderbilt. My mother, too, was a talented writer, having had a short story published in *Seventeen* when she was at Vanderbilt.

When my grandmother read her teenage daughter's telegram, she was livid. She immediately contacted her cousin Nora Hampton, who worked as a journalist in Washington, to ask for her help. To allay her cousin's fears, Nora tracked down my mother and invited her and her groom for dinner.

Nora was won over by the newlyweds. Later that night she wrote to her Nashville cousin. "Helen, honey, no need to worry. Jean's new husband is not a cad. He's an intelligent young man and is head over heels in love with her."

My grandmother's qualms were barely allayed. Yet knowing she could do nothing to alter the situation, she fired off a telegram of her own to her daughter.

"Bring husband to meet the family."

The wedding reception photos, taken in her parents' elegant Old Hickory home, show my mother and father posing alongside her parents, her college-age brother, Jimmy, and the Tennessee uncles, aunts, and cousins. My mother gazes at the camera with a wide, mischievous grin, beaming at the treasure she's snagged. In the pictures, my father is debonair in a light-gray suit with a large white carnation in the lapel. A black pencil mustache lines his upper lip, and his silky black hair ripples away from his forehead above his sparkling dark eyes. My mother stands nearly as tall as he in her white high heels, knee-length white organza dress, and drop pearl earrings, her face exuding joyous assurance. Although some of the relatives were rumored to have glanced discreetly at my mother's belly, wondering whether there was a pressing reason for her hasty marriage, everyone looks happy.

A year later, on a February day in 1952, I was born in Washington, DC. Within a year, my father was carrying his redheaded daughter on his shoulders as we three braved the cold January day to stand on the mall to watch the inauguration of President Dwight D. Eisenhower.

My father worked at the Department of the Interior. The year I turned four, the Department of Defense was searching for a capable candidate to send to Tehran to establish an English-language school for Iranian military officers. The candidate would go there as part of a US government team to set up the project's infrastructure and oversee the new school for two years. With my mother's enthused encouragement, my father applied for the position in Tehran.

two

Iran, 1956

IN A LETTER HOME IN 1956, MY MOTHER DESCRIBED THE sprawling city she saw for the first time from the airplane.

"Set at the foot of a very high range of snowcapped mountains, Tehran looks like a giant town in South Texas, scurrying in every direction across the plains."

Tehran was very different from Jerusalem and Beirut, the two other Middle Eastern cities my mother had recently visited. A month earlier, while my father had gone to Tehran ahead of us to settle in, she had flown with me from Washington to Beirut, Lebanon, home to my father's mother's family. Then we flew to Jerusalem to meet my father's Palestinian family.

Beirut and Jerusalem were compact, picturesque cities with Mediterranean-style red roofs and white limestone architecture. My mother was struck by the much larger Tehran, a concrete city with wide boulevards and gardens hidden behind high, forbidding walls.

By then, my father was an American citizen. Although he was ethnically Arab rather than Persian, because he was Muslim and understood the culture, religion, and politics of the Middle East, Washington considered him an ideal candidate for the Tehran job. Although Persians and Arabs had a history of long-standing problems with one another, this fact didn't seem to be a concern to Washington. While Arabic and Farsi are different languages, after a course of study, my father became nearly fluent in Farsi.

The expansive Iranian-style home and surrounding garden my father was given was located in Shemiran, a suburb near the heart of Tehran. Along with a car and driver, it reflected his official civilian rank in the US military. It also signified the interest America was taking to help the Iranian military achieve its goal of establishing English education for its officers. The house had a large garden planted with cherry trees, strawberries, chrysanthemums, and asters still blooming in the cold weather.

The first time we arrived at our new home, my father parked his army jeep on the gravel driveway within the high garden walls. The driveway was flanked by yellow pansies and rows of cherry trees. I jumped out of the jeep and ran toward the large house.

"Where's my bedroom, Daddy?"

My father showed me my room, which was downstairs, across from the dining room, and looked out onto the garden and the swimming pool. Then he showed us my parents' room with its wide second-floor balcony that embraced views of the snowcapped Alborz Mountains in the distance. From this balcony, I could survey the backyard, driveway, and cherry trees. The kitchen was at the front of the house, where grocery deliveries could easily be brought in.

My mother, finally embarking on her dream life of travel to distant lands, was fascinated by her surroundings. She wrote to her mother: "Mama, you'd be amazed. A recent snow in the mountains has caused packs of jackals to come down to the edge of town at night, howling and baying and looking for food."

In another letter, she wrote: "The women are not veiled here, a practice outlawed by the current Shah of Iran's father. They wear the *chador,* a large black cloth draped from the head and reaching to their feet like a giant cloak. Most striking is the vast difference in the social classes here. Very rich and very poor."

Outside the high walls of the Tehran houses similar to ours ran the *jube,* an open-ditch, cemented waterway on the side of the road that provided water for most of Tehran. As the snow melted from the icy tops of the Alborz mountain range in the distance, the resulting water was channeled into huge mountain creeks that led toward town. These creeks traversed the city, distributing water down each street by means of these concrete *jubes.* Women washed clothes, vegetables, and fruit, as well as dirty dinner dishes in the constantly running water; men washed oil and grease off their metal working tools in the same water. Our own water for plumbing and irrigation came from our garden well rather than from the *jube,* while the drinking water was specially delivered from the American embassy in case our well water wasn't pure enough to drink.

Those first months in Tehran, as I went about the business of being a four-year-old in a new and unfamiliar place, my parents settled in, hiring a female housekeeper and a gardener. My mother sewed curtains for the long windows and typed letters to her mother describing with delight her new home. She also listed much-needed items to be sent to us via the US

Army postal service: a coffee percolator, tubes of Dupont glue, and bed pillows, since the only ones she found in Tehran were straw and much too uncomfortable. In another letter home, my mother noted it was good the Persian army had supplied us with a driver since it appeared traffic regulations were completely unknown.

Iran was emerging from turbulent times. Several years earlier, there had been a power struggle between the now deposed prime minister, Mohammad Mossadegh, and the British-backed monarch, or Shah, Mohammad Reza Pahlavi. In 1951, Prime Minister Mossadegh had attempted to seize control of the country's oil from the British Petroleum Company. To protect its interests, Britain had secured the backing of the young shah against the prime minister. Britain had also sought the aid of the United States. In 1953, after his attempt to nationalize Iran's oil, Mohammad Mossadegh was removed from power.

My parents and their fellow American expats, undoubtedly aware of the Iranian government's turmoil of a few years earlier and of America's clandestine role in Iranian politics, did not consider it their place to question their country's involvement or their own temporary sojourn in Tehran as part of US policy. It certainly didn't affect my father's focus on his job of setting up the language school. He was already making plans to open similar schools in the cities of Isfahan and Shiraz.

It was a good time to be an American in Iran. Compared to three years earlier, the government appeared to be stable. Many upper- and middle-class Iranians were already adopting much of the social culture and many mores of the West.

Barely a month after we moved to Tehran, my parents

were thrust into a demanding social life of formal functions. An outgoing young couple, they socialized with Americans, internationals, Iranian professionals, and the military officers who worked with my father. I frequently overheard them talk of meeting certain Iranian princes and princesses as well as the urbane young shah and his beautiful half-German wife, Queen Soraya. And there was always the music and dancing, whether my parents were entertaining at home on the weekend or relaxing alone after dinner in the evenings.

By the time I grew to awareness in the late 1950s, Latin music—particularly the Cuban mambo and Caribbean calypso—was in full bloom both in America and in our expat-filled living room in Tehran. Arthur Murray records, with diagrammed footprints on the back of the album covers explaining how to dance the tango, samba, mambo, rumba, or cha-cha, were part of my parents' record collection. Because the Middle East had been exposed to Western influences, whether through decades of colonialism or travel, many in the urban middle classes were open to change and were enthusiastically absorbing Western art and music. With the Middle Eastern general fondness for things Spanish, Italian, and French, it was practically inevitable that the Latin American music craze spreading internationally would be welcomed.

In Washington, my parents had discovered the newly popular calypso music. Now the melodies, drums, and flutes of the Caribbean islands regularly cascaded through our Tehran house and out to the garden where guests gathered around the swimming pool. My father aptly found a kindred spirit in the singer Harry Belafonte, a man striving to preserve his Jamaican island heritage in the New World. Around the same age as Harry, my father was similarly nostalgic for the warmth of his family, culture, and all that was familiar back in his homeland of Jerusalem. He easily identified with the sentimental lyrics of Harry's songs.

My father was a talented dancer, and the ballroom dance lessons he'd taken in college made him a much sought-after partner at parties. My mother danced, too, and by her own account did a "pretty good jitterbug." But it was my father's passion that impressed me. I memorized the lyrics to most of the calypso and Latin tunes he played on our record player: "Quizas, Quizas, Quizas" and "Mambo Italiano" along with his favorite Belafonte songs, "Jamaica Farewell" and "Banana Boat Song."

"Day-o . . . da-a-a-o," my father would intone along with Harry. He swayed his hips and rocked in time to the drums as he took my hand so I could join him in a rumba.

He'd smile as he modulated his voice and accent to match Harry's island croons; then his mood would turn wistful to sing "Jamaica Farewell," a song lamenting a lost love. That one made me sad even though I loved it. My father would wink at me as Harry sang about leaving a little girl in Kingston Town. I knew I was that "little girl" for whom he and Harry pined. Although I was dancing with my father in that very moment, I sensed he was looking into the future at a time when I would no longer be his little girl, and we would have to part.

My mother wholly embraced the role of expatriate wife, hosting and attending ladies' luncheons and bridge parties as well as my father's career-related cocktail parties. Lazy white plumes drifted up from the cigarette at her fingertips, her fingernails immaculately polished a deep blaze of red. Whether she sipped coffee or a martini, there was the perennial cigarette poised at the end of her slender white fingers. The pungent scent of tobacco also infused her purse, where a green pack of Salems or red Pall Malls mixed with the floral scent of lipstick-blotted tissues. Sneaking peeks into her purse, I would inhale the glamour. To me my mother was rose and jasmine perfume, lipstick, and the rich smell of raw tobacco. It denoted the thrill of a grown-up woman's life.

Everyone smoked. I particularly liked the pungent smell of the tobacco smoke from my father's pipe. His collection of carved wooden pipes was displayed on a special stand on the bookcase in the living room, my favorite being a curved one with the face of a gargoyle.

On summer evenings, when my parents hosted their friends around our pool amid the fruiting trees, my father would pluck the maraschino cherry from his gin and tonic for me to taste or hand me a cracker spread with butter and tangy black Iranian caviar. I savored the tiny, salty fish eggs, mellowed by the sweetness of the butter, as they softly popped and disintegrated on my tongue. As the music flowed from the indoor stereo out to the garden, its hypnotic rhythms pulsing through a delicate veil of cigarette and pipe smoke, the grown-ups began to dance.

I wanted those evenings to last forever while I grew sleepy under the stars, watching my parents and their guests rock to the music. The kaleidoscope of figures came together and moved apart to the thrumming beat; the tinkle of their laughter spilled into the cool night air. I drowsily reached out to my father, wanting him to take me in his arms to dance. But he was too far away to notice me, surrounded by the other guests. I was finally lifted from the chair and carried back into the house to be tucked into bed.

three

In the East

THE MOVE FROM WASHINGTON AND ALL I HAD PREVIOUSLY known to distant Tehran was a seismic shift for me. It caused me to finally abandon "Tima," my meddlesome, imaginary playmate who was always getting herself, and me, into trouble.

My birth certificate read, "Kathryn Elizabeth Karjawally." My mother named me after her favorite cousin, Kathryn, and had given me her own mother's middle name, Elizabeth. Unofficially, my name was Kathryn Elizabeth *Fatima* Karjawally. Fatima was the name of my father's mother, and it's customary in Arab culture for the eldest son to name his firstborn daughter after his mother.

From my earliest memories, the foreignness of the name Fatima frightened me. I invented Tima, an abbreviation of Fatima, who was a part of me and yet alien to me . . . an alter ego to blame.

"Tima did it," was my constant defense if I broke something or did something I knew I wasn't allowed to do, like sneak a candy before mealtime. Unlike me, with my red hair and green eyes, Tima was dark haired and dark eyed, like my father.

Tima was more than an imaginary friend. She was a part of me I didn't know what to do with. Even at the age of four, I was aware of having two distinctly different halves, although Western and Eastern still had no clear meaning for me. My mother, too, seemed aware of my two halves.

She would affectionately put a palm beneath her nose and say with a chuckle, "From here up, she's all Kal," because I had my father's broader nose and wide, Arab eyes. My mother's eyes were smaller and bright blue, and her nose was narrow and upturned, an American nose. My mouth, though, was like hers, ready to break into an easy, American grin.

I never heard my parents talk of any racial or cultural biases or discrimination they may have experienced being married in the United States in the 1950s. Yet I unconsciously held this cultural conflict within myself. I was two people: one was Western, redheaded, and sensible, like my mother; one was dark, tempestuous, and Eastern, like my father. Kathy and Tima. Perhaps even then the burden of carrying those two conflicting parts within me was too great. Our move was the perfect excuse to discard that irksome, "other" part.

"Where's Tima?" my father asked me shortly after my mother and I joined him in Tehran.

"She took the slow boat from Washington," I answered without hesitation.

Nothing more was said about her. The American part of me was all I knew or felt safe with, leaving me skeptical of anything that placed me outside of being a thoroughly American girl. On our first Christmas in Tehran, my parents gave me a female collie I named Betsy after a favorite doll. Now that I had a pet, there was never a need for any imaginary playmates.

My mother, with her sunny demeanor, auburn hair, and

melodic southern drawl, took easily to the new Iranian setting. She helped Abbas, the gardener, plant celery, peppers, and cucumbers in the yard, adding to the strawberries and cherries already there.

Abbas was a soft-spoken elderly man with sad eyes and sunken, creased cheeks permanently coated with gray stubble. He brought along his young son, Akbar, to play with me outside and from whom I quickly learned Farsi.

In addition to gardening, Abbas was wondrous at knitting his own socks. Whenever he took a break from his raking and digging, he sat in the garden tool shed and picked up his knitting. As he diligently manipulated the four needles, looping coarse, gray wool over each, he calmly drank from a little glass of tea, a sugar lump in his mouth to sweeten it. I was as impressed by Abbas's ability to slurp hot tea with a lump of sugar in his mouth without choking as I was by his knitting with four needles.

My mother continued to avidly detail her impressions and experiences of Iran in letters to Tennessee, many intended for publication in the Old Hickory newspapers. With her family's ties to Middle Tennessee, her reports from faraway Tehran were of great interest to local readers:

"Prices at the American army co-op, which sells canned foods, cosmetics, and liquor, are outrageously high, so we have vowed to deal with them as little as possible," she wrote. "Liquor and cigarettes are dirt cheap, but one can't live on those." She also described how my father had bought popcorn from the co-op one day, and when she popped some in a skillet on the stove, the baffled Iranian housekeeper was convinced she was some sort of witch who could turn hard, dry kernels into white fluff with a mere shake of the pan.

Having been expertly coached by our Iranian chauffeur on the ways of doing business in the teeming Tehran bazaars, my mother learned how to bargain. She started by rolling her eyes in disbelief and walking out of the shop at the first price the shop owner quoted her, no matter what the price was. This went on several more times, the vendor good-naturedly summoning her back inside for more tea and haggling each time she walked out, until she was convinced she was being given a fair price and made her purchase.

While the driver nodded and exclaimed, *"Bali!"* ("Yes!") to my mother all the way home, she settled in the car with her new purchase, smiling with pride at having stood her ground. I, too, felt proud that she was so happy, although I was sorry for the vanquished vendor who had to settle for so much less than he'd originally asked for.

MUCH OF OUR family's social life revolved around the Officers' Club, the hub of recreational activity for American military personnel in Tehran, as well as for civilian personnel like my father. This club was an expat's home away from home. Every American holiday—Christmas, Easter, Thanksgiving, and the Fourth of July—was celebrated with parties where Western-style bands played on the outdoor terrace around the club's swimming pool. Once, during the Easter family luncheon, a drummer tapped out a jaunty rhythm while my mother and some other women paraded their homemade Easter bonnets around the swimming pool. I shook my hips to the drummers' enticing raps until I noticed some of the other children pointing at me. My mother's hat won first place in the contest.

My favorite club event was the weekly Friday brunch—Friday being the Muslim Sabbath—when the Riding Club members, of whom my father was one, returned from their long morning horseback ride. My father clearly relished galloping across the rugged Iranian countryside, perhaps missing his college days on the ranch in New Mexico.

My mother wasn't part of this horse group, so she and I would arrive at the club just as martinis were being served around the pool for the returning riders. There would be other children for me to play with on the swings or in the swimming pool while the adults socialized.

"Why don't you ride with us, Jean?" I heard one of the male riders ask my mother once.

My mother chuckled, the sunlight dancing in her red hair as she shook her head. "Oh, Lordy! I grew up with farm horses in Tennessee. I've had my fill."

I ran up to my father, who stood striking in his jodhpurs, high boots, and a red checkered Arab *kaffiyeh* and black *igal* cord on his head like a Bedouin, rather than the usual equestrian riding cap. He hugged me and then brought my mother a martini, smiling at the suggestion of his pretty, nonathletic wife on a horse. Photos showed him tall and handsome, hoisting a martini alongside the other riders. My father, although Muslim, drank occasionally, and in the days of the Pahlavi rule, Iran had relaxed the Muslim prohibition against alcohol.

In one photo, my mother sat on the lap of a kneeling American male friend as they playfully toasted each other with their stemmed glasses. The world was their playground.

QUEEN SORAYA, THE daughter of a nobleman of the Bakhtiari tribe and the shah's second wife, had been handpicked to be his consort after he divorced his first wife, Princess Fawzia, sister of King Farouk of Egypt. In photographs in newspapers and magazines, the beautiful Soraya, her dark hair swirled up in a chignon under her royal tiara, smiled up at her husband, the young shah. I fancied a resemblance between Queen Soraya and my mother, who was about the same age as the queen and also wore her hair swept off her neck whenever she and my father attended formal functions. I thought of my mother gazing up at my father the way the queen gazed at the shah. Like subtle perfume, the shah and Queen Soraya's names hovered over us with a phantom presence, as if they actually attended and took part in my parents' gatherings.

Each time I watched my parents leave the house for an official event, my mother wearing a cocktail dress and with her hair up, I knew they'd be seeing important people, perhaps even the shah and Queen Soraya in their Golestan Palace. I imagined the queen and my mother were friends. I pictured them talking together, presuming the queen spoke better English than my mother spoke the few words of Farsi she'd learned from the gardener and housekeeper. I wondered whether Queen Soraya and the shah danced, and whether my mother ever got to dance with the shah.

Decades later, whenever I dressed to go out, as I applied my makeup and fastened my necklace, the cold metal against my chest, a sound burst into memory: the clink of my mother's heavy, gold charm bracelet, the one she always put on first as she prepared for one of her soirees. She floated through the hallway from bathroom to bedroom half-dressed, her skin flushed from her bath, swathed in the jangling of gold and a floral swirl of perfume. I trailed behind her during this ritual preparation for the cocktail and dinner parties, a magical time when the three of us were suspended in exquisite anticipation of the night to come. As my mother adorned herself with additional pieces of jewelry, wriggled into her girdle, and slipped into a fitted dress and high heels, my father would gaze into the mirror to adjust his tie, smiling and winking at me.

Often, he would sing the words to "Jamaica Farewell" and twirl me under his arm. After taking a final look at himself in the mirror, he'd kiss me and pat my cheeks with his palms to share some of his piquant aftershave. He was eager to begin the outing with his lovely wife at his side. This, I was certain, was what lay ahead for me in adult life—tasteful evenings of dinner and dancing, as the curling, intertwining smells of my mother's perfume and my father's Old Spice reached around me to whisk me off with them into their enchanted world.

In those later years, hearing the jingling of my own jewelry as I kissed my children before leaving the house for a New Year's party or an office celebration, I wondered whether Caribbean music would be played that night. Even more, I hoped someone there would dance with the same passion my father once did.

four

Zena

OUR HOUSEKEEPER, ZENA, A YOUNG TURKIC WOMAN FROM Tabriz, lived with us to escape life with her abusive husband. Once, after returning from a weekend visit home, she showed my parents small knife wounds on her arm, recounting her troubles with him. I overheard my mother urge my father to report Zena's husband to the police. I loved Zena, with her shiny black hair fixed in two pretty, fluffy rolls on either side of her face. The thought of anyone harming her was unbearable.

I have a memory of accompanying Zena to visit her mother in her house in Tehran. Unlike her energetic daughter, Zena's mother was a thin, sickly woman with a sad face. Once, Zena brought an X-ray of her mother's hand to show to my parents, who then took it to a doctor. The X-ray, I was certain, showed a sewing needle floating above the bones of Zena's mother's hand, as if it had somehow entered her palm and was lost inside her flesh. This must have been a fantasy of mine. Perhaps the "needle" was a fracture on her forearm. But for years, whenever I threaded a needle, I imagined the white bones of Zena's mother's palm with the floating, trapped needle.

At the time, it made me aware of the dangers in everyday reality to people less fortunate than we were, such as the destitute women wrapped in *chadors* who sat on the Tehran streets, begging for money to feed their children. How could anyone not have enough food to eat? I was always glad when my mother reached into her purse for some change to give them.

One chilly morning as we walked along one of these alleys, we came across an injured dog lying against a wall. It was a day or so after Thanksgiving, and instead of going to the produce stall as planned, my mother took me back home where we gathered scraps of leftover turkey in the refrigerator to take to feed the weak dog. She showed me how to gently coax it to take the cold meat from our fingers. This tender gesture, taking time out of her busy day to care for the stray dog, would always remain with me.

IN OUR QUIET Shemiran neighborhood, there were other occasional unsettling signs of danger. Some nights we heard raucous sounds from the next-door neighbors' backyard— loud laughter and men's voices yelling out in Farsi. One night when my parents were out, there was a loud knock at our front gate. I came up behind Zena, who struggled to shut the door of the garden wall against men attempting to push their way into our yard. I was paralyzed with fear; it was the first time I felt the terror of someone I loved being hurt. Yet I couldn't make a sound as I watched Zena heave the door shut against them. I clearly remember her struggle but never knew whether the men were dangerous robbers or the drunken, noisy next-door neighbors, or even Zena's husband trying to break in and drag her away.

Soon after, my father acquired a hulking Iranian army-trained German shepherd named Wolf to guard the house so we would never have an intruder again. Wolf proved adept at scaring away any would-be intruders, simply by prowling the garden. He also patrolled the swimming pool whenever I was in it, attentively pacing along the edges, alert to any hint that I might be in trouble in the water. However, when Betsy, my collie, and Wolf produced several litters of droopy-eared, half-breed puppies, the normally docile Betsy turned into a fierce watchdog, growling as she protected her brood from the rest of us.

ONE NEW YEAR'S morning brought a dusting of snow on the gravel drive between the rows of fruit trees where my father's jeep was parked. My parents, Zena told me, had come home very late from their New Year's Eve party, and she warned me to be quiet since they would sleep late.

Lonely and bored while Zena also slept, I watched the white snow blanket the pool and pansies outside. I thought back to a night months before in early spring, when the warming fires of Nowruz had glowed throughout the city.

Fire was symbolically important in Tehran. The previous March, my parents and I had celebrated Nowruz, the ancient Zoroastrian holiday and Iran's most important festival commemorating the first day of spring. We ran together to jump over the ritual bonfires set for good luck and purification. My parents had each held one of my hands, and, in the time-honored tradition, we ran together, along with our Iranian friends, to leap over the flames. The fire night was such a mystical and distinct memory with the three of us skimming over the sparkling blaze that I wanted to recreate the fire in order to leap over it as I had so happily done with my parents. With some matches and paper, I managed to start one.

I remember both my fascination at the way the fire I'd set instantly devoured the paper in my bedroom, and my shock at the severe scolding my father gave me when he discovered the black-and-red embers soon after. I tried to explain that I'd wanted to repeat the good times he and my mother and I had together on Nowruz, but he frowned in anger, telling me it was dangerous to set a fire, that I could have burned myself and burned our house down. He didn't seem to understand the connection I'd made between the fires and our night of fun together.

MY MOTHER, LOOKING for something to do in addition to being an expat wife in Tehran, found administrative work at the American army office in the city. With her regularly out of the house for the first time, I spent the mornings in the kitchen with Zena, watching her do her chores. Zena also took over some of the cooking. The sweet aromas of saffron and frying onions filled our Tehran kitchen whenever Zena cooked. At lunchtime, she often made us *adas polow*, white rice mixed with brown lentils and served with a layer of crispy, caramelized onions on top, a popular dish across the Middle East. I first learned to love this lentil dish in Iran, called *mujadarra* in Arabic, which was cooked scented with saffron. Knowing how much I liked it, Zena made it often, carrying the platter into the dining room in a dramatic display, the aroma of browned onions blooming into the air.

It is cheap, easy to prepare, and a staple in households across the Arab Levant and Egypt. Whenever I cooked it at home in the United States when my children were growing up, my son would eat a few bites, then discreetly forage for any leftover meat from the refrigerator. My two daughters, while enjoying the dish, eschewed the best part—the topping of crisped onions. Zena would have been puzzled to see my girls pushing the onions aside. Onions are a staple in Middle Eastern cooking, and this dish is impossible to present without its crowning, caramelized glory, as Zena had so lovingly done.

In Tehran each noon, I would run to open the kitchen door when the Iranian bread, *sangak*, was delivered from the bakery. The warm, freshly baked slabs, nearly the size of Zena's ironing board, were puffed up in spongy black bubbles I couldn't wait to chew into. My mother and I sometimes went to the bakery to watch the bread baking in the hot stone ovens. In a letter to Nashville, my mother likened the fiery bread ovens where the elongated dough was shoved onto the hot stones with long paddles as "the gates of hell." She was particularly fascinated by one man's job of shaking off the pebbles sticking to the fresh, hot loaves once they were done.

For my favorite Iranian dish, *chelo kebab*, we always went out to a restaurant. The thin skewered patties of ground lamb were grilled and served piping hot, with a sprinkling of sumac, alongside steaming white rice. A raw egg was cracked and mixed into the hot rice at our table right before serving so that the moistened kernels glistened as we dug in. I loved this dish so much that on the way to the restaurant, I chanted happily in Farsi in famished anticipation, *"Khaili khob chelo kebab!"* ("Chelo kebab is very good!")

Amid the delicious, spicy Iranian flavors of *chelo kebab* and *adas polow* intruded the horrid daily dose of cod-liver oil my mother insisted on spooning out for me. Although she tried to make the fishy taste more palatable by mixing it into a glass of orange juice, nothing could disguise the sickening stench, and I gagged each morning as it slithered down my throat. I was sure no Iranian child was ever made to drink this revolting tonic, and I never gave it to my own children. The flavors of the Iranian foods that Zena cooked never contained such offensive tastes. It was almost like the difference between my mother and father: the science and practicality of the West, which included the foul-tasting medicines and periodic frightful injections in the clinic to protect me, crashing up against the softer, enticing ways of the East.

And yet the Western lifestyle our family lived in Tehran had much to offer in the way of fun. I enjoyed watching my parents prepare for the seasonal masquerade parties where they dressed in elaborate costumes. One night for a Halloween party, my father put on his Arab robes—a gold-embroidered brown *abaya* cloak and the *hatta* and *igal* men's white head-dress with a black cord holding it in place. Since he no longer had a mustache, he drew a thin black one above his mouth along with a dark goatee to complete the look. My mother wore a Greek village woman's outfit—a long embroidered skirt and white chemise with a sheer, white shawl draped over a flat, round Greek woman's cap on her head. I found pictures of them dancing, my father's arm held high as he clasped my mother's hand, her head tilted back, her mouth open in an expansive smile. I imagined her laughter flowing through the room.

This lighthearted, adult play would have seemed anathema to the more conservative Iranians. Many might have been shocked by such play-parties where members of the opposite sex, expats as well as upper-class Iranians, freely mixed and danced together.

ONE EVENING, MY father came home, disturbed as he put a new record an Iranian colleague had given to him on the phonograph. The song was in Farsi, the haunting tune sung by a man's sorrowful voice. It was called "*Mara Beboos*" ("Kiss Me").

I must have overheard my father telling my mother—for I can't imagine him saying this outright to a child—that the words were those of a prisoner's letter of farewell to his daughter on the eve of his execution. The condemned man had been rumored to have been a supporter of ousted prime minister Mohammad Mossadegh.

"*Mara beboos*," the singer intoned sadly.

I hummed the irresistibly hypnotic tune along with the singer, although thinking of my father having to say goodbye to me for the last time and under such wretched circumstances made me sob. It was far sadder than Harry Belafonte having to leave his little girl in Kingston Town.

I still hear the somber male voice singing the words of a distraught father, as I'd heard it on that long-ago night in our Tehran living room when it had made me so sad. I regret never asking my father in later years whether he'd felt conflicted when he arrived in Iran only a few years after Prime Minister

Mossadegh had been ousted with the help of the United States. At the time doing a job for the American Department of Defense, my father's daily frustrations had to do more with the red tape involved in setting up a cutting-edge military language school, obstacles he faced from both the head office in Washington and the bribe-riddled Iranian bureaucracy. And yet, as a man of Middle Eastern heritage and sensibilities, the plight of the poverty-stricken Iranians, along with the political oppression he must have been aware of, had to have weighed on him.

Many years later, when the shah was overthrown, several of the notorious generals in his army, along with the chief of the secret police, the SAVAK, were tried and executed by the new revolutionary government. My father had known some of those generals when they were young, committed men forging careers and devoted to their country. He was shaken to hear they had been shot by a firing squad, convinced they had been innocent of their alleged crimes. Perhaps, though, he had also wondered whether their youthful idealism could have veered into something vile.

five

Mommy

THE SEPTEMBER THAT I WAS FIVE, THE LONG-AWAITED DAY arrived—my first day of school. All summer I'd been counting the days until I could start first grade at the Tehran American School.

My class was taught in a large tent on the school's lawn where I, along with the other American children, first learned how to write the alphabet. The teacher wrote on a large blackboard and instructed us to repeat aloud after her.

"*W*," she said, writing the letter. "*E*," she said, showing us how to write that letter. "We."

"We," we repeated after her.

"We, We," she said again, and I giggled uncontrollably at the naughty reference.

With my mother working mornings, the job of walking me home from school at noon fell to the gardener, Abbas.

"*Biya*," he'd say as he took my hand to walk along the sidewalk in the midday Tehran sun. "Come." I was often so hot and sleepy that I closed my eyes as I walked, once painfully colliding with a telephone pole.

Some of my friends rode the big school bus to and from their homes, since they lived farther away. Each day, while walking with Abbas, I watched them climb onto the bus. I wished we lived farther away so I could ride the bus with them. I couldn't wait to move up a class so I could carry a load of books like the older students and get to complain about homework as I heard them do.

I was a fearful child. Whether it was due to things I overheard the adults talking about, stories read to me, or my lively imagination, I created frightening scenarios of being kidnapped or chased by ghosts. I was especially afraid of being alone whenever my mother or Zena went into a part of the large house without me. When my mother went into the bathroom and shut the door behind her, I was terrified and begged to be let inside with her. Her way of dealing with my fear was to play a game where we were army rangers and could connect through the closed door by calling out to each other and answering, "Roger."

"Kathy," she called out from inside the bathroom.

"Roger," I responded.

Then it was my turn. "M–Mommy," I called back, tentatively.

"Roger," she cheerfully answered, and so forth, until she emerged from the bathroom.

My mother had a solution to everything to quell my constant, unwarranted anxieties.

Not one to be intimidated by the foreign surroundings or by not speaking Farsi, my mother loved to walk up and down the backstreets where the Iranians lived, away from the larger expatriate houses on the main streets. She often took me with her to buy vegetables from the stalls along the back alleys where lilacs, roses, and jasmine spilled over the high walls of the enclosed gardens.

Once when she and I were walking home at night from a neighbor's house, I grew frightened that someone was following us. I gripped her hand and pressed against her. Perhaps I'd overheard something on the radio. My parents regularly listened to Voice of America and read the American newspapers, and I sometimes heard them comment to each other on some violent story. Perhaps I was remembering the frightening night of the intruders trying to force their way past Zena through our gate. My mother had comforted me that night by teaching me the words to "You'll Never Walk Alone" from the musical *Carousel*. We sang it the rest of the way home in the dark.

My mother was mystified by my timidity, unable to understand why the world, so abundant and welcoming to her, was such a daunting place for her child. Once, while spending the afternoon at a friend's house, my friend's mother offered to French braid my hair as she did her own daughter's. I'd never heard of it before and refused. When my mother picked me up, and I proudly told her that I had not allowed my friend's mother to French braid my hair, instead of approving she was visibly disappointed.

"You should have let her, Kathy, so I could have learned how to do it," she said.

I was baffled by her reproachful tone. I never seemed able to please my confident mother, who expected me to be more like her, outgoing and bold. I was keenly aware of my own vulnerability, of how little power I had to control things around me. I longed to be fearless like her. Yet she and I were so different.

WHILE THEY DIDN'T seem to pay much attention to my fears, my parents were concerned about my health and my manners. The piquant smell of menthol from a jar of Vicks VapoRub always transports me back to a time in Tehran when I was in bed with a respiratory infection, while my parents took turns warming cloths on the kerosene heater in my bedroom and then spreading them on my Vicks-slathered chest to steam out the congestion. This memory of being nurtured while in bed brought me comfort throughout my childhood. It was something I did with my children whenever they had a chest cold. I would rub Vicks onto their chest and then place a heating pad on top, remembering the smell of kerosene from our Tehran heater and my parents' look of concern.

While they were loving when they treated my illnesses, both of them were sterner when it came to good manners. On one occasion, for no reason that I could discern, my mother pulled me into the bathroom, rubbed a wet washcloth with soap, and rubbed it against my tongue as I gagged from the bitterness.

"Do not talk back!" she admonished.

I understood neither what "talk back" meant nor what I had done to incur this strange punishment. I was left crying and bewildered, vaguely aware I'd said something I shouldn't have but not understanding what it was. My parents, I learned, had a stringent set of rules I had to adhere to. These rules were the opposite side of the same lifestyle that allowed me to enjoy the luscious gin-soaked cherry from my father's drink and the happy calypso music we danced to. Much of the time, the adult world seemed contradictory and confusing to me.

Although she was serious about many things, my mother had a keen sense of humor and a vivid imagination. My favorite bedtime stories were the ones she made up in which I was the heroine who set off on a multitude of adventures.

"Once upon a time," she'd begin, "a brave girl named Kathy went with her uncle Hungus on an important mission." My fictitious uncle Hungus and I encountered witches or goblins along the jasmine-strewn Tehran alleys and quickly overpowered them. No fairy tale from a book captivated me like an Uncle Hungus story my mother wove for me.

Occasionally, my father took over the storytelling. His fanciful tales involved a girl named Fatima and her magical winged horse.

"One night, Fatima got onto her white horse and flew across the night sky to a distant, enchanted land," he would begin.

Listening to his voice, I imagined the horse's powerful, flapping wings lifting Fatima into the moonlit sky above the Tehran rooftops. I loved his stories as much as my mother's, loved being the active heroine in them, aware that the girl, Fatima, riding the magnificent steed, was *me* bent on some magical quest.

In Tehran, I also first became aware of the different roles my father and mother held when it came to raising me. My mother was mostly the disciplinarian, while my father gave my opinions more sway. Besides playfully teasing me, he sang me songs when we were driving together, like "Que Sera, Sera," and Dean Martin's "That's Amore." He had perfect pitch, and music and singing, as much as dancing, were an inherent part of his nature.

One day, he was in charge of getting me ready to go out

to meet my mother. He stood beside me at the bathroom sink and carefully parted my hair down the middle, as I instructed him to, brushing my bangs off my forehead on either side the way I liked. He even wet my hair as I asked him to, the way Zena wet her own thick hair whenever she combed it, but which my mother never let me do, saying I'd catch cold. I liked the image staring back at me from the mirror, my wetted bangs neatly parted in the middle like Zena's. I had a growing awareness of my power with my father, an awareness that his way of loving me was often by giving in to my wishes. It was also my first insight into the depth and unconditional quality of his love.

six

Patriarch

ONE AFTERNOON, I WENT UP TO MY PARENTS' BEDROOM ON the second floor of our house to find my father sitting alone on the edge of his bed with his head cradled in his hands. Never having seen him so hunched over and in such obvious distress, I went over to him.

"Daddy?"

He raised his head, his eyes red and wet.

"What's wrong?" I asked.

Composing himself, he said, simply, "Baba has died." Baba. His father.

My shadowy memories of Baba were few, but I understood something terrible had happened to him. Though I'd seen him only once, he loomed large in our home.

We met him when my mother and I went to Jerusalem to meet my father's family before coming to Tehran. We also met my father's stepmother, Om Hassan, and his three brothers and three sisters, as well as his larger clan of aunts, uncles, cousins, and in-laws.

Baba and Om Hassan lived on the Mount of Olives overlooking Jerusalem, along with my father's older sister, Aisha, and his two youngest brothers, Shafiq and Basil.

Om Hassan was my grandfather's third wife. Baba's first marriage to his cousin, a brief, troubled union, had ended in divorce not long after the birth of their only son, Ahmad. Wanting to get away from Jerusalem after his divorce, my grandfather ventured to Lebanon where he started a trading business in Beirut.

Some years later, he was introduced to the Lebanese Zaidan family, which had an eligible daughter, Fatima, who became his second wife. After the birth of their daughter, Aisha, and my father, Khalil, in Beirut, Baba and Grandmother Fatima moved back to Jerusalem where Fatima soon had two more daughters. I've never seen any photographs of my grandmother. Although reputed to have been a woman of considerable dark beauty with long, luxuriant black braids, Fatima had refused to have her photograph taken, adhering to the pious belief that it was blasphemous to reproduce a human image, which only God could do.

When my father was four, his mother suddenly took ill. Fatima went back to Beirut to stay with her family while she sought more advanced medical care than what Jerusalem could offer. She left her three daughters in her husband's care but insisted on taking her son to Beirut with her. A few days after arriving in Beirut, my father woke in his grandfather's home to find his mother lying next to him in bed, unresponsive. Frightened, he ran to tell his aunt that his mother was not waking up.

It was never clear what had killed Fatima at the age of thirty. Witnessing this early loss of his mother would stay with my father throughout his life as a lingering melancholy that frequently cast its aching shadow over him.

My distraught grandfather traveled to Beirut to bury his

young wife and bring his son back home to Jerusalem. With the help of his mother and sister, Baba managed for a while to care for all four of his young children. But it soon became apparent that the children—the youngest, Sameera, was barely a year—needed a full-time caretaker. Still grieving for Fatima, my grandfather finally decided to remarry for the sake of his children. He asked his female relatives to look for a suitable, mature woman to be his wife.

When Baba wed a third time, it was to a demure widow with two grown children of her own. Om Hassan, or mother of Hassan, was barely forty, with delicate features and skin like fresh milk. Yet everyone presumed Baba had selected an "older" woman for the sole purpose of caring for his motherless children. The good-natured Om Hassan soon got tired of people saying she was too old to have been chosen as a wife for anything other than to look after her husband's offspring. Discarding her birth control, she surprised everyone by becoming pregnant twice, giving Baba two more sons, my uncles Shafiq and Basil.

BABA'S RED-ROOFED, stone house on the crest of the Mount of Olives was visible from miles away, jutting up between tall pines. Baba's original family property had been inside Jerusalem's walled Old City, in a section known as the Karjawally Corner. He and his young family had first moved out of the crowded Old City to a newer, modern section of Jerusalem. Then, as he looked for a larger home to accommodate his growing brood, the open vistas of the nearby Mount of Olives drew him.

Baba was a tall, slender man with piercing eyes who

oversaw his large clan with a quiet assertiveness. His eldest unmarried daughter, Aisha, serious and reserved, was now a seamstress and lived and worked at home. She also helped to run the household. His two younger daughters, Suad and Sameera, were married and settled with their respective families families nearby. His two youngest sons, Shafiq and Basil, were finishing post–high school training and also lived at home. His oldest son, Ahmad, from his first marriage, was the manager of a bank in Jerusalem. He lived nine miles away in the town of Ramallah with his pretty, red-haired wife, Khadija, and their seven children.

A temperamental firebrand in his youth, my grandfather had mellowed into a thoughtful patriarch. He had grudgingly agreed to my father's going to study so far away in America and had been upset by the news—which was every Arab parent's nightmare—that his son had married an American.

"There are so many eligible young Jerusalem women who would have made Khalil a fine wife," he'd lamented. "Nobody in Jerusalem can vouch for the virtue or good name of an unknown *Amercaniya*."

It was nearly ten years before my father could travel back home to Jerusalem to see his father on his way to his new job in Tehran.

My father was unable to remain in Jerusalem until my mother and I arrived from America. But he had faith that his wife's charms could assuage any lingering doubts his father might have about her being an unknown American woman of questionable background.

Although Baba had been dubious about his new American daughter-in-law, once we were due to arrive, the grandfather of fifteen led a delegation of relatives to the airport to welcome us. As my father had suspected, it didn't take Baba long to be won over by the sunny American his son had married. He wholeheartedly gathered us into his fold.

BABA'S FOREBEAR HAD been an Albanian soldier who came to Jerusalem as a conscript in the Ottoman army around 1805. Albanian army recruits from the Balkans, known to be tough fighters, had been favored by the Ottomans and were referred to as *Arnaut* in reference to their Albanian lineage. All three generations of Baba's ancestors had been Arnaut soldiers of rank in Jerusalem, then part of the Ottoman Empire. Our surname, Karjawally, is said to be an Arabized version of Karachooli, the original Albanian.

Baba, too, had been an Ottoman soldier in Palestine during the First World War. But the Ottoman defeat by Britain and France gave Britain control over Palestine in the mandate that was to last for nearly three tumultuous decades. The local Palestinian Arabs and the minority Jewish population had resisted the British Mandate imposed on them, and each formed local militias to combat the British authorities. Like many Palestinians, Baba had become a political activist during that time, agitating against the imposed British rule. In the mid-1930s, he was forced to flee to Lebanon to avoid arrest. He returned to Jerusalem only in 1938, after Britain granted a general amnesty for Palestinian dissidents ensuring his safe return.

In the decades leading up to the Second World War, as Jews were persecuted and killed in Europe, there was an influx of Jewish refugees into Palestine, a move opposed by the Arab population. In the ensuing war of 1947–1948, armies from the neighboring Arab states fought alongside the local Palestinian forces for control of the British-held territory against the Jewish militias but were defeated. The land long held by the Ottomans and then by the British was subsequently partitioned into separate Arab and Jewish states. The Jewish state became Israel, and the Palestinian lands remaining under Arab rule were joined to the Kingdom of Jordan.

Although he rarely discussed it, Baba's disappointment at the failure for an independent Arab Palestine to materialize for his people after their years-long resistance against British rule had spiritually diminished him.

With his rabble-rousing days over, what seemed to trouble my grandfather most, as we sat around the dining table for lunch in his Mount of Olives home, was that his lanky American daughter-in-law looked too thin to bear sons. In Baba's eyes, extra pounds on a woman meant sturdier health and enhanced fertility. He would glance from his buxom, olive-skinned daughters to my mother's translucent cheeks and slim shoulders and sigh.

"Eat, Jean, eat," he'd gently prod, nudging the platters of food toward her.

My mother would finally grasp her stomach, her blue eyes pleading. "Baba, I simply cannot eat another bite, no matter how delicious the food is or how much you want grandsons."

Once, as I lay screaming on the stone floor of the sitting room in one of my temper tantrums, Baba asked my mother why I was making such a fuss.

"I'm an old man," he said, irritably, "and it disturbs me to hear such noise."

My mother, generally easygoing and respectful, but exhausted with trying to placate her stubborn four-year-old, glared at her father-in-law. None of the mild-mannered southern men she'd grown up with in Tennessee had my Arab father's quick temper or his father's brazen imperiousness.

"Nobody in *my* family behaves this way, Baba," she quipped. "This is pure Karjawally."

Baba smiled, his annoyance melting into pride that I, his granddaughter, had inherited his rebellious genes. (Over the years, the accusation was proven right repeatedly as I earned a reputation for being an intense and moody child, a fact attributed to the impulsive Karjawally blood flowing through me.)

Later, as Baba sat on the couch in the foyer smoking his bubbling *narguile* hookah pipe, he patiently rubbed my back to soothe me when I cried because my mother had left for an evening out with some of my uncles and aunts.

"It's good, it's good," he said in his halting English as he patted my back. For all his claims to being an old man with little tolerance for loud noise, he knew life could be unsettling for a child in an alien place amid so many unfamiliar people, all speaking an incomprehensible language. He understood that, although surrounded by family, I felt isolated and alone.

In Tehran, that afternoon, when my father lifted his face from his hands and said somberly, "Baba has died," I had no idea how devastating the loss was to him. It was the first death in our family that I remember. Even though I'd seen Baba only once, I had felt a deep connection to him and could barely comprehend that I'd never see him again.

In later years, whenever my father spoke lovingly of his own father, I began to understand how deeply Baba's death had affected him and how close they had been in that short time before he left as a teenager for America. He would always regret those ten years spent away from his father—years that could never be replaced.

In time, I would relate to his great feeling of loss. But then, what most bewildered me and shattered my sense of safety was that my strong, adult father could break down in tears.

I take my first belly dancing class when I am twenty-one and living in Westchester, New York. In the evenings, while my husband watches our infant daughter, I drive from our apartment in Harrison to the apartment of Saleema, a professional belly dancer. Saleema—Silvia Goldstein is her real name—is from Queens. Ethnically Russian and Jewish, Silvia has a beautiful, chiseled face, dark hair and eyes, and a small, taut body. She looks like a woman from Yemen. I imagine the Queen of Sheba. It surprises me, at first, to learn a woman who has never been out of the United States—nor even out of New York much—can do a Middle Eastern dance so authentically and naturally. When she touches her hand to her forehead and shimmies her hips, she is a woman from Cairo or Istanbul. More to my surprise, Silvia attaches no shame to belly dancing.

Although I've grown up watching Arab women belly dancing among each other, I've associated professional belly dancing with a degree of disrepute because of its cabaret nature and sensuality. But to Silvia, belly dancing is the supreme female art form, and she holds it in great reverence. In her classes, we become temple goddesses, shimmying our hips to the vigorous drumbeats in sensual, rippling waves, our shoulders daintily seducing the air. In those evenings in New York, where I am the only student with any true Middle Eastern ties, I begin to reconnect to my Eastern roots and to Arab womanhood with all its soft yet strong, joyful femininity. In her classes, we are playful, we are tender, we are erotic, we are powerful. We are dancing!

seven

My Palestinian Family

MY MOTHER HAD TAKEN TO HER HUSBAND'S LARGE ARAB family as eagerly as it did to her. Her mother's Hopkins family from Columbia, Tennessee, was small. However, her father, being one of ten farm children, boasted a tightly knit Pedigo clan that spread across several towns in Middle Tennessee, with an affectionate, close kinship similar to my father's Arab family.

Although not brought up to be particularly religious, my mother enjoyed touring Jerusalem's legendary biblical sights with my Muslim uncles and aunts. They, having grown up amid the legacy of three monotheistic religions, had been exposed over the years to scores of multinational pilgrims. They knew every church and bit of biblical lore she'd grown up with in Tennessee. The ground they walked on each day echoed the names familiar to her: Judea, Hebron, Jericho, Mount Moriah.

From Baba's kitchen window, we could look down the slope of the Mount of Olives to the Old City walls. They had been built, my uncles explained, by the Ottoman sultan Suleiman the Magnificent in the sixteenth century along the remains of the Roman walls built in the second century. Within the walls, and visible from our kitchen, was the Dome of the Rock mosque. At that time, the dome was a facade of aging mosaics, later replaced by the bright, golden one of today. Outside the city walls was the white Rockefeller Archaeological Museum and below it the Kidron Valley, known in Arabic as the Valley of Walnuts.

My uncles also took my mother on excursions to sites farther away such as Hebron, to the tombs of the prophet Abraham and his wife, Sarah. Sarah's tomb was where women often prayed to be granted a son, as Sarah had been, late in life.

In a letter home to Tennessee, my mother wrote wryly, "I suspect I'm being taken to the tombs in Hebron for reasons other than their cultural and historical significance."

Yet she prayed there, as encouraged by my aunts, to be rewarded with a son. Despite what must have seemed an absurd notion to her—male children so prized above female ones—my mother accepted how important it was to my father's family, and in Arab culture, that he have a son.

MOST DAYS, WHILE my mother went on her sightseeing expeditions, I stayed at Baba's to play with my cousins—Aunt Suad's toddler daughter, Maha, and her two older sons, Talal and Adham, who were my age.

Aunt Suad, my father's hardy, gregarious younger sister, arrived early each morning. Like her older sister, Aisha, Suad was olive skinned and dark haired.

"*Marhaba*!" ("Hello!") she announced loudly, blowing into her father's house like a gust of Mount of Olives wind. After sharing the family breakfast of hummus, falafel, chopped tomatoes, cucumbers, olives, an omelet, bread, and za'atar— the tart dipping condiment of crushed oregano mixed with sesame seeds—she began to overhaul Baba's house. Suad's own house in another part of the village was small, so she'd already finished her housework there before we were even awake at Baba's.

While Aunt Aisha sewed for clients, Om Hassan and Baba retired to their bedroom, and the remaining adults went sightseeing, Aunt Suad cleaned. She hoisted the small tables and stools onto the couches, knotted up the curtains to get them off the floor, and flung the small rug over the balcony railing to beat the dust out of it. Then she turned on the radio loud enough for the music to resound throughout the house.

With her favorite music divas belting out their hits, Aunt Suad bustled through all the rooms as she sang along in her strong, earthy voice. Sometimes she'd pause in her cleaning long enough to shimmy her shoulders and hips to the beats of the drums and tambourines, as though dancing for a theater audience. I was fascinated by the way she rolled her belly . . . little ripples that started below her waist and floated upward. Belly dancing, she whispered to Maha and me, when her father was out of earshot, had been her dream. To dance profession-ally. If only Baba had allowed it. As Maha and I watched her, I shyly tried to shimmy my shoulders like she did.

After sweeping the floors, Aunt Suad flooded them with water and mopped them with a large cloth. Bent at the waist, she held the cloth and dragged it the length of the floor as she moved backward.

"Can we help, please, please?" Maha and I begged.

She gave us small rags to drench in her bucket and crawl

alongside her, crab-like, but then shooed us away so she could get on with her work. She was quick and efficient, and soon the puddles of water on the floor had dried, the curtains were unknotted, and the rug was brought back in after its flogging and placed in the foyer with the side tables.

I was fascinated by, yet somewhat fearful of, Aunt Suad's ferocious vitality. She had an innate need to scrub and did it with noisy delight, wanting to finish quickly so she could help Aunt Aisha and Om Hassan prepare the substantial lunch for everyone. All the while, Aunt Aisha sat quietly at her sewing machine, shaking her head at her sister's intensity.

Finally, she would call out in protest, "Suad, that radio is scalding my ears!"

Once the floors were clean, Aunt Suad went to the kitchen to make the pita bread for lunch. Forming a well within a large mound of flour and some salt, she'd call Maha and me over to slowly pour in the cup of warm water, then the small cup of yeast she'd fermented. As we poured, she kneaded the watery dough, folding it over and over until it thickened into a gleaming, silken lump, which she covered with a blanket to rest.

"Can we have some?" Maha and I would ask. She'd pinch off a few scraps for us to play with, and we'd roll the soft dough into long ropes that we wound into cakes or drooped above our upper lips like mustaches.

When the dough had risen sufficiently, Aunt Suad uncovered it, divided it into smaller rounds, and with a rolling pin and sprinkled flour, rolled each round into a perfect cylinder. These she again covered with the blanket to rise on a large wooden tray before she called one of her sons to carry it to the communal wood-burning oven across the street. When my cousin returned with the tray of freshly baked pita bread balanced on his head, its warm, yeasty fragrance made us clamor for a taste immediately.

When we sat down for lunch, Aunt Suad would shake her head and say with a sigh, "Life ends, but work never ends."

Although I believed her, I suspected if her work did happen to end, she would happily create more of it, just to keep busy. Sure enough, the next morning when she arrived at Baba's, it was as if a tornado had hit, and the frenetic crush of activity started all over again.

IN THE WINDY, chilly afternoons, after the big lunch Om Hassan and my aunts cooked each day and the ensuing afternoon nap, my mother and I were taken off to visit more of the endless stream of relatives living in Jerusalem and Ramallah. There were so many houses to go to, so many cousins to meet. And my father's cousins came in all shades. Some were olive skinned and dark haired; some were blond. There was even a family of second cousins, eight pretty sisters, several of whom had red hair and freckles like my mother. The eldest of these was Khadija, Uncle Ahmad's wife.

I dreaded these afternoon family visits, preferring to stay in the quiet of Baba's house and garden with Maha. But sometimes we had to go along with the grown-ups. Aunt Suad, by now done with housework, had taken a short nap, bathed, and dressed in one of her bright blouses and gathered skirts cinched at the waist. Although she and Aunt Aisha resembled each other in their complexion and black hair, unlike her modest older sister, Aunt Suad exuded a fearless determination and sensuality, especially when she was dressed to go out.

After applying her face powder and crimson lipstick, she would check herself in the mirror, pleased by her transformation from her morning labors.

Catching me staring at her image in the mirror, she'd smile and ask, in one of her few words of English, "Good?"

I'd nod, too timid to say anything, and she would glow at my approval.

She was unabashedly open in both her opinions and her love. Taking me by the hand, she'd set out from one cousin's house to the next, exclaiming, "Here's Khalil's American daughter!"

As an only child and shy by nature, being surrounded by so many new people speaking words I barely understood overwhelmed me. I would hang back, even when plied with candies by the benevolent cousins we visited.

I particularly dreaded the neighborhood where my youngest aunt, Sameera, lived—at the time she had six children, later to become nine—because it included the homes of several of her inlaws' families. Visiting this multigenerational neighborhood always entailed hordes of shrieking children racing up and down the alley like sentinels to announce our arrival. They would stand around and stare at me, the visitor from America.

My mother was unfazed by the multitude of cousins and relished both the clannish nature of her husband's complicated Arab family and its foreignness. Neither the unfamiliar Arabic nor the differing customs made her uncomfortable, especially since my uncles, her main guides, spoke English. She showed none of the terror I felt at new situations or unfamiliar people and saw no need to shield me from the mob of curious children at family gatherings.

"Go along and play, Kathy," she'd say, expecting me to adapt, just as she had.

When my aunts took us shopping in the narrow streets of the Old City, my mother never held her nose against the stench of the hanging carcasses of butchered lambs in the meat market or the wafting reek of sewage in an alley. She loved perusing the cavernous shops built into the walls of the ancient city and emulated my uncles as they haggled and bargained with the merchants. Although I couldn't understand her boldness, I assumed this was part of being a grown-up and that I'd someday attain a measure of her verve.

For now, I was most at ease in the sanctuary of Baba's house playing hide-and-seek in the garden where mysterious nooks amid the damp, cold stone provided good hiding spots. Aunt Aisha gave Maha and me scraps of cloth and threaded our needles so we could sew dresses for our dolls. We would sit at her feet and watch her furiously pedal up and down as her machine stitched her clients' skirts and blouses.

"*MARHABA*," CAME ANOTHER raspy voice each morning after breakfast.

Zareefa, the spry, elderly village grocer, poked her head in the front door. One of my aunts would pause in her work to make everyone Turkish coffee. Maha and I had coffee poured into glasses of hot milk, boiled by Aunt Aisha each morning from a neighbor's freshly milked cow. While the old lady enumerated her selection of fresh produce that day, my aunts decided on which vegetables and meat they wanted to cook for lunch.

Zareefa was nearly toothless, her chin marked with small

indigo tattoos in the shape of tiny stars. As she sipped her coffee and relayed the latest village news, I tried not to stare at them. Once she caught me looking at her and chuckled, telling me her tattoos had been put on her when she was a young girl, as a mark of beauty. But it was hard for me to imagine her as any age but old. She always wore her village *thobe*, a floor-length embroidered women's robe that was faded and patched in places and smelled of oregano, mint, or some other herb she'd been sorting earlier in her store. Although her eyes were glazed over with cataracts, Zareefa could remember my aunts' list of groceries as if she'd written them down in her head. Once she'd finished her coffee, she was off down the street to her store to dispatch the order to us with one of her small grandsons.

A less amiable daily visitor appeared in Baba's doorway, his silhouette highlighted by the morning sun behind him.

"*Salaam alaikum,*" he'd call out gruffly.

Great-Uncle Jalal, Baba's younger brother, always wore a suit and a red *tarbouche,* the Ottoman fez still worn by most older men. Short, stout, and grumpy, he was the physical antithesis of Baba. Since his wife had died and his marriage had produced no children, Baba's family was his closest kin. My clearest memory of him was when he scolded me loudly once for crawling across the floor with Maha on my back as we played horse, angrily telling me doing so would stunt my growth. Afterward, I mostly avoided him. As the only one in the family to own a car, though, he was the one usually depended upon to drive us on any lengthy excursions.

In his youth, Uncle Jalal, like Baba, had been a political agitator. During the British Mandate, both of them had defied the British policy prohibiting Arabs from carrying guns by carrying concealed pistols, despite the penalties. Jalal was the hothead of the two. Once in the 1930s, he organized Baba's daring escape to Lebanon when the British had put out a warrant for his arrest for participating in several insurrections against the authorities.

Unlike Baba, who was content to quietly puff on his *narguile* in the evenings and listen to the conversations of the younger family members, Uncle Jalal was a card shark and relished evening games with his nieces and nephews. My mother, too, loved to play cards, and she eagerly got into the family game one night.

But when she caught Uncle Jalal slipping a hidden card into his hand, she announced aloud, "Uncle Jalal, you're cheating!"

"What?" Uncle Jalal snapped.

My mother tried hard not to giggle at the old man's angry outburst; my uncles and aunts feigned ignorance. Aware that their uncle cheated at cards, they judiciously chose to ignore it.

"This *Amercaniya* is accusing me of cheating!" Uncle Jalal shouted, his chin jutting in indignation. He abruptly left the house.

The next day he returned, announcing his arrival as he walked into the foyer and sat on a chair, waiting to be served his usual cup of Turkish coffee. He died shortly after, so I never saw him again. Despite being cantankerous, Uncle Jalal was lovingly tolerated as the elder, if eccentric, uncle. Whenever anyone spoke of him in later years, it was always with an affectionate chuckle and respect for the heroic rebel he'd once been.

eight

The Families Meet

THE YEAR AFTER BABA DIED, TWO YEARS AFTER WE'D MOVED
to Tehran, my father's contract with the Department of Defense ended. Wanting to extend their foreign adventure
rather than return to what both he and my mother considered
the "humdrum of Washington," my father scouted around
and sent out his résumé for another overseas job.

For my mother, the colorful and hospitable environment of
the Middle East, with the importance placed on family life,
reminded her of growing up amid her extended family in Tennessee. Now that she'd experienced a more laid-back life in
Tehran and seen how my father's relatives lived in Beirut and
Jerusalem, she wasn't eager to trade this more relaxed lifestyle
for the unsparing, busy routine—"the sludge, drudge, and no
fun," as she put it—they'd left in the United States.

Soon, my father received the offer of an executive position
at Aminoil, the American Independent Oil Company, located
in Kuwait, a tiny desert sheikhdom on the tip of the Persian
Gulf. He would be chief personnel officer and the company's
liaison to the ruling Al-Sabah family. My father had come to
briefly know the current Sheikh of Kuwait, Abdullah Al-Salim
Al-Sabah, in Washington five years earlier. The company,

headquartered in New York, seemed to think this acquaintance would be an asset to them. All my father had to do was fly to Kuwait to make the final arrangements for his employment and for us to join him there.

My mother wrote to her mother about the little-known desert nation: "It is terribly hot there during the summer, but most people send their families back to Lebanon and Jordan for the hottest months. Housing is high, help cheap, goods very cheap because it is a free port, lovely beaches, and plenty of seafood. Yum, yum."

While my parents were looking forward to this next chapter of their lives, I was unhappy as I helped pack up my belong-ings and bid sad goodbyes to my beloved Zena, our dogs, Wolf and Betsy, our gardener, Abbas, and our American and Iranian friends. I couldn't grasp the finality of it, and I sensed a big change lay ahead. I was scared to leave my world behind for something new and unknown.

My mother and I headed to Jerusalem for a month while my father went to Kuwait to prepare for our arrival. Mean-while, Mammaw and Grandy, as I called my mother's parents, had taken their daughter's advice to travel out of Tennessee. In the summer of 1958, they were on a journey around the world. After Europe, they planned to meet us in Jerusalem on our way to Kuwait.

My grandparents' adventure had been duly written up in the Old Hickory newspapers. They were to fly first to Europe to visit France, Italy, Portugal, and Germany. There, they would buy a car and with little more than printed maps, drive the rest of the way across Germany, Austria, and other parts of Europe to Greece. They would continue their drive through Turkey and Syria to get to Jerusalem.

My mother and I had been on the Mount of Olives for several weeks, never sure when her parents would arrive. We knew they had purchased a Volkswagen in Germany and were driving to Jerusalem—a daring feat considering neither of them had ruggedly traveled before, and not outside of the United States. We were sitting in Baba's foyer on the Mount of Olives that summer afternoon when Aunt Aisha went down the outdoor stone steps to answer a loud knocking on the iron garden door.

Moments later, my aunt returned and announced, "Mama, Baba Jean!"

After a pause, my mother leaped up and dashed out the front door and down the steps to greet them.

The two years we'd been apart from my grandparents meant there was much to catch up on. My mother and I temporarily moved out of Baba's home to stay with them in the Ambassador Hotel in downtown Jerusalem.

"Good morning, shugar *shuuug*!" my grandmother would greet me in her deep southern accent each morning when I knocked at the door of their hotel room.

Each day she presented me with a small package wrapped in white tissue paper in which was a delicate new doll from a different European country they'd visited. The rest of the day, while I was taken to Baba's house, my mother and grandparents toured the Old City and other points of interest around Jerusalem, accompanied by my uncles. My Arab aunts were struck by my American grandparents' boundless stamina and curiosity to discover their new surroundings. In turn, my grandparents marveled at the bountiful lunches my aunts and Om Hassan prepared for them each day when they returned—the rolled grape leaves and stuffed zucchini and eggplant, roast lamb, and the variety of fresh plums, figs, apricots, and oranges for dessert.

We were all driven down to the Dead Sea one evening, the usual time Arabs ventured to Jericho to swim, away from the searing summer sun and heat. Tall date palms and lush citrus and banana groves lined both sides of the Jericho road leading to the sea. After setting out a picnic dinner of cheese, bread, and watermelon, the adults swam in the dark, still water. My most vivid memory of that night is of my grandmother holding me on her lap to soothe me as I wailed from the sulfuric salt water burning my eyes and skin.

My grandparents and my mother even made an arduous six-hour drive through the Jordan desert to Petra, the isolated, millennia-old Nabatean city. For centuries the rose-red city carved into towering red rocks had been mostly hidden from the outside world, except for the nomads living in the surrounding caves. In the 1950s, there were still very few Western tourists who made the trip there.

My mother and grandparents returned with vivid colored photos of entering the ancient city on muleback through the high, narrow crack in the red stone and of the gigantic Nabatean stone monuments and the rugged Bedouins.

NOW THAT MY father had finished preparing for my mother's and my arrival in Kuwait, he came to Jerusalem to fetch us back with him to our new home. My grandparents would briefly leave us to resume their trip for another month through Egypt and Morocco before meeting up with us again in Kuwait.

When it was time to leave them, I cried. By then, I was

familiar with what parting meant, and I was inconsolable at the idea I'd be separated from them yet again. I was learning departure meant loss, as I had lost Zena and my dogs. It seemed my life was piling up with saying goodbyes.

My grandmother comforted me with hugs and kisses before she left. She reminded me how exciting our new move would be. And she had a few important instructions.

"You promise to help Mommy and Daddy get everything ready for our arrival and not have any windows for me to wash once I get there?" she asked, coaxing a reluctant giggle and a promise out of me through my tears.

I nodded, still not convinced about this new journey to Kuwait, despite my parents' puzzling eagerness.

nine

Kuwait, 1958

A WEEK LATER, MY FATHER LEANED OVER TO POINT FROM the airplane window next to me.

"Look down there, Kathy. Do you see the sandbox I have for you? There it is—a great big sandbox just waiting for you!"

"Where?" I peered out but couldn't see anything remotely like a sandbox. Only an endless sweep of beige flatness below.

I kept looking for a defined, marked-off little square; one I imagined was painted a bright red or blue and filled with plastic molds and a spade, like the sandboxes I'd played in before. As the plane swooped closer to the ground, tiny moving cars and trucks glided on long black threads crisscrossing the vastness. No matter how hard I strained to locate anything resembling a sandbox, I was unable to. My excitement grew into impatience. Surely, I could see it if I kept looking!

"It's all of that," my father finally said, proudly gesturing to the vast landscape below. From now on, I'd be surrounded by an endless amount of it to play in, he explained. *That* was my new sandbox.

I'm certain my father had no idea how disappointed I'd been by this innocent deception, or how eagerly I'd been looking forward to a simple box big enough to have sand and plastic toys to make pies with. I was six. Being offered an entire desert to play in meant nothing to me.

To make things worse, during the two-hour plane ride, someone sitting in the row behind us reached between our seats several times and gently pulled a bit of my hair. When I turned around to see who was doing this, I saw a figure cloaked from head to toe in black, including a black mask around the eyes and nose.

"Mommy, is it the Lone Ranger?" I asked in surprise.

My mother smiled. "No, honey," she said softly, "it's just a lady who's curious about your hair color."

The hot wind blew on my face as we descended the plane's metal staircase and walked across the tarmac toward the small, sand-colored airport terminal. Our new home. Kuwait. None of my aunts in Jerusalem had heard of Kuwait. I now understood. It was in the middle of nowhere.

IN THE EARLY 1700s, nomadic clans from Saudi Arabia moved upward and settled around a fishing village that was to become Kuwait City. Having one of the best natural harbors in the Persian Gulf, Kuwait, over the next two centuries, became a commercial center for the transit of goods between India, Muscat, Baghdad, and Arabia, all the way to Aleppo, Syria.

It also became a boatbuilding center. Kuwaiti sailors became known as the best in the area, and demand for the delicate, coveted Kuwaiti pearls grew internationally. The British East India Company soon secured trade routes between India, Kuwait, and the east coast of Africa. In 1899, Kuwait beame a British protectorate to guard its independence from the encroaching Ottoman Empire.

In the first decades of the twentieth century, Kuwait's elite merchant families prospered from trading, shipbuilding, and pearling. The ruling Al-Sabah family, one of the tribes that originally migrated from Saudi Arabia, retained the country's political power, offering protection and political stability within the walled seaside city in exchange for income and taxes from the wealthy merchants.

But the worldwide economic depression of the early twentieth century halted the demand for goods traded through Kuwait. The country eventually became impoverished. Many of its leading families were forced to move elsewhere.

Then, in 1938, a British–American company drilling for oil under black patches of desert sand hit a gush. The black liquid flowed. And it flowed.

By 1952, Kuwait had become the largest oil exporter in the Persian Gulf. The new oil income enabled the ruling Al-Sabah clan to free itself from economic dependency on the merchants. To accommodate the burgeoning oil boom, the government initiated a massive public works program that attracted thousands of foreign workers to the country.

Several years earlier, an American company, Aminoil, had been granted by the Kuwaiti government a concession to explore for and extract oil and natural gas in Kuwait's Neutral Zone—a deserted area in the south that the country shared with Saudi Arabia. By 1958, Aminoil was operating a productive refinery in an isolated, seaside compound called Mina Abdullah. My father was sent to work in this new administrative and residential compound.

All was blinding bright sun and heat as we drove from the sand-colored city into the endless desert toward our new home, Mina Abdullah. *Mina* means "port" in Arabic. Mina Abdullah, or Abdullah's port, was named for the ruling Sheikh of Kuwait, Abdullah Al-Salim Al-Sabah.

Beige sand stretched in all directions to the horizon without a single hill, tree, or building anywhere in sight. Our only companion as we drove down the sole road was a thick black pipe snaking its way alongside us. Each time I looked out the window, the black pipe was still there.

"That's a pipeline," my father explained. "It carries oil to the refinery."

After our hour-long drive, a huge ball of fire appeared on the ground in the distance beside several tall metallic structures.

"That's the refinery and that's the flare," my father said proudly, as we drew closer to the buildings and the roiling fire. "The flare keeps burning off all the extra oil from the refinery."

We came to a guard post with a long pole that was lifted to let us drive into the fenced-in compound. As we passed the shiny towers of the refinery, I couldn't understand my father's excitement to be here. All I could see from the car's windows was sand, heat, and fire, with nothing green or beautiful to look at like the cherry trees and flowers we'd left behind in our Tehran garden or even the white stone houses on the Mount of Olives. So far, this was the strangest, bleakest landscape I'd ever seen.

As head local personnel officer, my father had been assigned one of eight identical, beige brick bungalows in the compound, newly built for the senior expat American execu-

tives and engineers. Ours was the third in the row, newly furnished with rattan furniture and appliances from the United
States.

The modest bungalows were not like our two-story
Tehran house with its view of the snowcapped mountains and
its formidable outer wall enclosing the fragrant fruit trees,
swimming pool, and driveway lined with yellow-and-purple
pansies. These houses stood a mere few yards apart from
each other, separated only by sand. In back of each house
was a cement patio. Ours had a low brick wall my father had
built to partition off a garden for my mother.

"Jean, I had a load of brown planting soil mixed into the
sand so you can plant your flowers," my father said with a
smile.

My mother appraised the brownish soil. "I love it!"

Beyond, on the horizon, was a wide, glittering sheet of
blue-green sea.

"That's the Persian Gulf, Kathy," my father explained.

OUR NEW HOUSE had two bedrooms, a bathroom, and a living
room with an attached dining room opening onto the small
kitchen. There was also a sunroom overlooking the patio.

I stared out the window and frowned at the vast swath of
sand—my sandbox—dotted with tufts of foot-high straw
grasses my father called "camel grass." The only other plants
were the dusty pink and white oleander bushes planted
around the houses. I missed our trees in Tehran and the cool
of their shade where I had played with Akbar while his father,
Abbas, raked around the vibrant beds of pansies, strawberries,
and vegetables.

Instead of Zena to help take care of the house and cook the Iranian dishes I loved, there was a taciturn houseboy named Ali, a Kuwaiti of Persian extraction, whose eyes drooped gloomily downward. He wore a white shirt and trousers and a white headdress flung about his head, the way my mother wrapped her towel after washing her hair. In addition to vacuuming and mopping twice a day, Ali would dust the shelves and tables, clucking in exasperation at the never-ending accumulation of fine sand on everything.

My mother appeared ecstatic. As she had in Tehran, she set about making our new surroundings feel like home. Since the house was already furnished, she began to conquer the outside by creating flower beds around the patio and planting seeds of marigolds, zinnias, petunias, and snapdragons from bright little packets. Each morning, before the sun got too strong, she would slip on her gardening pants and broad-brimmed straw hat and kneel, spade in hand, to dig, plant, and water the small seeds with the brown, brackish water from the garden hose.

With no natural freshwater springs under the sand, the Kuwaiti government had embarked on a large desalination project from seawater, so there was plenty of brown, brackish water for washing and watering the garden. The water wasn't directly drinkable, and at first it was dismaying to see our white shirts and underwear taking on a brownish tinge after being laundered. But the sight of the sprouting seeds burrowing up through the sand in my mother's flower beds made the brackish water precious and appreciated.

By now I'd forgotten my disappointment about the absent sandbox, especially since we had our very own beach only a short distance away. Late in the afternoon of my second day in Mina Abdullah, our next-door neighbor, Hugh Smith, took me there. Hugh was a stout Texan who always wore a cowboy hat and pointy-toed cowboy boots and strutted, teetering slightly side to side. His son, Erik, a skinny boy a few months younger than me, had white-blond hair cut in a short crew cut.

"Let's go, Kathy," Hugh Smith said in a gentle drawl as he handed me a beach towel.

I'd never been to a beach before. A few minutes' walk across the desert brought us to a large stretch of warm, soft sand to pillow my toes. The water, gray blue in the late afternoon, had at low tide seeped back to a mere few inches deep. The water had drawn so far away from the shore that entire reefs of mossy coral, like brown cotton wool, lay exposed, interspersed with large sandbars. It smelled salty and fetid, its scent mixing with the putrid odor of the refinery.

"Step carefully," Mr. Smith said, taking my hand as he, Erik, and I picked our way over the moss-covered rocks to get to the smooth sandbars and clear water beyond.

Once across the rocks, Erik and I raced around the soft sandbars playing tag.

"Erik, Kathy," Mr. Smith called, "let's build some sand-castles."

He showed us how to scoop up fistfuls of wet sand and let them trickle out of our hands in towering, wet spirals. The warm breeze blew as Erik and I knelt and oozed the soggy sand out of our closed palms. The sun sank low behind the refinery in the opposite direction from the shore, spilling its red-and-pink haze across the horizon. It was as though the giant flare had suddenly set everything on fire. I was beginning to see the fun of being here. Amid the beach and open spaces, it could be a wonderful place to play.

Beyond our compound's barbed-wire fence and guarded entry post near the refinery, endless open space was dotted with raised ridges of camel grass all the way to the flat line of the horizon. I would occasionally see a few dark tents appear outside the guard post. Sometimes there'd be a large American car parked alongside the tent and a few children tending black goats and woolly beige sheep.

"Who are those people, Daddy?" I asked the first time we drove past them.

"Bedouins," he said. "They live in the desert."

"Don't they have houses?"

"Their tents are their houses," my father replied. "They don't want to live inside a house."

"But it's so hot," I said, sorry for the children who couldn't come inside to an air-conditioned house like ours.

"They're used to it," my father said, with a reassuring smile. "In their tents they feel free."

The next day, these Bedouins would disappear without a trace. People, tents, sheep, and car—gone. As if they'd evaporated into the hot air.

Outside the compound, the lone black road that had brought us here ran parallel to the sea. It connected us back to Kuwait City, an hour away, as well as to the closer seaside villages of Shuaiba and Fahaheel and the larger inland town of Ahmadi. This road also continued in the other direction beyond our compound where there were no farther towns or villages, only desolate beaches and a few private beach houses belonging to various sheikhs of the ruling Al-Sabah family who went there on weekends to fish or relax.

ONE NIGHT IN our new house in Mina Abdullah, after my
mother had drawn my bathwater, and I'd taken off my clothes
to step into the tub, I was suddenly overcome by dizzying
thoughts that the world would one day end. There would be
nothing in it at all. No *us*. Not my parents or my grandparents
. . . nothing. Perhaps it was the new place itself—the vast,
barren desert—along with the huge change in my life, which
caused me to think, *One day even I will not be here. I'll be
dead. I'm going to die. Mommy and Daddy are going to die
too.* I tried to picture what the world would be like with none
of us here. Only total emptiness everywhere. The thought was
so strange and terrifying that I felt my head would explode. I
started to cry hysterically.

My mother rushed into the bathroom.

"What's wrong, Kathy?"

"You and Daddy are going to die!"

"Honey," she said, softly. "Nobody's going to die for a
very, very long time. There's no need to be afraid."

I kept sobbing. Hearing the commotion, my father came
into the bathroom.

"What's wrong?" he asked, looking worried.

I blurted out my fears again. Seeing my mother was getting
nowhere with her reassurances, he tried to soothe me himself.
But I was crying so loud I could barely hear a word he said.

Finally losing patience, he snapped at me, "Kathy, stop
this nonsense right now!"

I eventually got into the tub, still shaking in terror of
what was to come.

For some reason, neither of my parents seemed upset by

the terrifying knowledge that our lives would someday end. That there would only be a huge, meaningless void instead of our current life. Was I the only one with these fears? How could they not be afraid of their—and my—death? Why were they so sure that everything would be all right, even though we would all be gone? We would be nothing. *Nothing.* Didn't they care for me as much as I did for them? I couldn't fathom losing them. How could they be okay with losing *me*?

Looking back, I understand my parents' frustration with trying to calm their high-strung child's newly discovered awareness of death. They had no real answer to give to reassure me. Yet their lack of acknowledging my fears that night made me feel I was suffocating. More than ever, I sensed I was alone.

ERIK SMITH'S PARENTS were older than mine. His mother, Pat, a Texan like her husband, already had a deeply lined face. She was tall and, like my mother, had a southern accent, but her voice was deep and gravelly. She and my mother became close friends.

At Erik's house, I first tasted chili con carne, which Erik requested from his mother nearly every night. Pat would open a can of Chef Boyardee chili, and out spilled ground meat and brown beans in a spicy brown sauce. After heating it up, she spooned some in a bowl for each of us and gave us some saltine crackers to go with it. I savored the cumin and chili powder spicing the velvety beans. It tasted almost as delicious as Zena's *adas polow*.

There were a few other children besides Erik and me living in our row of eight houses. Since I was the oldest, though by only a few months, I assumed leadership, deciding what and where we would play and who would be on each other's teams.

Then, that summer, the most exciting thing happened: the arrival on our street of several American teenagers visiting their parents from their boarding schools in Switzerland and the United States. Immediately, the quiet road of our drab Mina Abdullah compound came alive with the roaring, sporty cars of teenage boys and pretty young girls in bright clothes and sunglasses riding beside them. They were a species unto themselves, neither adults nor children, bursting with energy. They whizzed down the tar-paved road of our compound as though they owned the desert, oblivious to us children and too removed from our lives to acknowledge or interact with us.

I watched in fascination as they came out of their houses in the cool of the late afternoons, their laughter spreading across the sand to where Erik and I played. I was certain I'd never seen a teenager before, certainly nobody who acted this boldly and inhabited such a splendid, magical world. There was something magnetic about their imperious confidence as they proudly sped by us.

These teenagers' exuberance at being in Mina Abdullah echoed my own growing feelings that life here wouldn't be so bad after all. We could roam between each other's houses unsupervised, play outside where there wasn't much traffic, and swim in our own private sea. I was beginning to see, in these few early weeks in Kuwait, there were exciting adventures to be found despite the dreary sand and smelly refinery, as though we could mold our new home into whatever we wanted it to be.

ten

Shuaiba

AS MY GRANDMOTHER HAD PROMISED, A FEW WEEKS AFTER
we'd settled in Mina Abdullah, she and my grandfather and
the Volkswagen they called "Trek" arrived on a freighter from
Africa. They planned to stay for a month or two to help us
settle in before resuming their trip.

The tan Volkswagen was the exact color of the desert, a
little ball rolling along the road as my grandfather immediately
set about running errands for my mother to the nearby food
markets and Indian-run stores in Shuaiba and Fahaheel. Our
backyard patio had finally been emptied of the large wooden
crates from our household shipment from Tehran, but one
crate had been purposely left in the yard so Grandy could
build me a playhouse. With my father's help, my grandfather
turned the crate upside down and sawed open a door and a
window. He hammered and painted for a few days until I had
my own perfect retreat on one side of the patio. Inside my
"house," I could be in charge of everything, inviting my
friends in to play house or school, the small, confined space
making me feel I had finally set down roots in Kuwait. The
arid desert was beginning to replace the green gardens of
Tehran as my concept of where I wanted to be.

Once September came and it was time for the school year to start, my mother made a decision that would forever impact my life. She gave me the means to truly enter the Arab world. With no formal English schools nearby, the parents of the other American children in Mina Abdullah homeschooled their children in the Calvert Correspondence Course based out of Baltimore, Maryland. Although there was a small British school in Ahmadi, a twenty-minute drive away, most American parents wanted their children to study an American curriculum to be able to adapt when they returned to the United States. My mother, however, wanted me to also learn Arabic. Knowing I'd never learn my father's language at home where we spoke only English, she decided to put the Calvert lessons aside for a while and enroll me in the public Kuwaiti girls' school in the seaside village of Shuaiba, a ten-minute drive from our compound.

Besides being home to the village's indigenous Kuwaiti fishermen and pearl divers, Shuaiba, a village of mud and cement houses, was now the regional port for the oil tankers. It was also home to some expatriates working in the various oil companies. There was an older, walled compound on the sea built before our Mina Abdullah compound to house Aminoil's employees who worked at the port and on the oil tankers. Indian and Pakistani merchants operated the village's laundry, tailor, and grocery shops.

I started my first day of Arabic school on a blistering September morning in an old cement building in the middle of the village. The rooms were barely cooled by open windows and whirling ceiling fans. Since there were as yet no female Kuwaiti teachers, the teachers were Palestinian women from towns near Jerusalem, hired on work contracts by the Kuwaiti government. They were housed in the school, under the protection and strict supervision of the Kuwait Department of Education. They mostly kept to themselves, not mingling with the Shuaiba villagers.

My parents and the headmistress took me to my classroom that first morning. All the girls looked so different from me with their amber skin and jet-black hair. Except for the teachers, nobody at the school spoke any English, and despite my visits to Jerusalem to visit my father's family, my Arabic was still weak. To make it more confusing, the Kuwaiti dialect the other girls spoke sounded very different from the Palestinian Arabic I was accustomed to.

Terrified of being alone among strangers, and unable to understand or communicate with my classmates, I broke down in tears. Seeing my fear, at recess the classroom teacher summoned a tall older girl with a long ponytail to take me around the schoolyard by the hand.

"Shh, shh," the girl said gently, patting my head.

Although she couldn't have been more than fourteen, since the school only went up to the eighth grade, to me she seemed enormously tall and grown-up.

"I want to go home," I said tearfully, clinging to her for safety.

"Shh," she whispered, not understanding me, as she fed me glazed animal crackers from a box to keep me from crying.

The school's headmistress was a short, middle-aged woman from Nablus, a town not far from Jerusalem. When she came into our classroom after recess, the girls stood up and were silent. Sit (Miss) Abu-Ghazaleh was always referred to by her last name because of her status as headmistress. She clumped into our classroom, the click of her high heels on the stone tile alerting us before she appeared. Her short, black hair and bangs accentuated her overall square body.

After greeting us, she took two pieces of chalk, one yellow and one pink, in her right hand and wrote out our first lesson on the blackboard: *D-A* in Arabic. Da da. Unlike English, she wrote from right to left, the colored pieces of chalk swirling in parallel unison like a rainbow, screeching across the blackboard to form the short, pretty word. She sounded out the letters *d,* which looked like half a triangle, and *a,* which was a straight line pointing up, and then told us to repeat it after her. The bright letters were left to dance on the blackboard all morning. I tried to memorize the word so I could draw it at home to show my parents.

Our classroom teacher, Sit Salwa, was a soft-spoken young woman with light-brown hair so long it double-coiled around itself in a ropelike ponytail. I was fascinated by her hairstyle and wanted to describe it to my mother so she could fix my hair like that. After our classwork was done, Sit Salwa took down the board game Snakes and Ladders from the shelf and gathered us around her.

"Katty," she said, "you can play first." She and the girls called me Katty, which was easier for them to pronounce than "Kathy" with the "th," but I was too shy to correct them.

After several days, though, the alluring novelty of the headmistress's handwriting and Sit Salwa's pretty ponytail wore off. Since I could barely communicate with the other girls, having to sit and listen in the hot classroom became frustrating and tedious. I went from being afraid of the new school to being angry at my mother for putting me there.

"I'm not going to that school anymore!" I shouted when I got home, stomping into the kitchen where she was making lunch. "All they ever speak is Arabic! And they call me Katty!"

My mother stared at me. Despite her blue eyes softening, she dismissed my sullen mood with a good-natured chuckle. "Well, you'd better learn to speak it quick or you're going to feel pretty stupid."

I glared at her. "I won't go back!"

I was furious at her refusal to acknowledge the isolation I'd been through the past few days. She didn't seem to empathize with how lonely I felt, and instead of being concerned that I was floundering, she seemed certain I'd adapt, just as she would have. Rather than feeling confident from her expectation that I would manage to adjust, I was upset she didn't have to go through what I endured at school each day. She never seemed to understand that I was so different from her. I wanted to be like her, brave and strong. But I just wasn't.

SOME WEEKS LATER, our Shuaiba school was swept up in an exciting event. We moved! Instead of the drab gray building in the center of the hot village, our school was now housed in a new complex on the turquoise beach next door to a new boys' school. The new building had two floors. The classrooms and dining room were downstairs, and the teachers' living quarters were upstairs. It was an airy, fairy-tale confection with an outward facade of bold pink-and-blue cement latticework. It didn't look like a school at all. Outside and facing the sea was a dirt playground where we could draw hopscotch squares with a rock, play tag, or link arms with each other as we walked and chanted out the day's lessons to memorize them.

When the morning bell rang, we'd line up in rows of two,

according to the pink-and-white square tiles of the central courtyard. We'd sing the Kuwaiti national anthem, accompanied by a teacher playing the accordion, after which we'd lower our eyes to recite the Islamic *Fatiha* prayer. Then, we held out our hands as the teachers walked down the rows of girls to make sure our nails were clean and trimmed. The teachers also confirmed that our blue-and-white-checked uniforms were clean and pressed and our hair was tied back or braided with crisp, white ribbons. Finally, we were led away row by row to our classrooms.

Once a week, the teachers poked around our scalps with pencils for any signs of lice or their nits, immediately sending off any girl found to have them to the bathroom to have her hair fumigated. Several times a week a girl would be crouching in a corner of the bathroom, her hair saturated with smelly disinfectant. I'd shudder at her shame.

Each midmorning, I looked forward to filing into the dining room with my classmates for a bowl of cumin-scented lentil soup, along with a choice of a cheese or jam sandwich and a piece of fruit for dessert. We ravenously slurped the warm, fragrant soup ladled into tin cups by Abu Omar, the round-bellied cook. Two Shuaiba village women, in loose robes and long head shawls, were hired to clean the school and assist him.

The rules of the school were strict. Along with teaching the curriculum, the teachers considered it their duty to enforce stringent discipline. I was horrified to find the punishment for not memorizing our lessons or completing our homework was a brisk slap on our open palms with a wooden ruler. The scowling teachers didn't hesitate to dispense these raps, and I watched in fear each time the ruler slammed down on a girl's open palm.

When I told my mother of these punishments, she looked surprised but didn't appear concerned. She even told me of a time when her teacher back in Old Hickory had doled out a similar punishment on a rowdy classmate. What she didn't tell me then was that my parents had made it clear to the headmistress on my first day that no teacher was to ever lay a hand on me. Even when the entire class was meted out a summary punishment of a slap with the ruler for whatever misbehavior we'd cumulatively been accused of, the teacher would pass me by and mumble, "You didn't take part in this, Katty, did you?"

"No, miss," I'd answer sheepishly.

Even though I knew I wouldn't be punished, I was riddled with guilt at being singled out. I was grateful for being saved by my parents, but being treated differently from my friends deepened my sense of isolation. Although I accepted I wouldn't be touched by any of the teachers, I still flinched whenever the ruler came down on a girl's palm, wanting to run and put my arms around her to protect her.

AT FIRST, MY grandfather drove me to school each morning in Trek. Tall, robust Grandy loaded me and my book satchel into the Volkswagen. Dressed in shorts and a sleeveless white undershirt for the heat, as though he were in Tennessee, he drove me from Mina Abdullah to Shuaiba. Only interminable desert stretched between our compound and the village—sand and camel grass, home to black scorpions, honey-colored camel spiders, and iguana-like lizards. The Bedouins outside their black tents stared at us as we sped by in the little egg-shaped car.

Back and forth my grandfather and I went as he dropped me off to school each morning and picked me up each early afternoon, to the gleeful curiosity of my Arab schoolmates— and my embarrassment—at his exposed pale skin in shorts and undershirt. Except for the bare-chested fishermen wearing long loincloths, the Kuwaiti men wore *dishdashas,* the men's white cotton robes that covered their entire bodies.

When my grandparents left Kuwait a month after I started school, they bequeathed my mother their Volkswagen. They had no more use for the little car now that they were continuing their expedition for another month through the Far East on their homeward journey back to Tennessee. They had one final stop planned in Honolulu to visit my grandmother's cousin Nora Hampton, whose husband, John, had been relocated there by the Marine Corps from the Pentagon in Washington.

For years, my grandmother, like her daughter, had wanted to explore beyond Tennessee. She and my grandfather had considered moving to Mexico once he sold his dental practice. But Grandy had suffered a stroke the year before he retired, which required they live within reach of more reliable medical facilities. Hawaii immediately captured my grandmother's heart on that homeward trip. After some deliberation, they decided to take up residency in Honolulu.

Over the next few years, our contact with Tennessee would almost entirely cease, other than my mother's tireless correspondence with her extended family there. Our new American "home" was now officially Honolulu, where we would travel each summer to visit my grandparents during my father's month-long home leave.

With my grandfather gone, a company driver was assigned to drive me to and from Shuaiba each day. Although by now I'd learned to speak passable Kuwaiti Arabic, living in the Mina Abdullah compound where only employees and outsiders with special permits were allowed to enter, I was still an outsider in Shuaiba. I was the only red-haired and half-American girl in the school, and I was not a part of the village life of my friends. I never got to walk home with the other girls who lived along those dusty alleys, purchase groceries from the stores, or pick up the family's laundry from the Indian-run laundry shops like they did. Chauffeured alone in the air-conditioned car between the Arab village and our isolated Western compound, I inhabited a cocoon. Each day as I was driven away from school in the car, I watched enviously as my classmates clustered together to walk home, linking arms or stopping at the store to buy something. I had very few girls to play with in Mina Abdullah, and I wanted to belong to the group of Shuaiba friends I could visit in the afternoons after school.

My mother, too, was totally different from the other mothers of my Shuaiba school friends who, with the exception of the mothers of a few Lebanese and Palestinian girls, were Kuwaiti. When it was time at the end of the school term to put on our first school performance, all of the mothers were asked to attend. Parents were rarely seen at our school, so we eagerly anticipated having our mothers come to our play.

We'd been rehearsing for weeks. The girls in the upper classes were to perform a traditional dance in honor of the fishermen who spent grueling months at sea diving for oysters from which to extract the prized Kuwaiti pearls. The older girls wore festive sequined gowns and swayed back and forth as they sang of lonely days at sea, mimicking the rocking of the boats. Periodically, they threw their heads forward in a rhythmic shake, their luxuriant, long black hair falling toward the floor.

We first graders were putting on a performance about plants to show what we'd learned in science class. Our teacher made us costumes out of crepe paper, and each of us had to sing a short song about a certain kind of flower, dressed in a costume the color of the particular blossom. Because I was tall, I was chosen to be the stem and leaf, my costume a deep green. My friend Mariam, a Lebanese girl with dark hair and ruddy cheeks, was to be a red rose. We had rehearsed our lines for days on the school's dining room stage. Our teachers were as enthusiastic as we were to show off our accomplishments and their hard work.

On the afternoon of the performance, the long tables in the dining room were removed and the chairs set up in rows facing the stage. We nervously rushed about backstage, the teachers shushing us to maintain order. A few of my friends stuck their heads out from behind the heavy curtains and announced they'd seen someone's mother. Finally, I took a peek from behind the curtain.

The sunny dining room had transformed into a sea of inky black. The mothers were all sitting quietly, wearing silken black abayas that covered their heads and draped around their bodies. Some were wearing the Zorro-like black or gold-colored masks, *yashmaks,* that covered their eyes and noses, as if they were attending a masquerade ball. Since there were only women present, some had let their abayas drop to their shoulders, revealing their shiny black hair. By now, I was accustomed to seeing the women in the Shuaiba roads dressed in abayas and yashmaks, with only their eyes visible, so this masked display no longer surprised me.

As my gaze darted along the rows, I spotted my mother in a bright, sleeveless dress sitting between two darkly clad women. Although aware of the conservative mode of Shuaiba and of our school, she hadn't covered up her arms like the other women. Mothers of my Palestinian and Lebanese friends didn't cover their hair or wear abayas, and some of our teachers also wore shorter sleeves in the heat. But none of them had my mother's pale, freckled limbs or red hair, now brazenly exposed. Among the ebony-haired, amber-faced mothers of my school friends sitting on either side of her, my mother's hair blazed as her crystal-blue eyes gazed ahead. There was no question whose mother she was!

She smiled up at the stage, utterly at ease. Despite my initial embarrassment, I couldn't help being swept with a feeling of pride at my mother's obvious lack of discomfort at being so uniquely different from everyone else in the room. I admired her. I yearned to be like her, unapologetic, courageous, and free of shame, doing as I wished without worrying about what others might think. Yet I also desperately wanted to fit in and be exactly like all the other girls.

Finally, my excitement overtook me, and I reached out my hand and waved to her, acknowledging I'd seen her. I was her daughter.

Whenever Paul Anka's song "Diana" is played, it's once again 1959, and I'm nearly eight years old, watching a teenage girl and her boyfriend dancing rock and roll to those poignant words of unrequited love. When my childhood friends and I listen to the song on our small portable record players, our shoulders and heads irrepressibly sway to the beat. I'm sad to hear Paul can't love Diana because he's only fifteen and she is several years older—too old for him.

But along with the sadness for his plight, there is also a feeling of wonder, a breathless anticipation of what lies ahead for me—when I'm old enough to dance rock and roll with a teenage boy who loves me as much as Paul loves Diana. I can still feel that moment of childhood and giddy exhilaration. There is so much mystery and excitement that lies ahead for me. Through the popular songs we play and dance to, I start to get a glimpse of my future and all the coming joys that await me.

eleven

My World Expands

TOWARD THE END OF THE SCHOOL YEAR, A NEW GIRL MOVED into the house next door to us. Cynthia Dawson was the daughter of Eugene Dawson, the new general manager of Aminoil, and Ray Dawson, a woman with auburn hair even deeper than my mother's. Like Pat, Erik's mother, Ray was older than my mother. The three women became good friends.

The family was from Long Beach, California, and Cynthia, at nine years old, displayed a confidence in herself as the senior girl in the compound, undermining my previous status as oldest of the children on the road.

"I'm a tomboy," she proudly proclaimed the moment we met.

"What's a tomboy?" I asked.

"I can do anything as good as a boy can," she answered.

This declaration of male strength further anointed her with the status of being our new leader. Being like a boy was of supreme importance, even though I'd always regarded Erik, a real boy but younger than me, as less skillful than me at many things.

Cynthia had short brown hair, olive skin, and velvet, doe eyes. She, Erik, and I now formed a trio, playing at our three houses, constantly reconfiguring our shifting alliances—two ganging up on the third—depending on our mood. I soon followed Cynthia's tomboy example, wearing the most boyish clothing I had and shunning anything girlish.

Occasionally, Cynthia would do an about-face, deciding on a whim that we'd be "sophisticated." She'd insist we sit with our legs crossed in prissy poses or practice walking with books balanced on our heads to develop good posture. Whenever we began our sophisticated phases, Erik was shunned. Feeling guilty, we'd include him in our game for a while. But it wasn't long before we were once again casting him off and sequestering ourselves in girlie things.

I never questioned these whimsical reversals of Cynthia's. Perhaps I enjoyed this first notion of the differences between the sexes or the variety of aliases we could assume or else being happy to have a sole link to Cynthia that Erik couldn't be part of. Yet I felt somewhat confused whenever we changed roles, often preferring to be a tomboy rather than girlish, with its implication of girls being less tough than boys. I already knew from my Arabic school that boys were off-limits to us girls. To Arabs, there was something powerful and special about being a boy. But I also loved dressing up and being girlie, with its implication that we were objects to be admired.

Erik and I were each only children, but Cynthia had a younger brother, Roger, who was a year old and just learning to walk. I was fascinated by his curly brown hair and baby talk and enjoyed taking turns with Cynthia holding his hands and coaxing him forward as he teetered along.

I tried to copy Cynthia in almost everything. I was introduced to an array of different foods I'd never tasted before, like corn tortillas and beans, something her mother made for her and showed me how to eat with the beans rolled up in the soft tortilla. She ate these a lot in California, Cynthia told me. I found the taste of the corn tortilla intriguing, unlike any other bread I'd tasted. But I wasn't sure I liked it.

Since we weren't allowed to go to the beach by ourselves, the three of us ambled in the opposite direction across the sand toward the refinery to a large, lone tree. The tree's wide, ancient trunk seemed to have sprung spontaneously from the ground eons ago. It possessed a reverent, mystical quality. Unlike our relatively new compound with its refinery, modern houses, and newly planted oleanders, this tree appeared to have been in that spot forever, intrinsic to the desert like the Bedouins and the camel grass. It also bore tiny crab apples, which we enjoyed eating. We'd head for the tree, sit on its sturdy, gnarled trunk, and make believe it was our fort. Since I wasn't good at climbing high like Cynthia or Erik could, I perched on the part of the crooked trunk that formed a natural ledge, content to collect and munch on the tiny fallen fruit at its base. The tree symbolized a reassuring permanence and I latched onto it, finding it a welcoming anchor binding us to this place that was now our home.

SOON ENOUGH, CYNTHIA and I had a real-life, sophisticated role model to emulate. Donnie Dinkle was one of the teenagers who descended like deities on Mina Abdullah from their Swiss boarding schools each Christmas, Easter, and summer. We couldn't wait for these vacations when the teenagers suddenly showed up in our compound. The boys with their slicked-back hair looked like Ricky Nelson, Elvis Presley, and Paul Anka, the teen idols Cynthia introduced me to through her records.

Donnie was fifteen, with snow-white skin and black hair to her chin styled in a flip. Even the usually cynical Cynthia was mesmerized. We'd knock on Donnie's front door, and she would allow us to watch her curl her hair, apply her makeup, or simply read a book. Everything she did was graceful, and Cynthia and I followed her around her house like worshipping devotees, copying her every move. Donnie didn't object to our hanging around her so much. Our expatriate community was tightly knit, like one big family, so nobody, including Donnie, would have thought it strange that two little neighbor girls visited her so often.

One evening, we were allowed to stay at Donnie's later than usual while she got dressed to go to a party with her boyfriend, Kelly. Kelly also attended the American boarding school in Switzerland. A hulking boy of seventeen, he had a blond crew cut and drove a red MG convertible.

"Donnie and Kelly are going steady," Cynthia whispered to me.

"What's that?"

"They give each other rings and kiss a lot," Cynthia said, with a knowing nod.

When Donnie was ready to leave, dressed in a bare-shouldered yellow dress with a puffy skirt that accented her tiny waist, Cynthia and I ran to the Dinkles' doorway. We watched her walk down the cement sidewalk in her high heels, the breeze ruffling her skirt, sand gently blowing across her ankles. Kelly was waiting for her at the end of the sidewalk, parked in his MG. They were going to a party at the recreation club in Aminoil's Shuaiba compound.

Once, when I went to the recreation club with my parents, I saw Donnie and Kelly dancing rock and roll to a catchy song, "Be-Bop-a-Lula." At the end of the song, Kelly slipped his arm around Donnie and dipped her low. As she bent backward, her head nearly touched the floor, and her eyes closed as though she had fainted.

"Mommy!" I gasped.

My mother smiled. "They're just having fun," she said.

I couldn't stop staring at them. When Donnie stood back up and smoothed her hair, I wanted to run up to Kelly so he could dip me just the way he had her. But I just sat at the table with my parents while we finished dinner.

At nine, Cynthia was already aware of the American teenage world Donnie and her friends inhabited—that mysterious realm of near adulthood. Being a teenager seemed fascinating. Donnie was our goddess. To acquire her ethereal beauty and grace became our new obsession. I could already see myself wearing my hair in a flip like hers and being driven off in a red convertible by a young man with whom I was going steady. Someone with whom I'd dance rock and roll and who'd gallantly dip me as I closed my eyes in bliss, just as Donnie had.

When Donnie and the other teenagers went back to Switzerland, Cynthia and I were bereft. We moped. We were bored. We missed Donnie and the thrill spun around her, and we imagined she missed us. Finally, as the excitement of those summer weeks waned, Cynthia and I resumed our tomboy ways. Erik was once more admitted into our fold, part of our threesome bent on adventure.

Cynthia's revelations about teenage life opened up my world. Having led a relatively sheltered existence in Mina Abdullah and Shuaiba before her arrival, I now began to see my own potential as a future young woman. She knew all about the exciting things that would become part of our lives as American teenagers. I never questioned her expertise, grateful she considered me important enough to pass on her knowledge to.

EARLY IN SEPTEMBER, Erik, Cynthia, and I started English school through the Calvert Correspondence Course. I'd been attending my Arabic Shuaiba school for a year and was now going into second grade. Cynthia was going into fourth grade, and Erik was starting first. Our English school was also in Shuaiba, but unlike my large, multihued Arabic girls' school down the road, this school was in the Shuaiba Aminoil compound and was situated around the dining table of Mrs. Howe, the British wife of an Aminoil employee.

Mrs. Howe, a certified teacher, oversaw our lessons in the Calvert curriculum designed mainly for homeschooled American expats in the absence of formal American schools. The coursework was followed until the seventh or eighth grade, after which kids were sent away to Lebanon, Switzerland, or the United States for high school. The Calvert curriculum was especially useful for the children of the oil company employees who lived in trailer compounds near the oil rigs in remote parts of the Kuwait desert, such as Wafra and Mina Saud, where there weren't schools of any kind.

I enjoyed the relaxed environment of our English lessons, which I joined every day at lunchtime after my morning sessions at the Arabic school. The three of us worked at Mrs. Howe's table independently, each pursuing our own grade-level work and without the regimentation or strictness of my larger Arabic classes. Mrs. Howe was a kind woman who never lashed at our hands with rulers for not doing our homework; instead, she relied on a stern gaze to show her displeasure.

On our first day of class, Erik, Cynthia, and I sauntered into Mrs. Howe's house and, as coached by Cynthia, solemnly saluted her with raised palms, Indian style, saying, "Howe."

She smiled at us.

Then, we sang "The Battle of New Orleans" to her as Cynthia had taught Erik and me to—schooling us in tumultuous British–American history. We happily chanted that we'd caught the "bloody British" in the town of New Orleans.

"Well, then," Mrs. Howe said, with another stoic smile. "I suppose I'll have to make up a nasty little song about Americans for you now."

Later, when she gave us a break and served us tea in pretty English teacups along with warm, buttered toast spread with honey, I was ashamed of our earlier prank.

Because I only did about an hour of work with Mrs. Howe, the time I missed in English lessons had to be fortified by my mother's extra tutoring at home. She and I curled up in her bed in the afternoons, where she always retreated to read a book or do crossword puzzles before taking her nap. We'd go over my homework together. I read to her, and she constructed a history time line on a roll of paper, according to the instructions from Calvert, for me to study and memorize. We did arithmetic and read Greek mythology together, as well as stories from American history. The required testing was done each month by Mrs. Howe and was sent back to Baltimore for grading by our assigned teachers there.

The company driver drove Cynthia, Erik, and me to Shuaiba each morning in a minibus. He first picked me up at seven and dropped me off at the Arabic girls' school; then, an hour later, he picked up Erik and Cynthia and drove them to Mrs. Howe's. The driver returned to Shuaiba before noon to pick me up from the Arabic school and take me to Mrs. Howe's a few minutes away for another hour. Finally, he drove all three of us back to Mina Abdullah in time for a late lunch. It was much more fun to ride home from school with Cynthia and Erik on our own school bus.

One day, the driver was in a hurry to do other work and wanted to drop me off in front of Erik's house instead of my own. Erik's house was next door to mine, but I wanted to be considered important enough to be dropped off directly in front of my own house. I refused to get off at Erik's. I insisted the driver pull up in front of my house. When the driver refused, saying he had to get somewhere else, I started to cry. I walked into our house for lunch and told my parents the driver had dropped us off back at the entrance to Mina Abdullah near the refinery and guard post, a ten-minute walk away.

My parents were alarmed that a trusted driver had let children walk home alone so far and in the midday heat. When my father went back to the office that afternoon, he contacted the transportation department and insisted the driver be fired.

Later in the afternoon, my mother interrupted my play outside and called me into the living room. She asked me to relay again what had happened with the bus driver, and I again concocted the lie. Only this time, she told me my father had heard from the driver that I had been dropped off in front of the Smiths' house next door and not near the refinery as I'd claimed. When I admitted my lie, not having thought my bruised ego would cause such harm to our driver, my mother spanked me. Later, when my father came home, he spanked me. My fabrication had nearly cost a man his job.

Although I promised never to fib again, my father walked me down the road to Donnie Dinkle's house. Mr. Dinkle was in charge of Aminoil's transportation services, and since the bus driver was one of his employees, I was made to apologize to him in person at his front door. I blubbered an apology, eternally thankful that Donnie, my idol, was away at her boarding school and not a witness to my disgrace.

Mr. Dinkle, a kind-looking man, graciously accepted my apology. The lesson was learned. Truth and integrity were important in our family, and like the mouth washing with soap that was threatened if I ever spoke back to my parents or used bad language, the threat of a spanking and public humiliation if I ever strayed from the truth was a strong deterrent. Although we were a family of storytellers, there were to be strong limits put on the kind of inventive stories I was allowed to tell.

twelve

Sabha and Captain

LIVING IN OUT-OF-THE-WAY MINA ABDULLAH, THE ADULT expats had few recreational activities. The nearby towns had several cinemas that featured Indian or Egyptian films, which the expats didn't frequent. The club in Aminoil's Shuaiba compound showed American movies several times a week, held occasional dance parties, and had a canteen that served milkshakes and smoky American hamburgers. But other than swimming in the long stretch of beach with its shimmering water, there was not much else to do for amusement. So, my father and Erik's father came up with the idea of buying horses.

My father, eager to resume the riding he'd enjoyed in New Mexico and Tehran, put out the word they were interested in purchasing horses. Soon, some horse-breeding Bedouins near Saudi Arabia brought two to Mina Abdullah—a four-year-old red mare and a slightly older gray stallion. The mare was named Sabha, meaning "beautiful," for the broad streak of white down the center of her nose; she was tall, slender, and frisky, with a strength and speed that made her suitable only for experienced riders. My father was immediately smitten and picked the elegant mare. Hugh Smith acquired the stocky gray stallion and renamed him Captain.

They had a stable built for the horses, surrounded by a large pen topped with barbed wire. They called it the horse house. It was close enough that Cynthia, Erik, and I could run over there each afternoon to watch the newly installed animals feeding in their stalls or ambling around the pen. We admired the new riding gear that had been expressly ordered. For Hugh, there was a bulky, embossed Western saddle from Texas with covered stirrups that squeaked and smelled funny because the leather was so new . . . for my father, a lighter English saddle with open metal stirrups, like the ones he'd ridden in Tehran.

Two young cousins from Baluchistan, Iran, who were employed by Aminoil as houseboys, were soon hired to feed, groom, and exercise the horses. Jalal and Mohammad, slight in stature, were already expert horsemen in their village. Jalal was the handsomer of the two, with smooth, jet-black hair styled like Elvis's. When Jalal approached Sabha for the first time, gently slipping her bridle over her head and patting her affectionately on her neck, he spoke to her in Farsi in a soft, melodic, and romantic tone, as though he were speaking to a sweetheart.

Not bothering to saddle her, he sprang onto her bare back, his body coiled agile and elastic. With only the bridle to guide her and his legs gripping her belly, he cantered her around the pen a few times, leaning back as though relaxing into an easy chair. Sabha didn't resist his lead like she sometimes did with my father; whenever he slid the bridle's bit into her mouth, she would friskily jerk her head up, determined to resist all authority. Sabha seemed to hardly feel Jalal on her at all, intuitively submitting to his guidance, seeming to share some secret language only the two of them knew. Then, as though she'd sprouted wings, the mare was out of the pen's gate and galloping across the sand toward the beach with Jalal bent forward over her head, urging her on. It seemed at any moment the two of them would soar into the air. Erik, Cynthia, and I ran after them, whooping. We watched them disappear over a slight ridge and down onto the soft sand of the beach.

My father and Hugh began training Sabha and Captain to jump over horizontal jumping poles held on either side by special stands. It was thrilling to watch our fathers leaning forward on the leaping horses who seemed to catapult through the air to gingerly land on the ground beyond the pole. In home movies taken by my mother, my father and Hugh, both much taller and heftier than either Jalal or Mohammad, galloped across the sand on Sabha and Captain as each horse lurched forward to clear the wooden pole.

Both Hugh and my father were good riders, but when Jalal or Mohammad rode either horse, it was different. Whether riding them saddled or bareback, the Baluchis melded with the horses, their thighs soldered onto the animals' glistening coats. When Sabha lunged into her full gallop, both she and Jalal rocked to the same rhythm, as if they'd come out of the same womb.

The two cousins exercised Sabha and Captain daily, racing each other along the powdery beach. We could catch a glimpse of Jalal's and Mohammad's heads from the stables. Sabha invariably won, her neck straining forward, her tail jutting straight up behind her like a flag. Captain was no match for her ruthless lunging. Erik, Cynthia, and I would cheer them on, dreaming of riding like that someday on horses stretching their limbs like scissors to cut across the sand before them.

We were too inexperienced to ride unsupervised, and our parents had laid down specific instructions to Jalal and Mohammad that we were to be carefully monitored whenever we were around the horses. We were not allowed into the pen alone, for fear we'd get kicked. My father was especially aware of Sabha's strength, and I was only allowed to ride her if she was led on a training rope by *him*. But I secretly wanted to ride with Jalal, to hold onto his muscled torso on Sabha's back as she galloped across the wide sand, to feel I was an organic part of her just as he was. I began to fantasize that I would one day run away with him to his far-off village in Baluchistan, where we would ride horses all day long.

IN TIME, A few other expats got interested in raising rabbits and pigeons, which were also housed at the stable. We monitored and checked on which pigeons had laid eggs in their little wooden houses, and we petted the rabbits. Another neighbor got horse fever and acquired a slim filly a similar color to Sabha. Still too young to be ridden, the excitable young horse pranced skittishly around the pen, holding her head high, her unruly red mane whipping the air. We could imagine how it would be to ride her one day and were looking forward to the time when her owner deemed her old enough to break in and allow one of us children on her back.

One day, when Erik, Cynthia, and I reached the stable, we couldn't find the filly in the pen where she usually cantered or was led on a training rope by her owner. We wondered whether her owner had finally considered her ready to be ridden or whether Jalal or Mohammad had taken her down to the beach to give her a taste of wading in the cool sea, as they often did with Sabha and Captain.

"Jalal, where's the filly?" we asked when Jalal came out of the stall.

Jalal shook his head, his mouth twisting. "She is dead," he said softly.

I gasped. Cynthia, Erik, and I stared at each other.

In a sad voice, Jalal told us that while alone in the pen in the morning, the filly had caught her long mane in the barbed wire along the top of the fence and strangled. He and Mohammad had removed her limp carcass.

Tears welled in my eyes. I didn't know what to make of the fact that one moment something so lively and healthy was prancing around the pen and the next, dragged away, lifeless. I couldn't imagine this beautiful, younger version of Sabha, her head held high as she snorted and neighed, dying so senselessly. My heart tightened. It was my first experience of the death of a living thing I had come to know and care about and of the loss that followed. The sadness I saw on Jalal's face mirrored my own distress.

Over the past year, I'd learned to push my fears of death and oblivion out of my mind. My mother had told me none of us would die for a very long time. Her confident reassurances when responding to my anxious questions about death had made me feel safe. Perhaps, I'd begun to feel, my thoughts were exaggerated fears resulting from my overactive imagination. From my mother's nonchalant attitude, I had come to believe if something or someone did die, it would be a very rare thing and, most importantly, it wouldn't be any of us or anyone I loved. Yet here was evidence such deeply tragic things did occur. And they could profoundly touch me. Pierce my shield of safety. Beings I cared about, like this young filly, could vanish in an instant. People too. No amount of my mother's assurances could negate this cold, simple fact. People and animals did die. And it was painful to experience.

ONE AFTERNOON, NOT long after I started second grade, my mother called me into the living room where she sat alone, reading. She had some special news.

"Kathy, I'm having a baby."

"A baby? For us?"

My mother nodded and smiled.

"A real, live baby for me to play with?" I asked in disbelief. Cynthia had her toddler brother, Roger, whom we liked to spoon-feed and had taught to take his first steps. Having my own baby at home would be even better. I would be an older sister and be in Cynthia's league, with a bundle to cuddle and dress and push around in a carriage.

A month or so earlier, my mother had explained human reproduction to me, about seeds and eggs, and how a man and a woman had to put their wee-wees together to make babies. I had listened with mild disgust as she explained the strange act necessary to plant and grow a seed in a woman's stomach, a seed that eventually turned into a baby. It even had a name—intercourse.

I stared at her, now, incredulous.

"You and Daddy did intercourse?" I blurted out.

She nodded. "Yes."

I felt faintly sick at the thought my parents had to perform this distasteful task just to present me with a baby brother or sister. This was something I simply couldn't imagine them ever doing. I felt sorry for them.

Turning my attention back to the baby, I peppered my mother with questions.

"How big is the baby now?"

"It's still very small," she said.

"How fast will it grow?"

She chuckled. "Very slowly."

"Is it a boy or a girl?"

"We won't know until it's born."

"What are we going to call it?"

My mother laughed. With a droll smile, she said since we didn't yet know whether it was a he or a she, we could call it Little Ignatz until its birth.

"Little Ignatz?" I repeated, giggling. It was the funniest name I'd ever heard. I pictured a tiny, wizened dwarf—neither a he nor a she—floating in her belly.

Soon, instead of her usual reading and gardening, my mother spent her afternoons sitting in the living room armchair knitting. Slender knitting needles and bundles of soft wools appeared from which she produced wondrous woolen outfits for the baby: a tiny, delicate turquoise sweater with a matching baby cap and booties and another just like it in pale yellow. Nothing pink, probably not to deflate my father's hope for a little boy this time. Her knitting needles clacking away, she manipulated the wool into designs that grew each day, like her stomach.

I was amazed she could knit so well. Knitting seemed so out of character for her, something I associated with older Arab ladies in Jerusalem or with our gardener, Abbas, back in Tehran, meticulously knitting his coarse, gray socks. Had she magically acquired this ability in anticipation of the baby?

She had always sewn for herself and me, and her sewing skills had come in handy for all the cocktail functions she had to attend. Most of the expat women had their dresses tailored by the Indian tailors in Fahaheel, but sewing was my mother's hobby. She ordered patterns from the Sears catalog from which she fashioned stylish suits and dresses with matching wraps. She always made my holiday dresses, velvet reds or greens for Christmas, with delicate flowery buttons and silky white blouses and pinafores; my plain clothes, like my Christmas gifts, were ordered from the Sears and Roebuck catalog.

The wardrobe she knitted in those months for Little Ignatz was no less impressive, and in looking back, I find it incredible that a young woman, who only a few years earlier had been busy with college and sororities, could have found the time to learn this skill so proficiently. In those first years of marriage, my mother had been thrust head-on into the demanding social life of two expatriate communities in two different Middle Eastern countries. She had to attend countless cocktail parties and arrange dinners with ambassadors, business executives, and government officials in foreign cultures that had no resemblance to her past in Tennessee. Adaptability was obviously innate in my mother, and, true to her nature, she relished every novel experience.

thirteen

Dr. Midhat

ONE LATE SUMMER AFTERNOON, AS CYNTHIA, ERIK, AND I
played in our front yards, I ran in and out of our house several
times to retrieve things, each time banging the door loudly
behind me. My father was reading the newspaper in the living
room and had already called out to me several times for banging the door, warning me I would hurt myself. This last time,
I heard his warning too late. When I pulled the door and
heard it slam behind me, I simultaneously felt a sharp bite at
the tip of my middle finger. Blood spurted. I shrieked.

In an instant, my father had scooped me up in his arms
and was running with me to his car. As he furiously backed
out of our driveway, I caught a glimpse of my mother coming
out of Erik's front door where she had been visiting Pat, a
look of puzzlement on her face to see us madly dashing off.

I was soon sitting on a table in the compound's small clinic
near the horse stables, crying hysterically and holding my
bloody hand. Aminoil's American physician, Dr. Richards, a
slender man with sandy hair and a serious look on his face,
confirmed to my father the unbelievable.

"She's cut off her fingertip."

I started to scream louder, suddenly understanding what was causing all the blood and pain. Cynthia and Erik, having run after our car on foot, were pressing their faces against the clinic's screened window, trying to glean what was going on inside the examining room.

Meanwhile, I continued to hold up my hand as I screamed to them and to the world, "I cut off my finger!"

My mother, now heavily pregnant, pulled up to the clinic in Trek, fearing something awful had happened. By now, my finger was totally covered in blood. While my father cradled me, Dr. Richards told my mother to go back to the house and search for my missing fingertip.

She soon returned to the clinic, carefully carrying the small piece of bloody flesh in a Kleenex. As the preparations were made for sewing the tip back onto my finger, the doctor, with my father by his side, laid me down on the examining table and covered my nose with a giant wad of moist cotton that emitted a pungent smell.

"Ether," the doctor said, as he held the porous cotton in place.

I breathed in the sharp, noxious fumes that penetrated my nostrils and expanded through my head like an inflating balloon. My arms suddenly felt loose, and I saw myself floating above the anxious faces of my father and Dr. Richards. They grew smaller and more distant as the piercing smell filled my lungs and head like a huge, wet cloud, opening all my senses, carrying me high beyond the room.

When I woke up, I was still in the clinic, my left hand wrapped in a tidy gauze bandage the size of a boxing glove. As soon as I could walk steadily, I was taken home.

There was no more pain in my finger, so a day later I went back to my Arabic school and to Mrs. Howe, eager to show off my huge glove. My Arab girlfriends and teachers listened in disbelief as I relayed the unfortunate mishap.

"*Ya Allah*," they whispered, in sympathy and horror. ("Oh, my God!")

A WEEK LATER at the clinic, my parents and I sat in rapt attention as Dr. Richards unwound the boxing glove to take a look at my finger. He carefully turned my hand around a few times, peering closely at the bluish, sewn-on tip.

He sighed. "The severed tissue hasn't fused properly with the rest of her finger."

We stared at the darkened tip. It did look lifeless.

"It can't be left on or it'll rot," the doctor said.

I watched my parents look at each other. My mother seemed worried.

"What can be done?" my father asked.

Dr. Richards sighed. "My only option is to amputate the finger to the first knuckle."

I stared at my left middle finger, at the stubborn tip of flesh that had rejected the rest of me. Somehow, the idea of amputating it did not alarm me much—I was a tomboy much of the time and gave little thought to having pretty fingers. Besides, in the eyes of my friends, I was a hero, and my finger was a curiosity worthy of endless attention. Amputation would be another interesting twist.

My parents, however, looked devastated. I can imagine the thoughts racing through their minds at that moment: How was I going to manage with a shortened finger? I was a girl, and the aesthetics as well as the practical impact of an amputated finger concerned them. How would I be able to play the piano, something I'd been hankering to learn lately? And how would a decision they made now affect me later?

While I was resigned to going along with the amputation, my parents were less so and asked the doctor to give them a few days to think about it. Despite Dr. Richards's warning that waiting too long would allow gangrene to set in and force him to amputate even more of my finger, he was willing to give them a few days to come to terms with the idea.

Meanwhile, in a stroke of luck, my parents received an invitation to a dinner party in Fahaheel given by their friends Sa'eed and Widad Khoury. Sa'eed was a Palestinian engineer from the Eastern Galilee town of Safad who, in 1948, had fled his home with his family during the Arab–Israeli War. Now a successful businessman, Sa'eed had built his own walled compound in Fahaheel, the town beyond Shuaiba.

Sa'eed and his wife, Widad, often threw large dinner parties in their Fahaheel home. At this particular dinner, which they urged my parents to attend to take their minds off my finger calamity, my parents met a young Egyptian surgeon who had just completed his orthopedic training in England. He had been hired to work in Kuwait's large Sulaibikhat Hospital. When told about my finger, he asked to see me before any further decision on amputation was made. Grasping at this ray of hope, my parents eagerly agreed to take me to him.

Dr. Midhat's warm brown eyes focused on my now famous finger. Although he agreed the tip couldn't be salvaged and had to be removed as soon as possible, he suggested an alternative to amputation. He could perform a skin graft in which he would fuse tissue from my stomach onto the tip of my finger to cover the bone. He'd do this by inserting my finger into a slit made at my waist where it would stay for a week until enough new tissue bonded to create a viable fingertip. Hopefully, the skin would take, and a new fingernail might grow back as well.

This was cutting-edge medicine, and my parents agreed to the experiment. Dr. Midhat, while sounding confident of his abilities, cautioned them that he couldn't guarantee it would work, or that the new fingertip would match the others, or even that I would regain sensation in the tip. But it was worth a try to save the length. If the graft didn't work, there'd be no choice but to amputate.

The next time I saw Dr. Midhat, he gazed at me confidently from above his white surgical mask in the operating room. He placed a rubber mask over my nose and mouth to administer the anesthesia, and the noxious fumes once again filled my nose and head just as they had two weeks earlier in the Mina Abdullah clinic. As I sleepily watched him and the white-clad nurses recede into the distance, I felt a sudden surge of love for this gallant man who was about to rescue my finger. Then I slipped into the vast void of darkness.

While I was under the anesthesia, Dr. Midhat made a two-inch incision at my waist into which he inserted my fingertip, closing the wound so the new tissue would graft onto the bone. I had to remain in the hospital the entire week while the skin was grafting. To relieve my boredom, I walked along the ward with my finger tucked into the slit at my waist. I met a few other children who were hospitalized for various surgeries. Entire families seemed to be camping outside patients' doors, the women's black abayas pooled about them on the floor like puddles. Dr. Midhat cheerfully popped into my room each morning to ask how I was feeling and to check on my bandaged waist.

The best part of my hospital stay was that I shared a room with an Arab schoolteacher who had just had her gallbladder removed. As we recovered, she entertained me by teaching me some English songs she taught to her students. "Where Are You Going, My Pretty Maid?" and "Oh, Where Have You Been, Billy Boy, Billy Boy?" and "Que Sera, Sera," an old favorite of my father's. When my mother came to see me during the day, I sang them to her, and then to my father when they both returned in the evenings.

Days later, the final part of my finger surgery took place. My finger was removed from the incision in my waist and rebandaged in a small splint. A week later, the splint was removed, and my new fingertip was revealed for the first time.

It was a sight! Tissue, indeed, covered the bone, but my middle finger was almost a quarter inch shorter than the one on my right hand, and it was bluish and nubby rather than pink and tapered like my other fingers. It looked nothing like my old fingertip. Yet it was real skin and, like a normal middle finger, it was longer than the forefinger and ring finger on either side of it.

Dr. Midhat looked pleased. "The graft took well," he said. "I think a new fingernail will soon emerge."

I stared at the new tip, not too sure. There were some ugly black spots in a circle around the top.

"Those are just the stitches that I'll remove next week," he said. He also told me the bluish skin would lighten up in time to match the color of my other fingers.

I had an entire finger again. I also now had a two-inch

centipede-like scar at my waist from where the new skin had been grafted. I felt proud for having gone through the loss of my fingertip and the subsequent surgery so nonchalantly. Perhaps I was more adaptable and like my mother than I thought.

"Owwww!" I screamed from the shooting pain that suddenly coursed through my finger.

Dr. Midhat gave a sheepish, triumphant grin.

"Sorry, Miss Kathy. I had to give your finger a little prick to make sure the nerves are working."

AS WE DROVE away from the hospital, my parents announced we'd soon be getting a piano. Now that I had all my fingers intact, I was going to take lessons. I couldn't wait to get to Mina Abdullah to see Cynthia and Erik and show off my new finger. But instead of driving home, my father drove us to Fahaheel, to the guesthouse of Sa'eed and Widad Khoury. He said we had to stay in Fahaheel for a few days while work was being done on our house.

"What work?" I asked, disappointed.

Then they told me. While my mother was visiting me at the hospital one morning, our house had caught fire. Faulty electrical wiring, my father said. By the time the fire was put out, many household items, including furniture, clothing, and books, had been destroyed or damaged by flames, smoke, and water.

Sa'eed and Widad Khoury had come to our rescue, insisting we stay at their Fahaheel guesthouse until our house was fully repaired.

When we returned home some days later, I was shocked

to see the damage to parts of my bedroom and the living room. My mother began to mend wooden picture frames and put back together the crisped photo album covers with adhesive paper. Some of the dolls my grandparents had brought me from their trip were damaged, too, and had to be thrown out; others my mother was able to repair.

I cried when I saw my red-haired doll brown with soot, her satin dress singed. My mother quickly told me she could fix it and sew the doll a new dress to make it look like new. I tried to think that, although it was a loss, it was just a doll, as my mother said. But I could see for myself the terrible danger we'd escaped. There was even an undercurrent of unease I sensed when my parents talked in hushed voices about how lucky it was that we hadn't been home when the fire happened.

Years later, I learned there was more behind the fire in our house than a faulty wire. The fire had been deliberately set. Some people in Aminoil were unhappy an ethnic Arab held an executive position in the company. Once, my father had made it clear that, along with being a loyal employee of the American firm, as an Arab he felt a certain allegiance to the dictates of the Kuwaiti government when it came into conflict with the American oil company's interests. When the Kuwaiti government had recently been in negotiations for a higher royalty from Aminoil, my father had tried to mediate, explaining to Aminoil executives the government's position.

I'd been aware my father had made some enemies within Aminoil from overhearing him talking with my mother. Apparently, a few men had hatched the plan to have him leave on his own resolve by spooking him with the house fire.

They very nearly succeeded. Even my fearless mother

had been shaken. When she learned men had been paid to douse the house with kerosene and set it on fire to scare off my father, she wanted to leave Kuwait immediately.

"Kal, we have a young child and another on the way," she argued. "Keeping our family safe is more important to me than your current job."

He listened to her in silence, wavering.

"You can find other overseas employment that doesn't threaten your family," she said, her voice breaking.

Widad Khoury, who had been inadvertently instrumental in saving my finger, stepped in again and convinced my mother not to concede to the wishes of those who had tried to get rid of my father. It was just what the scoundrels wanted, she said, and she urged my mother to reconsider and let the matter be handled by the proper authorities. Eventually my mother was swayed, and we stayed in Mina Abdullah.

More of a surprise was that the perpetrator of the arson plan had been Clyde Dinkle, sweet Donnie Dinkle's father. The man to whom my father had made me apologize for lying about our bus driver. Even years later I felt a stab of betrayal to hear this. His home was where Cynthia and I had spent such pleasant times fixated on his beautiful daughter. I remembered his good-natured smile. Mr. Dinkle had seemed benevolent, incapable of planning something so sinister. I'd always assumed Donnie and her family had disappeared from the compound because Mr. Dinkle's contract had ended. He had, in fact, been fired as a result of the fire investigation.

I returned to the Shuaiba school and to my Calvert studies, where I recounted the bizarre story of how my new fingertip had been created out of skin from my stomach. Over and over, the Shuaiba girls asked me for the details. Each time I retold the story of the door slamming, the sharp pain, my mother retrieving the fingertip and rushing it to the clinic to be sewn back on, and the subsequent skin graft from my stomach, the girls' eyes grew wide. They would stare at my newly grafted fingertip and whisper, "*Bismillah*," invoking the name of Allah. The experience made me feel heroic. I could sense even my parents felt proud of my bravery.

fourteen

Baby Boy

MY NEWBORN BABY BROTHER—LITTLE IGNATZ—WAS finally home with us. My father was thrilled. He had a son.

Although I knew he adored me, it was evident from the way he held the baby that he had longed for a boy, a boy he could mold in his own image, who would one day look just like him. The baby was small, only five and a half pounds, and bald, except for a sparse ring of dark hair reaching around the back of his head. I was disappointed he couldn't yet wear any of the colorful outfits my mother had knitted for him but was instead swaddled in flannel receiving blankets, his arms and legs bundled tightly together so he resembled a caterpillar wearing a small elf hat.

The first time I saw my mother nursing him in her bed, I recoiled.

"What are you doing?" I asked.

"I'm feeding him, honey," she replied, fumbling with her breast as she held his small head in her other hand. He kept turning his head side to side, as though agitated, before finally making small, sucking sounds.

I'd only seen the Iranian women seated along the streets of Tehran in their billowy *chadors* nursing their babies, and a few women in our family in Jerusalem, whom I turned away from in embarrassment whenever they bared their breasts to feed their infants. I'd never thought this was something a modern American woman would consider doing and certainly not something my book-reading, elegant hostess-of-bridge-and-dinner-parties mother would even know *how* to do.

My mother had small, dainty breasts, and it seemed inconceivable and primitive for her to feed a baby from them. Wasn't she going to use a bottle like she had probably used for me? Was it possible she'd once fed me this way? I very much hoped not! Although I loved all that I perceived as the glamour of womanhood, this detail of feeding infants from breasts I considered beneath her.

I was allowed to hold the baby with supervision. I kissed his tiny forehead, sniffing the warm, salty scent of his tiny face, which had a dusky tint at first. I finally had a baby brother to help take care of. But when I nuzzled him and lovingly called him Little Ignatz, as my mother and I had done these past months, my father objected.

"What's this Ignatz?" he said with a reproachful smile. "His name is Munib." Pronounced "Muneeb." He was named after his father, Baba, whose middle name had been Munib. As the second-oldest son, it would not have been Arab custom for my father to use his father's first name for his firstborn son. That honor had gone to Uncle Ahmad, who had already named his oldest son Mohammad, after Baba.

Munib. It sounded strange and too serious a name for a tiny baby. I still called him Little Ignatz when my father wasn't around.

Erik and Cynthia ran over often to admire our new baby. I felt special as his big sister when I held him in my arms in the mornings before school and in the afternoons when I got home. He'd gaze back at me as I peered into his crib, and he clung to my finger when I laid it against his tiny fist. I couldn't wait to be allowed to carry him on my own and take him for a stroll in the new baby carriage.

SIX MONTHS AFTER Munib's birth, the school year ended, and it was time for our annual home leave to Hawaii to visit my grandparents.

The trip from Kuwait to Honolulu would take us through the Far East, with stops of a few days each in Karachi, Bangkok, and Hong Kong. It was a long trip, and I remember going to a zoo in Karachi before we flew to Bangkok. On one plane, Munib swung from a hammock hung from the airplane's ceiling, which served as the airline's infant seat. On that flight, I befriended an American girl sitting a few rows behind us. The girl told me she was traveling alone with her mother and brother because her father had died. I felt stunned that someone my age could lose a parent. I thought this only happened in scary fairy tales. Could this ever happen to me? I went back to my seat and told my father. He reassured me this would never happen. For a while, I didn't want to leave my parents' side, my pulse racing at the thought I could lose one of them like this girl had.

Bangkok was hot and humid, although not as hot as Kuwait. My parents hired a babysitter for Munib at the hotel, and the three of us rode on a boat along the floating market— a river running through town where narrow boats stocked with bright fruits and vegetables served as market stalls, and children and adults bathed in the river alongside women washing clothes. We wandered through large temples with pointed orange roofs shaped like flames and went into one with a giant statue of a sleeping Buddha inside. At night, we went to dinner at a restaurant and watched doll-like dancers with painted faces, jewel-studded costumes, and pointy, jeweled hats. The women's nails were as long and delicate as their fingers, which bent back so far when they danced that they nearly touched the backs of their wrists and looked as if they could break off like thin glass. I tried to practice this trick the next few days, bending my fingers backward and moving my hands in graceful circles, but my fingers didn't bend back much.

In Hong Kong, my parents had clothes tailored. My mother had a pair of shoes made to match each of her new outfits—lime green, purple, red, and beige. While they shopped, I watched people in the streets eating what looked like sparkling white rice from little bowls. By lunchtime, the delicious smells had me ravenous to eat whatever they were, and I begged to have lunch in a restaurant. But because Munib was so small, we had to return to our hotel for lunch where my parents ordered in room service. The Chinese food in gleaming silver platters on an elegant, cloth-covered rolling table did not remotely resemble the bowls of food or the mouthwatering white rice I'd seen the people in the street enjoying. I balked at trying any of the vegetables and meats bathed in thick sauces before finally swallowing a few mouthfuls.

When we finally arrived in Honolulu, my grandparents stood in the breezy outdoor arrival area of the airport. Their arms were laden with fragrant, fresh-flowered necklaces they hung over our necks as they hugged and kissed us and exclaimed, "Aloha!"

The breeze carried the sweet smell of the pink, white, and yellow plumeria flowers that made up our leis. I would forever come to associate the smell of plumerias with Hawaii.

My grandmother was wearing a long, flower-print dress like a robe.

"It's called a muumuu," she said. "They're the Hawaiian dresses we wear here."

From then on, I never saw her out of a muumuu in Honolulu. My grandfather, like most of the men I saw, wore shorts and a flower-printed aloha shirt in a brightly colored fabric like the muumuus. Almost everyone wore flip-flops, including my grandmother, although hers had elegant sparkles on them.

It was the first time my grandparents had seen Munib. They gawked lovingly at him, and Mammaw gently lifted him from my mother's arms. My grandfather hugged me close, repeating, "My sweet gal."

My grandmother now drove a spacious blue Oldsmobile. We all piled in as she drove us to their new house—a turquoise wooden bungalow nestled in a tidy residential neighborhood with other bungalows fronted by lawns with vibrant bushes and palm trees. Across the street was a much larger lawn that belonged to the high school, and beyond the school were lush, green hills.

My grandparents' backyard bloomed with flowers. My grandmother took us on a tour of the garden, telling us the names of all the bushes—pink hibiscus, orange birds-of-paradise, blazing red anthuriums, purple bougainvillea vines, and several white plumeria trees. I'd never seen so many flowers in one place. All were carefully tended by my grand-father, who had also planted papaya and mango trees that produced fresh fruit each morning for breakfast.

The covered porch was called a lanai, a shelter from the rain that came for short periods, day and night. There was always a light breeze blowing through the open windows, so there was no need for air-conditioning. The summer weather in Hawaii was so different from that of Kuwait, with its scalding winds and sandstorms.

My grandmother immediately arranged for me to meet the children on her street. She said I was to be outdoors most of the day, getting fresh air and exercise, and not lounging in front of the television as I wanted to do.

We didn't yet have television in Kuwait, nor in Jerusalem, so this was my first exposure, and I was enthralled by the cartoons and children's shows. I was intrigued, most of all, by the Japanese samurai soap operas that played all day, featuring episodes about feudal Japan, where men with their heads shaved down the center above black ponytails lashed at each other with swords. Although I couldn't understand anything they said, I loved the drama, the funny way they spit out their words in anger, and the heroic way the good men overcame the evil ones. But when I sat down to get absorbed in one, my grandmother would hustle me out the front door with her usual, "Get along outside now. Go and find your friends!"

She also signed me up for hula dancing lessons twice a week. These hula classes were my first experience with for-mal dance classes, and I enjoyed learning the swaying move-ments of the hips, arms, and hands. I learned the steps to the lyrics of "Little Brown Gal" and "Hukilau," which the hula teacher taught us, and I watched the hula dancers perform at the various restaurants we went to. I couldn't wait to finish learning the basic slow hula, so I could advance to learning the fiery Tahitian dancing. I loved the way the drums throbbed and the older girls' hips gyrated like propellers. I constantly put on shows for my parents and grandparents, copying with a budding sensuality what I had seen the older girls do.

MY GRANDMOTHER, LIKE my mother, was seldom without a book, although hers were mostly history books rather than the novels my mother favored. My grandmother was as adamant as my mother that I read as much as possible and took me on weekly trips to the library. She also bought me books on American history, along with illustrated books of Japanese and Chinese fairy tales and Hawaiian legends.

My grandfather's eyesight had deteriorated so he could no longer drive. Instead, my grandmother drove us on trips around the island. My favorite outing was to the pineapple fields and factory, where the pineapples were canned or turned into juice. We could smell the caramelized whiff of burnt sugar from the factory as we approached, and we were given fresh slices to sample. I'd never tasted fresh pineapple before, and I loved the revelation of its crunchiness.

Hawaii was so different from our stark desert. Hawaii's plush green grass grew abundantly. The supermarkets had more aisles than any of our markets in Fahaheel or Ahmadi. We could drink water directly out of a faucet rather than from the big filter we had in Kuwait, and we didn't have to wash the fruit and vegetables with soap. It seemed everything in Honolulu was clean before we even cleaned it. And dust didn't accumulate on anything in my grandparents' house as it did nonstop in Kuwait. I never saw any dust in Hawaii.

Once in Honolulu, my parents were content to hand over the child-rearing and rule-enforcing to my grandmother. I didn't have to do many household chores in Kuwait, since we had a houseboy to clean the house. My grandmother, however, drew up a list of tasks for me to complete each day before I could go out to play or watch television, which included making the beds and vacuuming the living room. Whenever I protested to my parents that I had no time to play because of all my chores, they smiled, telling me that while we were in Honolulu I had to mind whatever my grandmother told me.

Later I realized why my parents had turned me over to Mammaw. They had something more serious preoccupying them, which I sensed when they sat in private and talked for a long time without smiling.

MUNIB WAS NOW rolling around the floor of my grandparents' living room, attempting to scoot himself on his stomach. He was still mostly bald except for a tuft of black hair on top of his head. He had chubby cheeks and vivid blue eyes, and he would break into a happy grin whenever we made funny sounds for him. I often played with him to earn extra points for TV watching or fed him his bottle in the garden under my parents' supervision.

Munib looked totally healthy. Yet he wasn't as he seemed to be. Some months ago in Kuwait, his doctors found he had been born with a defective heart valve. The only clue my parents had that something was wrong was when he would occasionally gasp for breath. Although the doctors in Kuwait and even the specialists in Beirut had indicated the condition was not immediately dangerous, they all agreed surgery was needed to repair the valve. It was best to have it done in England or the United States. The doctors told my parents that, were it not corrected, at some point his condition might be life-threatening or impede his growth and ability to perform normal activities.

My parents were distraught at the thought of risky heart surgery on their baby, but the doctors said surgery was the only way to cure Munib's problem and recommended it in the following year when he would be almost two. My mother, the American pragmatist, believed in letting science do what it could for her son. She wanted Munib to have the benefit of the progress being made in life-saving procedures.

My father, though, was not convinced it was safe to do the surgery on a child so young, especially since Munib showed all the outward signs of being a perfectly healthy baby. But it was still too early to make a decision. So far, Munib was growing well and had good energy. The surgery would be something to consider in a year's time.

One of the leading hospitals pioneering the newest techniques in open-heart surgery for children was Children's Hospital in San Francisco. The hospital, coincidentally, was near Orinda, the village where my grandmother's cousins, Nora and John Hampton, now lived. On our way back home to Kuwait, we were to pass through San Francisco and stay with them while the doctors at Children's Hospital examined Munib to determine the best time to perform his surgery.

None of this was a major concern of mine when the days pulled me into the balmy Honolulu sunshine to do cartwheels and headstands on the lawn with the neighborhood children, Georgie and Debbie. Other times, one of the parents drove us to the little shopping town of Aina Haina five minutes away to go to the convenience store where we could buy drippy snow cones or sour *li hing mui,* the dried Asian plums that made our mouths pucker. So many people in Hawaii walked around barefoot, something people never did in Kuwait, where the sand was scorching hot, or in Jerusalem, where it would have been deemed improper.

Aina Haina was also where my grandmother took me for my dreaded dental appointments. A fun summer afternoon would be marred by prickly Novocain shots and drilling. So many things had to be scheduled before we returned home to the desert.

BECAUSE OF THE heat, schools in Kuwait didn't start until late September, but Honolulu schools started in August. With still a month to go before we returned to Kuwait, my parents decided I should attend the public elementary school in Aina Haina with the neighborhood children.

In 1960, I started third grade in an American public school, but with so many students of Japanese and Chinese descent that it was hardly typical of mainland schools. None of my neighborhood friends were in my class, so I faced a roomful of strangers.

The boys at the Aina Haina school were brash and loud and often made fun of me because I was new, calling me "Red" because of my hair. One large, mean blond boy persisted in calling me "Carhead," making fun of my last name, Karjawally. I had sometimes been teased by the boys in the road outside the Shuaiba girls' school while I waited to be picked up. The Kuwaiti boys, who had never seen red hair or light eyes before, were more playful than unkind, calling out "meow" as though I were a cat.

The routine of this school was leagues away from my girls' school in Kuwait. Here, in the mornings, we stood inside the classroom and placed our hands on our hearts as we said the Pledge of Allegiance, rather than recite a prayer and have our nails and hair inspected as we did in Shuaiba. I had never learned the Pledge in the Calvert curriculum. In Aina Haina, we wore casual dresses rather than uniforms and could style our hair any way we wanted without the white ribbons required in Shuaiba.

Most surprising was that, on one of the first days of school, the class reviewed what actions to take if there was an air raid signaling an atomic bomb attack. When the teacher asked us what we should do in the event of a missile strike, various students raised their hands to suggest we hide under desks or, as one boy smartly advised, "Hit the deck." It was said almost in jest, as though we were playing a game, each one trying to come up with a cleverer way of hiding from the bomb.

In Kuwait we never talked about bombs or air raids. The idea of being totally obliterated was like something out of a horror movie, for I had yet to study about the real bombing of Hiroshima and Nagasaki. Nothing in my carefree life in Mina Abdullah could have prepared me for the possibility of anything like a nuclear blast that my classmates in Aina Haina were being prepared to save themselves from. I was glad I was only there temporarily.

Even lunchtime was different. Here, we ate in a large cafeteria where we picked our milk cartons and juice and got to choose between fried chicken and macaroni and cheese, rather than sitting to be served by Abu Omar. Although I liked the food at the Aina Haina school well enough, especially the ice cream cups for dessert, nothing here tasted as satisfying or delicious as Abu Omar's warm, cumin-scented lentil soup.

Learning Japanese was mandatory in the Aina Haina school because of the large Japanese population on the island. The teacher who taught it was our homeroom teacher, who was of Japanese descent and greeted us each period with the word Konnichiwa, which she said with a slight bow, her hands placed on her knees. She brought us recordings of Japanese children that we sang along with, and I learned to write Japanese numbers and letters from top to bottom rather than from left to right as in English or right to left as in Arabic. I liked the Japanese classes. The hour I spent in an environment other than a purely American one made me almost feel I was back in Kuwait.

We hardly memorized in the Aina Haina school. We learned about the Hawaiian Islands and how to make tapa, the ancient Hawaiian cloth, by each pounding a square of special paper until it grew soft and pliant, which we then painted with Hawaiian designs in red and brown. We learned about King Kamehameha, the ruler who unified all the islands, and Queen Liliuokalani, who composed the popular "Aloha 'Oe" song of farewell while in prison.

I yearned to be included in the girls' games, but my classmates seemed distant and not interested in making a new friend. Instinctively, I also held back, knowing I wouldn't be staying in Honolulu very long. Although I loved being in Hawaii, I couldn't wait for the month to end. When it was time for us to return to Kuwait and to my other schools, I was relieved.

fifteen

The Enigma of Religion

MY AGNOSTIC MOTHER AND MINIMALLY OBSERVANT MUSLIM father sailed along on the currents of their respective beliefs without conflict. Their personal faiths, or lack of it in my mother's case, glided seamlessly on parallel tracks. I don't recall any religious discussions between them. I, on the other hand, was fascinated by religion, one of my favorite subjects at the Shuaiba school because of the stories we were told.

We had *deen,* the Arabic word for religion, in twice-weekly sessions. Unlike the strict morning classes, there was something relaxing about these afternoon lessons when we would sit slumped at our desks, hypnotized by the whirling blades of the ceiling fans slicing into the hot air. We had to memorize the short verses of the Qur'an, the *surahs,* along with the *tafseer,* which was the explanation of the seventh-century Arabic language of the holy book, after which the teacher usually told a story to go along with the lesson. I looked forward to the colorful drawing she would create for us on large white poster board to illustrate it.

One memorable drawing was of a beautiful, winged angel floating down from an azure sky above an old man and a little boy kneeling over a large boulder. In her arms the angel carried a white lamb as the boy and father stared up at her in awe. Despite the colorful drawing, the teacher's explanation was frightening. It was a rendition of the angel Gabriel, *Gibreel*, bringing the prophet Abraham, *Ibraheem*, the lamb to sacrifice instead of his son, *Ismaeel*. God had instructed Ibraheem to sacrifice his young son in a test of his love and obedience, our teacher told us. Ibraheem, although grief-stricken at the thought of killing his own son, had been ready to comply with God's request, holding down Ismaeel and raising his hand with the knife above a stone. At the last minute, the boy was spared from death when Gibreel appeared with a lamb, which Ibraheem was instructed to sacrifice instead, now that his devotion to his creator had been proven.

For a long time afterward, I remembered the drawing of the angel carrying the lamb in her arms to save the terrified boy staring up at her. God had tricked Abraham to test his love. But what, I wondered, if the angel hadn't arrived on time, and Abraham had killed his son? Would God have been happy? I knew my father believed in this same God. Would he agree to sacrifice me or Munib, if asked, just to prove his devotion?

As an adult, I'm perplexed that these lessons were taught to such young children, although none of my classmates seemed to question or be disturbed by this story. Perhaps they were better able than me to accept God's strange rules. Yet the point had been made to us: God was to be obeyed—or else.

Another illustration the teacher presented to us in deen

class was of a faceless man riding a fanciful winged steed that appeared to be half horse and half cow. The rider, we were told, was the Prophet Mohammad, who was never to be portrayed in art, and whose face was always left blank, as though he wore a white veil. The winged steed was the *Buraq*, a mythical creature sent by God to transport the Prophet from Mecca to Jerusalem and up to heaven to encounter God and back to Mecca in a single night.

This story, unlike that of Abraham, reminded me of the fictional Sinbad's adventures, with no hint of difficult moral dilemmas. I envisioned the glorious journey through the night sky among the stars on the back of a magical winged being. It was like my father's made-up stories of Fatima riding her white, winged horse.

Like my Shuaiba classmates, I felt proud to be learning the Qur'an. I memorized the verses aloud at home as I paced between the kitchen and living room while my mother cooked dinner. I recited them for my father to show off my new knowledge of his Islamic heritage. Although my mother didn't object to the religious classes, she must have found it odd to have her child swept up in such fervor.

The only Islamic practice my father observed was the month-long fasting during *Ramadan*. Like most other Muslim adults, he neither ate nor drank anything from sunrise to sunset, when he'd break his fast with an elaborate dinner. To show my adherence to his faith, I'd sometimes fast half the day, and he praised my effort.

Otherwise, he wholeheartedly participated in my mother's cultural celebrations—putting up the Christmas tree and lights, playing Frank Sinatra and Bing Crosby Christmas carols on the stereo, and enjoying the fruitcakes she spent weeks soaking in brandy. He and my mother filled my Easter basket with assorted chocolate eggs and bunnies each spring, and he joined in the Fourth of July celebrations of barbeque, hot dogs, and fireworks with our American friends. Each November and December, he made sure we got one of the frozen turkeys flown in from the States in time for my mother to make her elaborate Thanksgiving and Christmas dinners.

On the Muslim religious festivals, or *Eids*, an Arab chef would prepare a big lunch of roasted lamb over rice to be served in our home to our Arab friends and some of my father's cousins, who had recently moved from Jerusalem to Kuwait. I remember my mother's embarrassment after one of these Eid gatherings when, once our guests had left, my father gently reminded her she had served them a rum cake for dessert when Muslims didn't drink alcohol on religious holidays. The guests hadn't declined the dessert, perhaps hadn't even known it had alcohol in it when they ate the cake, he said with a mischievous smile, but it was something to keep in mind for future Eid holidays.

IN THE EARLY sixties, with Aminoil continuing to expand, my circle of Anglo friends in Mina Abdullah grew as more British and American families moved into the compound. Six new prefab houses were built nearer the beach to accommodate this growth. Cynthia's father, as the general manager, had a large new complex on the water. Cynthia had previously lived in one of the brick houses identical to ours, but her new house was much grander than any of the others, with two large sitting rooms for official entertaining, a separate bedroom wing, and a large formal dining room and kitchen.

There were also separate quarters for two houseboys, a room for Roger's Lebanese nanny, and another one for a French-trained Lebanese chef. There was also a guest cottage to host occasional executives visiting from Aminoil's head office in New York.

We were given a new yellow house next door to Cynthia's. It was larger than our first house, with three bedrooms, a bath, an open living and dining room, and a separate kitchen. To my mother's complete joy, we had a large garden that wrapped around the entire house. I was pleased to have a shorter walk to the beach.

Expansions were being made for the entire compound. A new hospital closer to the refinery replaced Dr. Richards's small clinic, with rooms for patients to sleep in and a complete hospital staff of British and Indian nurses. A new recreational club included a restaurant, a party room with pool tables, a small library, and an outdoor movie theater with a huge screen and descending steps lined with plastic chairs. There was even a room with standing hair dryers for a hairdresser to cut and style women's hair.

WITH MORE EXPAT children in the camp, some of the parents thought it a good idea to start an informal Sunday school one afternoon a week. The classes consisted of a storytelling hour taught in the new club by Betty McClure, an energetic British woman with rosy skin and a prominent, pointy nose. My friends and I would race across the sand the short distance to the club, where Mrs. McClure had us gather around her at a table so she could read to us from her book of illustrated Bible stories. Her crisp voice brought the biblical characters to life, her face lighting up whenever she read an intense passage. We learned of Noah's ark, of Samson with his long hair and extraordinary strength, of Joseph and his brothers who sold him into slavery, and how Moses fled the Pharaoh's army by charging into the parted Red Sea. Whenever Mrs. McClure finished a page, she passed the book around for us to look at the pictures.

I heard some of the same stories I'd already learned in my Islamic deen classes in Shuaiba, albeit with slight alterations. Jesus was the Son of God, according to Mrs. McClure, not simply a revered prophet, as Muslims believed; and it was not Ismaeel, but Isaac, according to the Bible, who was nearly sacrificed by Abraham. Although I never discussed it with either of my parents, I began to form my own image and belief in God. I feared the punishments He seemed ready to mete out to any who disobeyed Him, and yet I believed that if I behaved and prayed enough, He'd grant my wishes in times of need.

My mother allowed me to go along with my friends to the Bible classes, perhaps feeling a little extra moral instruction was advantageous. My father never objected to my going, either, even though as the child of a Muslim father, I was considered a Muslim by other Arabs. Perhaps it was one of those things they'd worked out together in private and agreed on. The religious classes were an added dimension to my education, and I would eventually make up my own mind which path, if any, to take.

For me, aside from the camaraderie of my friends as we listened to the stories, the religious classes provided reassuring—though hardly logical—explanations for why things were the way they were. I felt safer with religion's more concrete answers for my questions that neither of my parents were able to answer. I liked the idea that a God in heaven had a clear plan and was looking out for each of us.

WITH MORE CHILDREN in Mina Abdullah, part of a new one-floor building near the hospital was designated as our new school. It was one large room with a dozen desks, since we were now six or seven studying the American Calvert course and three or four British children studying a similar British correspondence course. Mrs. Howe had left Kuwait, so another British teacher, Mrs. Tremmel, whose husband also worked for Aminoil, took over as our teacher.

We each worked individually, since no two of us were in the same grade. Mrs. Tremmel ran the class with the strict discipline of a regular British school. She was a tall, voluptuous woman with a firm, authoritarian air, and she was particularly interested in the arts, regularly creating plays for us to perform. Like our Sunday school teacher, she was a talented reader who read to us for fifteen minutes before the end of class each day—A. A. Milne's *Winnie-the-Pooh*, Daniel Defoe's *Robinson Crusoe*, and Robert Louis Stevenson's *Treasure Island*, deftly playing each character as though she were performing on a London stage. Even the normally fidgety boys listened in rapt attention for those minutes before we were dismissed to walk home across the sand.

The other half of our school building was the new commissary. This was the first time there was a store of any kind in Mina Abdullah. More of a convenience store than a market, it carried an assortment of frozen and canned foods, American TV dinners, and a few fresh vegetables and fruit, as well as cleaning products and toiletries. Best of all was the row of candy, cookies, and boxes of cake mix. For the first time, we kids had a store in the compound we could walk to on our own to purchase a snack or a chocolate bar.

That same year telephone service for the compound was installed, so each house got a telephone, something we'd lived for years without. I could finally pick up the telephone to call Cynthia and my other friends. There were still no overseas lines available, so our only communication with my grandparents in Honolulu or with our family in Jerusalem still had to be through letters and tape recordings.

Several months after the telephones were installed, we finally got a television. We now had evening entertainment at home. Television was new to all of Kuwait, so the programming was still limited to a single Arabic channel starting at six o'clock each evening with a few American cartoons, followed by the news in Arabic. There would be a single imported British or American show, such as the Western *Bonanza*, followed by an Egyptian film. As soon as I finished dinner, I propped myself in front of the screen and waited for the American cartoons to begin. My Mina Abdullah life was, at last, catching up to Honolulu.

sixteen

The Fall

ERIK, MY FIRST FRIEND IN MINA ABDULLAH, WAS LEAVING after three years. Hugh Smith's contract with Aminoil had ended. I couldn't imagine Erik no longer being a part of Cynthia's and my world. I'd miss Pat's chili and Hugh's comforting laid-back Texas drawl and smile and the familiar clip of his cowboy boots whenever he dropped by. Everything, it seemed, would be different with the Smiths gone. They were moving to Honolulu, which was good news. Hugh, who had retired from the oil business, would be teaching mathematics at the University of Hawaii. We would still get to see them each summer.

Before they left, Hugh sold his gray stallion, Captain, who was moved out of Mina Abdullah. With his riding companion now gone, my father stopped riding as much. Even Sabha looked forlorn as she wandered alone in the pen, sniffing the air for the scent of her lost stablemate. Her main riders were now Jalal or Mohammad. My friends and I still made almost daily trips to the horse house to watch her nibbling her oats or trotting around the pen, but some of her friskiness diminished without Captain nearby.

One late January afternoon, shortly before my ninth birthday, a few friends and I walked to the horse house. Jalal was not there, but seeing his cousin Mohammad about to remove Sabha's saddle, I ran up to him.

"Let me ride her," I said, breathless.

Mohammad held out some barley for the mare, who nibbled peacefully. "Your father is not here," he said.

"Just for a minute, Mohammad," I begged. "Please, please!"

Although under strict orders that I was not to ride Sabha unless my father was present, Mohammad, perhaps feeling she was sufficiently tired after her morning exercise, gave in to my pleading. He helped me onto her back and led her by the reins around the pen a few times; then, after my continued pestering, he led us outside the fence. Excited to show off in front of my friends, I again begged him to hand me the reins. I walked her slowly around on the open sand, calling out to my friends to watch me. Encouraged by her calmer than usual demeanor that afternoon, I spurred her into a trot.

I pulled on the reins, and Sabha stopped. Without waiting for Mohammad's help, I started to dismount. As I heaved my leg over Sabha's back, my other foot slid through my father's wide English stirrup, trapping my knee so that I lost my balance and fell backward, one foot hooked in the stirrup. I came down hard, knocking against Sabha's leg, my head hitting the ground. Startled, the mare shot off into the desert, dragging me alongside her. None of us ever wore riding helmets—Hugh and my father had donned cowboy hats, but only as protection from the sun—so my bare head bumped along the ground behind Sabha's galloping hooves.

Mohammad frantically ran after us, sharply calling out to Sabha as she continued to bolt across the sand. When she finally slowed and stopped, he caught up to her and grabbed the reins. By then she had dragged me enough of a distance that I was unconscious.

I WOKE UP in a bright hospital room to female voices chattering in Hindi. The Indian nurses were changing my urine-soaked sheets, stretching the crisp, dry ones tightly under me. The Kuwaiti hospitals were almost entirely staffed by Indian and Pakistani nurses, as well as many Indian or Egyptian physicians, since there were still very few trained Kuwaiti medical personnel. The nurses' voices came through my semiconscious fog like the cheerful sound of twittering birds; I copied them, my mouth mimicking the unfamiliar words. The nurses would giggle softly at my groggy attempts to emulate their Hindi, but they kept burbling while changing more of my wet sheets.

I remember nothing of my going to the stable with my friends that afternoon, asking Mohammad to ride, or anything about my fall. I only learned what I was told afterward by my father and, later still, by Mohammad who, scared out of his wits by what had happened, had sent my friends scurrying across the sand to my house to tell my parents of my accident. I can only assume the panic I had as I lost my balance and realized I was falling. Did I feel my head hit the ground?

A week later, I became lucid enough to learn I was in the Ahmadi hospital, bigger than our Mina Abdullah one. I had suffered a severe concussion and, for the first few days, had been unconscious and unresponsive. The doctors, having studied the X-rays of my head and finding nothing abnormal, tried to allay my parents' fears, assuring them I'd soon regain full consciousness. Meanwhile, whenever I briefly awoke in the evenings, I was aware only of my father standing beside me, his hand gently touching my head or bending over me to feed me something I had asked for—jars of Munib's Gerber baby desserts, which I had often sneaked from the kitchen cabinet at home.

Throughout the day, the nurses changed my sheets, giggling good-naturedly when I tried to copy their melodic conversation. I never saw my mother, only my father in the evenings, spooning me soft pudding.

It was now February. One evening, the mother of one of the new American boys in the compound—rakishly handsome James Graves, who was two years older than me and on whom I had a severe crush—came along with my father to the hospital. Her name was Marcella, and she brought me a chocolate-frosted cake she'd baked for my ninth birthday.

"Mommy, do you have new glasses?" I mumbled in confusion as Marcella Graves bent over my hospital bed to say hello. Although my mother wore glasses, too, Mrs. Graves's glasses had a gold necklace attached to them around her neck. Mrs. Graves smiled and introduced herself.

I confessed something I'd held in my heart for most of the year. "Mrs. Graves, I love your son."

Mrs. Graves smiled gently. "That's all right, honey."

She probably wasn't surprised by my admission, since most of us girls constantly vied for James's affection. But immediately after I confessed my feelings, I regretted it, fearing she'd tell James, or my father would scold me for saying something so silly. But it was too late. My secret was out. Mrs. Graves stayed a while and then left with my father.

Because I didn't remember my mother visiting me, I began

to think she had died. When my father told me she hadn't come because she had to stay home with Munib, I didn't believe him. I was convinced she was dead. Then, one morning, as the sun lit up the stark hospital room, a woman in a bright blaze of turquoise entered.

I thought I was dreaming. "Mommy?"

"Hi, honey!" she answered brightly.

I was puzzled. "Mommy, are you a ghost?"

"Not at all," she said with a laugh. "I'm as real as can be."

I have no recollection of her kissing me after what I perceived as her long absence, although she surely must have, nor any memory of an explanation as to why she hadn't visited me sooner. I only remember the loosely knitted fuzziness of the turquoise sweater as she sat beside me in a chair, telling me the latest Mina Abdullah news. She was alive! I had only imagined she was dead. An immense relief washed over me as it did whenever I woke up from a nightmare to find that whatever horrible event I'd just gone through was merely a dream.

Later I learned my mother hadn't come to see me in the hospital as often as my father because she'd been in the early stages of a pregnancy and had miscarried days after my fall. While I was lying unconscious in Ahmadi, she was hospitalized. Not wanting to frighten or upset me during my recovery, no one said anything to me. They couldn't have known that shielding me from reality would cause me to conjure up an even more terrifying explanation for her absence.

SOON, I WAS well enough to be moved to the new Mina Abdullah hospital, where a jovial British head nurse cared for me. Still unable to walk, I was bathed and fed in bed. Each morning, the nurse came into my room to give me a sponge bath and then vigorously rubbed my arms and legs with alcohol.

"It's too cold, and it hurts," I complained about the cold alcohol and her brisk rubbing.

But the nurse merely smiled and asserted, "Good for the circulation!"

My mother now came to visit me regularly, but her visits never came soon enough for me, since I was now stronger and getting bored. Her visits each morning and afternoon were my sole relief from the dull routine of the hospital. I missed Munib, too, who had never been brought to the hospital.

One day I grew grumpy when she was late. "Where were you?" I demanded when she arrived.

"Sweetie, I overslept during my nap," she said with her usual good-natured dismissal of my moodiness. "When I woke up, I jumped into my shoes and flew right over."

To my mother, nothing was ever as dramatic as I made it out to be.

Before I could go home, I had to start walking on my own. So far, the times I'd been out of bed, I was so wobbly I had to be supported, as though my legs had lost their bones and were nothing but jelly encased in skin. The head nurse reassured me this was only because I'd been in bed for several weeks. But I had never felt this challenged just to hold myself steady on my feet. Over the next few days, and with the aid of the nurse and my mother, I put weight on each foot and powered the next one in front of it. I had no idea how hard it was to step for the first time without support. Now, I was learning, just like Munib was when he teetered around the tabletops, fearful of letting go, not understanding how to shift his weight from one foot to the next without falling. I began to feel I'd never master this basic skill again or do my hula steps or dance to Harry Belafonte.

Days later, when I got out of the hospital, my mother gave me a proper ninth birthday party at home. She showed our collection of eight-millimeter cartoons, deftly moving from the movie projector to the organized games as my friends and I ran around our living room.

I can barely remember this birthday in detail, other than watching the cartoons and my mother's shadowy figure manning the projector. I rifle through my head for a slice of a memory, but I don't know what kind of cake she baked me or what games we played, whether she was wearing one of her bright cotton dresses or pedal pushers, whether her hair was pulled up in a bun or held back in her casual, bushy ponytail; I only remember my relief at her not being dead as I'd imagined in my earlier delirium.

I'm saddened by the lack of more specific memories of that afternoon, the absence of a specific photograph or image I can hold onto for clarity and comfort. For although I couldn't have known it then, it would be the last party she'd ever give me.

seventeen

Uncle Jimmy

I WAS BACK TO ATTENDING BOTH OF MY SCHOOLS. MY FATHER made it clear I wasn't to go near the stables. He'd nearly fired Mohammad for letting me ride Sabha against his express orders. With the days of fading in and out of consciousness still fresh in my mind, I had no desire to go riding anyway. I wasn't exactly afraid of horses, since I didn't remember anything about my fall. But riding no longer held the same excitement with only Sabha there.

It was soon the summer of 1961 and time to return to Honolulu to see my grandparents. We again traveled through the Far East, along our previous route of Karachi, Bangkok, and Hong Kong, but this time when we arrived in Honolulu, there was another person at the airport along with my grandparents to greet us. I heard him before I saw him, a shrill, roguish whistle that pierced the air.

My mother shrieked in delight, "It's Uncle Jimmy!"

I'd been waiting a long time to see my legendary "Uncle Jimmy", who was two years younger than my mother. There were pictures of him holding me as an infant and of me playing with him as a toddler on our trips from Washington to Tennessee before we moved to Tehran. We hadn't seen each other since then. With his parents now in Honolulu, he had chosen to complete his residency in psychiatry there.

Uncle Jimmy's face was familiar to me from family photographs, especially those of his wedding to his pretty blonde bride, Toni, whom I couldn't wait to meet in person. To say that Uncle Jimmy was handsome would be an understatement. He had a chiseled movie star's jaw, blue eyes, and a dazzling smile. A thin goatee ran from his jawline to below his chin. And he was tall—as tall as Uncle Basil, my father's youngest brother.

He walked toward us ahead of my grandparents, his arms outstretched with leis. Bending down to my level, he garnished me with one, calling me his "favorite redheaded niece," and he crooned softly to Munib.

At eighteen months old, Munib was a sweet, moon-faced toddler with my father's black hair and my mother's deep-blue eyes. He was walking and saying his first words and understood how to roll a ball back and forth with me between our outstretched legs. I would play hide-and-seek with him and wait for his delighted giggle whenever he found me in my hiding place. And he laughed out loud when I zoomed down the neighborhood sidewalk with him in his stroller, eager to finish my job of taking him around the block to earn my nickel for ice cream. He also followed me around when I vacuumed the living room, turning the vacuum on and off and wanting to examine the long metal pipe and suction attachment, while I hurried to finish the dreaded chore so I could run out and play.

Our summer in Honolulu fell into its rhythm, which included my hula lessons. My grandmother insisted I start each day with a big breakfast consisting of half a papaya picked from our tree, a fried egg, buttered toast, smoky sausages, and a tall glass of milk. It was as though she intended to replenish my body with all the fresh, vital nutrients she guessed it was missing in Kuwait.

Although my grandmother had refurnished her Honolulu home with island rattan furniture and Asian accessories, she'd kept a part of Tennessee in her southern cooking—fried chicken, pot roasts, and casseroles. Although I complained about having leftovers for dinner, she had a knack for turning the previous night's meats and vegetables into appealing new dishes the next day.

My grandfather and my father spent part of most afternoons on the lanai playing chess, something they'd started doing when Grandy visited us in Kuwait. They sat for hours, studying and endlessly strategizing, each too skilled to fall in quick defeat. My grandmother played chess, too, but mostly she spent her afternoons reading books of places she wanted to visit or know more about—the Middle East, Africa, the Pacific Islands.

She loved secondhand bookstores and bought books for both of us that smelled of age and held the mystery of their previous owners' lives. I loved these used books because they were as much a sensual delight as an intellectual one with their velvety, yellowed pages and tidy inscriptions on the first page. I enjoyed picturing the people who'd owned and read these books before us—imagining what their lives had been like, whether they were now alive or dead. I learned to find a cozy escape in the refuge of books, a comfort that would rescue me in those tough moments soon to shake my world to its core.

UNCLE JIMMY AND Toni lived in a cottage on the beach in a windswept part of the island called Waimanalo. Unlike on my grandparents' manicured Kanau Street, the houses on Uncle Jimmy's road were set amid wild dunes on a turbulent beach.

Aunt Toni was indeed blonde and attractive, just as in her wedding pictures. Like my grandmother, she wore muumuus; hers were off the shoulder, showing her soft, bronzed skin. But from the start, I sensed a strange tension between Toni and my grandmother. Sometimes I overheard my grandmother discussing her with my parents, shaking her head at something Toni had said or done. But I never knew what they were talking about.

When I saw the Smiths, our old neighbors, I barely recognized Hugh wearing an aloha shirt and flip-flops instead of his usual cowboy boots. Erik looked the same, except he'd grown taller and now peppered his speech with Hawaiian words such as *mahalo* for thank you, and *pau* when he was finished.

One day they came with us to visit Uncle Jimmy and Toni in Waimanalo. The frothy Hawaiian surf was nothing like our clear beach in Mina Abdullah where Erik and I had learned to swim. When we waded into the water in Waimanalo, a whitecap promptly smashed into us, knocking us both over. Before I could stand up, I was dragged all the way back to shore, somersaulting and thrust about in a swirl of sandy water. I quickly saw this wasn't going to be the same kind of swimming experience we were used to in Kuwait. All we could do here was stay close to shore and try to resist being whacked down by the waves.

After lunch, Uncle Jimmy brought out a guitar and strolled on the grassy dunes, strumming tunes. Erik and I ran after him, dancing in the sand as though we were back in Kuwait.

Later, I stayed for dinner at Uncle Jimmy's after everyone else had left. When Uncle Jimmy and Toni drove me home, Toni handed me a small gold charm bracelet with a dog and an Eiffel Tower that had been hers.

"I want you to have this, Kathy," she said.

I put it on and felt special. I was unsettled by the friction I sensed between my grandparents and Toni. Perhaps it was not directed at Toni but simply their observation of their son and his wife having marital issues. But I wanted everyone to like Toni as much as I did. I needed the connectedness of my family because I'd begun to sense the crack starting to form under me. The grown-up world was not as safe or solid as it appeared.

DURING THAT SUMMER, my mother began going into the hospital. This wasn't particularly alarming to me since she'd gone into the hospital a few times recently in Kuwait due to several miscarriages. I'd often heard her casually talk of her miscarriages with her Mina Abdullah women friends over coffee, although I hadn't paid much attention to the details. I was told the purpose of her hospital stays in Honolulu was to run some tests; after a few days, she returned home and resumed her usual activities of sightseeing or going out to lunch with the rest of us. But her mood was distant, and her smooth brow was often wrinkled with concern.

She had a Japanese doctor, Doctor Terada, who had a

daughter my age, also named Kathy, who often came over to visit or spend the night. I'd heard Kathy's father was a cancer specialist, and I gradually became aware my mother was being tested for cancer, a dangerous disease I'd heard about. It didn't scare me too much, since Kathy's family frequently came over, and I didn't associate her father with hospitals or illness. The notion that something as life-threatening as cancer would ever strike our family—especially my daring, upbeat mother—seemed impossible. My previous existential worries had faded somewhat, and in my childish optimism, denial was strong. I was sure cancer only happened to others and that my mother would eventually be fine.

On a warm summer night, we five women are tying printed island wraps around our waists and putting silk flowers in our hair and around our necks and ankles. We're performing a hula show, "Little Brown Gal" and "Hukilau," that I've trained my students to do, swaying to the melody of the ukulele and guitar as I'd learned in my Honolulu hula classes.

We're a diverse group—a German, a Chinese woman from Hong Kong, a woman from Kazakhstan, an African American woman, and me. We're checking last-minute touches, helping each other finish applying makeup and pin flowers. It's the first performance for the other women who have spent months learning the delicate hand gestures of the hula that express the heart and soul of the Hawaiian people. Now, eager to perform and show all they've learned, they check themselves in the mirrors, animated and excited. A few of them go over the steps we've practiced for weeks, beaming the Hawaiian smiles that animate this dance.

I grow silent. Despite my joy to be sharing this sensuous island dance I had fun learning as a child, the hula makes me think of that long-ago summer in Honolulu when all was perfect, before my world changed.

— ❦ —

eighteen

Western Science, Eastern Instinct

MY BROTHER WAS SCHEDULED TO HAVE HIS HEART SURGERY performed in a few weeks. The doctors had decided he was old enough, and it had been timed to coincide with our summer visit to Honolulu. My father, having finally been persuaded to let Munib have the surgery, was to fly with him from Honolulu to San Francisco where it would take place at Children's Hospital. My mother couldn't go with them because she was scheduled to be in the hospital for more tests. Her illness, of which I knew very little, would keep her in Honolulu with her parents while my father stayed with our cousins, Nora and John Hampton, during Munib's surgery. A week later, my father and Munib would return to Honolulu, and we'd all fly back to Kuwait.

When the day came for my father to take Munib to San Francisco, we were all optimistic. It was exciting to think Munib would be part of a new wave of advanced heart surgery. He'd come home with his heart mended and would grow stronger as a result. Although to us he was a bubbly, healthy eighteen-month-old, the doctors made it clear the surgery was necessary for him to continue to grow at a normal rate and to live a healthy life.

As soon as Munib and my father left, I missed my brother's chubby face and infectious smile. I was even a little jealous he'd get to be with Nora and John Hampton, our fun cousins, who lived a magical life in their mountaintop house in Orinda, overlooking cloud-shrouded Mount Diablo.

Once my father and Munib arrived in San Francisco, we received word that all Munib's preliminary hospital tests had gone well, and plans had been made for the surgery. Right away, my little brother became a local celebrity. He was photographed by several of the San Francisco and Oakland newspapers that published stories about the "little boy from Arabia" about to undergo experimental heart surgery in San Francisco's own Children's Hospital. We received copies of the newspaper articles with the close-up photographs of Munib standing in his hospital crib, smiling at the nurse as she reached out with a spoon to feed him. Such a handsome little boy, everyone said, with those flirtatious blue eyes. And that smile! My mother, still in the hospital having tests, was as pleased as we were with the articles and photographs. She and my grandmother joked about Munib charming the nurses with his "seductive Arab glances." His eyes were indeed wide and beautiful in the photographs as he opened his mouth for the nurse's spoon.

The next day, my father called to tell us Munib's surgery had been a complete success, and he was resting and doing well. They would be returning in a week, as planned.

A day later, on a breezy, sunny day, my grandmother called me in from where I was playing across the street. I ran across the road and into the house, surprised to find my mother standing in the living room.

"Mommy!" I shouted in surprise. "You're back from the hospital!"

"Yes, sweetie," she said, opening her arms wide to hug me. Then she took my hand and led me into her bedroom. The rest is a blur, but in those next few minutes, she managed to tell me that Munib had died.

I stared at her, confused.

"But he's fine," I insisted. "Daddy said so!"

My mother's upper lip quivered despite her calm tone.

I imagine she took me in her arms, but I remember nothing except my howling as the meaning of what she'd just told me began to become clear.

"No!" I screamed in disbelief. "I want my brother!"

I screamed over and over that I wanted Munib. I can't remember whether my mother was crying, only that she tried to console me as I continued to wail.

I could hardly breathe between sobs. The air around me was closing in, squeezing my heart, which pounded so hard I could barely stand the pain. Everything in the world was collapsing. I wanted this horrible moment to disappear, to wake up and find this was all a nightmare and that everything was fine and Munib would be coming home with my father.

My grandmother may have come into the bedroom; perhaps she was crying too. I remember nothing except my own numbing, horrible pain when I realized everything in my life was crumbling. Horrible things did happen, even to my very own family. To *me*.

"Where's Daddy?" I cried, suddenly wanting the comfort of his strong, loving arms.

"He's coming home," my mother said softly, "after the burial."

Burial? A burial for my little brother? How was that possible? He would be put in the ground where we would never see him again? No! I couldn't fathom it. Only a few days ago, he'd been laughing as we rolled the ball back and forth, chuckling hysterically as I raced him in his stroller around the block as quickly as I could so I could get back home and earn my nickel for ice cream.

All I could think of in those awful moments was how much I wanted Munib home. If we could just have him back with us, I promised God, I would *never* complain again when I was asked to take him for a walk in his stroller. I would kiss his round cheeks over and over, breathe in his sweet scent of baby shampoo. I felt horribly guilty for the times I'd grumbled about having to entertain him or for getting impatient when he tried to take the vacuum cleaner hose from me, making it hard for me to finish the chore I hated but which fascinated him. I felt guilty for the times I'd complained about having to take him for a walk when I wanted to be out playing with my friends instead.

"I want my brother now!" I screamed into the afternoon. Each time I'd begin to quiet down, I'd imagine his happy blue eyes, round cheeks, and giggling smile and burst into a new round of crying.

None of us traveled to San Francisco for the unimaginably sad event. Islamic custom dictates that a burial be carried out as soon after death as possible. Transporting Munib's body back to Honolulu for burial wasn't an option. My mother was too weak from her hospitalization to fly to San Francisco to be with my father, and my grandmother couldn't leave my mother, me, and Grandy to attend the burial herself.

I'm sure there were discussions between my parents about the best way to proceed, and my mother would have been practical. As torn and anguished as she was, wanting to be at her husband's side for their son's burial, to glimpse or touch her child's little body one last time before he was lost to her forever, she also must have wanted to spare my father any additional distress by going along with his custom of an immediate burial. Nora and John, her dear cousins, were there to support him, she would have reasoned, and he'd be back in Honolulu in a few days so they could comfort each other.

When my father returned, he looked solemn, broken. He told us Munib's surgery had been a success, but later one of the stitches had broken loose, traveled through his bloodstream, and gone to his brain, causing a stroke. It had been a freak occurrence, something the doctors could not have foreseen. He described his grief as he carried his son for the last time at the cemetery. John Hampton had offered to carry Munib to lessen the blow on him, but my father had insisted he carry his son himself and lay his small, shrouded, coffinless body in the grave, facing Mecca, as is Islamic custom. He cried quietly as he said this, his face grimacing at the memory, the way it had that day in Tehran when he told me Baba had died.

MY FATHER LEFT for Kuwait. My mother and I stayed an extra two months in Honolulu until November, so she could continue with her tests and treatments and have her parents' support after the unbearable agony of losing her son. I was to continue as usual, returning to the Aina Haina school and spending Halloween in Hawaii. My mother took me to pick out a jack-o'-lantern and a gypsy costume from the Aina Haina store, and together we set out candy for trick-or-treaters. Halloween in Honolulu is the last memory I have of that summer.

Many years later, Nora Hampton recalled my father's anguish in the days leading up to Munib's surgery in San Francisco. Once word had spread in the local newspapers about the experimental procedure, well-meaning strangers called Nora's home to urge my father not to have Munib's surgery done. Several people claimed they had the same condition and had lived for years without significant impairment. And yet, as my father and I would much later reminisce about those times, he went through with Munib's surgery, despite his deep reservations, because my mother had felt so strongly about having it done. Since she had been ill at the time, he'd wanted to lessen her worries. I finally learned just how skeptical he had been about it all, and yet he'd agreed to it because he wanted to give his wife whatever peace of mind he could while she was fighting her own battle. He had acquiesced to her wishes and gone forward with something he wasn't confident about, despite having been reassured by the experts that the outcome would be favorable.

My father never forgave himself for going against his instincts. He would shut his eyes whenever he remembered that time and turn his gaze inward. Yet I never heard him blame anyone other than himself or display any anger toward my mother for her staunch belief in the surgery. He had acted out of love for her, wanting to lessen her anxiety, but he had paid the price of knowing he should have heeded his own skeptical feelings. The guilt he felt must have been unbearable. If he'd acted more selfishly, we might still have Munib.

nineteen

Recovery

IN KUWAIT, OUR LIVES LIMPED BACK ON TRACK DESPITE THE
crushing heartbreak we'd just been through. I began fourth
grade and was challenged by both my Arabic schoolwork and
my English studies in the classroom in Mina Abdullah, which
only got about an hour and a half of my attention each day
after my first half day in Shuaiba. My mother had to step in
more to help me with my English homework, and we spent
afternoons sitting in her bed making European history time
lines on long rolls of paper for me to memorize; she put in
Julius Caesar, Hannibal, Charlemagne, Magellan, and Christo-
pher Columbus, among others.

My parents put up a valiant front despite their blinding
sorrow, clinging to those elusive shards of happiness we'd had
before losing Munib, moments that now seemed like a blissful
dream. Several of my father's Arab male friends dropped by
in the evenings to cheer him up with a game of backgammon.
It would liven his mood, and I enjoyed watching the men roll
the dice and slap their pieces on the wooden board as they
sparred, chuckling genially at each other's wins and losses.

My parents had bought me the latest Elvis and Beach Boys records in Honolulu, and I played them over and over on the new console they had shipped from the States. They also bought me a record by Chubby Checker, featuring the popular "Let's Twist Again," and I would practice the twist that I'd learned in Honolulu. Sometimes my parents played their own music again, Mantovani's hits or Harry Belafonte's calypsos. I would tear up whenever I heard "Jamaica Farewell," having experienced, through Munib's death, just how painful a parting was. But I would perk up when the jubilant "Jump in the Line" came on, as I pranced around the living room, my sadness evaporating into the joyful Caribbean tune. Eventually, my parents began to entertain a few friends again and were even dressing up and going out at night.

I found solace being back among my Arab girlfriends and the routine of the Shuaiba school, where the girls were happy to see me after the longer than usual summer vacation. In Shuaiba, my best friend was Aisha Rashid, a tall, slim village girl with a long black braid and brown streaks across her front teeth. The daughter of a fisherman, Aisha was a year older than the rest of us and the smartest girl in our class. She had a sensible, almost maternal, demeanor, studied hard, and never got into trouble or answered back to the teachers as some girls did. The teachers, in turn, never needed to reprimand her, but her obedience seemed to be out of intelligence rather than meekness.

We all looked up to Aisha and took it for granted she'd be the one to do well in all the tests and recitations. She took me under her wing, and I joined her group of five or six girls in the mornings before the bell rang, linking arms and walking around the playground, memorizing the day's lessons to be ready for class. We never talked about what we would do or be in the future, but had Aisha declared she wanted to be a doctor or an engineer, none of us would have doubted her, although for a village girl from a humble, conservative family, these were practically unimaginable options. I often yearned to be able to visit Aisha in her home in Shuaiba, to see how she did errands for her mother and helped take care of her younger siblings. I was told by some of the other girls that she lived in one of the village's old mud houses, a traditional house with a wind tower at the top that drew in the air to cool it rather than an air conditioner. But it would have been impossible for me to stay after school. I always had to leave class before the end of the morning session to make it to my English school on time.

An added loss that year was that Cynthia, having finished sixth grade, had gone away to an Italian girls' boarding school in Beirut. The absence of my good friend and mentor for most of the year left me feeling the loss deeply. Her brother, Roger, now four, missed his older sister too. Looking lonely, he would appear at our front door to hang around me for company. Although I sometimes feigned indifference to his presence, with Munib no longer pitter-pattering after me, it gave me a certain comfort to have Roger nearby.

LUCKILY, ANOTHER GIRL had just moved to Mina Abdullah. Margaret Arroyo, a year younger than me, was half Spanish and half American, with chocolate-colored hair and eyes like her tall, striking father, Carlos, originally from Panama. Her mother, Estelle, some years older than my mother, wore her brown hair in a loose bun at the nape of her neck and reminded me of the bold pioneer women in cowboy movies. Margaret had a teenage brother in high school in the States, but her younger brother, Robby, who was five, was a cherubic-faced blond boy her parents had adopted. He walked with a limp from having contracted polio as a baby, before he could be immunized. He was impishly cute and mischievous, and his limp made him even more endearing.

Margaret and her family had moved to Mina Abdullah from Saudi Arabia, where her father, a petroleum engineer, had worked. Her parents were somewhat unconventional, and upon hearing that I attended the Shuaiba Arabic girls' school in the mornings, enrolled Margaret there to learn Arabic too. I was happy to have someone riding in the car to Shuaiba with me and waiting with me at the Shuaiba school gate so we could be driven back to our compound for our Calvert lessons.

Mr. Arroyo was an avid horseman, and we Mina Abdullah kids were excited when Margaret told us their two horses were being brought up from Saudi Arabia. Since Sabha was now the only horse in the stable, we couldn't wait for the two horses to arrive and liven things up. My father, deeply grieving the loss of Munib, seldom rode Sabha, and since my accident, I'd been forbidden to ride without his personal supervision. Even then, he was careful to keep his hands on the reins, leading me around himself as he walked alongside me. Although Jalal and Mohammad continued to exercise Sabha, things had grown quiet around the horse house.

When the Arroyo horses arrived, things changed. There was a white mare named Hediya, "gift" in Arabic, which was Mr. Arroyo's, and a smaller brown pony named Abaya, after the black cloak worn by the Saudi and Kuwaiti women, which was Margaret's. Both horses were more docile than Sabha.

Mr. Arroyo was eager to go riding with Margaret, especially with the wide expanse of near-empty beach available in Mina Abdullah. Aware of my riding accident the year before, as well as my parents' recent loss of their son and their increased fears for my safety, Mr. Arroyo proposed that he take Margaret and me on rides, where I could ride his gentle horse, Hediya, and he would ride the more spirited Sabha.

My mother did not want me to ride any horse at all. But a combination of my begging and Mr. Arroyo's assurances that Hediya's compliant nature would pose no threat to me swayed her to allow me to ride again, provided I didn't ever ride Sabha. She must have continued to struggle with the idea of my riding each afternoon when I ran out of the house to go to the stables; she also must have told herself that it was best to let me do something I loved so much, and that Mr. Arroyo would keep me safe.

I harbored some gut fear of riding after my accident, but it was outweighed by my desire for adventure with Margaret and her father. As soon as the afternoon cooled down and my homework was done, I'd pull on my cowboy boots and wait for them to pick me up to go to the horse house.

The first time I pressed my foot into the stirrup and took the reins, hoisting myself onto the white mare's back, a shiver rippled through me, and my legs trembled.

Mr. Arroyo nodded encouragingly. "You'll be fine, Kathy," he said.

Indeed, Hediya patiently stood still, as if to prove she was up to the job of calming my fears. Despite her size, she was, as Mr. Arroyo had promised, easy to control. The three of us headed out of the fenced stables toward the softer sand of the beach, and I relaxed into Hediya's even gait. Margaret's smaller Abaya trotted along beside me. Sabha, frisky as ever, took the lead, but was capably reined in by Mr. Arroyo.

We would start toward Shuaiba, several miles away, and after a few minutes of steady walking on the soft sand, Margaret and I were allowed to trot our horses and then spur them into a canter. Our horses' hooves splashed in the silvery-gray sea that had receded with the low afternoon tide to expose the mossy corals and sandbars, while the sun sank lower behind the distant refinery in fluid streams of pink and magenta. I was finally transported to another world free of any hint of illness or death. I was grateful to Carlos Arroyo for realizing this was what I desperately needed to lift me from the heavy sadness enveloping our family.

Whenever we approached Shuaiba, where the fishermen were cleaning their nets alongside boys swimming near the shore, Margaret and I urged our horses into a gallop to show off, hoping some of our schoolmates would see us. Although the fear of falling occasionally still gripped me, if Hediya galloped faster to try to keep up with Sabha, I'd rein her in, and she would slow down. Each time we rode out of the stable, my courage grew, and I settled more comfortably into Hediya's predictable stride until I was finally no longer afraid.

Sometimes our afternoon rides took us in the opposite direction, to the stretch of public beach south of the Mina Abdullah compound. Here there were no buildings, just occasional cars parked on the dunes where Kuwaiti families came to swim or picnic. During the week, this beach was usually deserted. We'd ride until we reached Riyah palace, the beach house bungalow that belonged to Kuwait's crown prince. I kept hoping to glimpse the prince on one of his visits, but we never saw anyone other than the watchman guarding the property. The beach was mostly ours to roam.

Occasionally, especially after a storm, we'd slide off our horses to inspect the abundant dead sea life that had been churned up on shore by the raging waves—thick clumps of brown seaweed entangled with shells, huge purple jellyfish the size of platters, dead sea cucumbers, and carcasses of crabs with claws as large as my mother's garden shears. As fascinating as I found it, at times I had to turn away, unable to bear the weak sensation in my stomach at the blatant evidence of decay, reminders of Munib's death. I was becoming more courageous in riding, feeling almost invincible now that Hediya followed my every command; still, I could easily be pulled back into a swamp of grief and fear whenever I saw something dead, some animal or bird, reminding me of the fragility of life and of our terrible loss.

SEVERAL OF MY father's cousins had recently moved from Jerusalem to Kuwait for work, and they began to drive the hour from the city to Mina Abdullah on Fridays to have lunch with us and swim at our private beach. I liked his cousin Malak, a stylish woman with caramel skin, black hair, and piercing dark eyes. Her tall, slim husband, Rasheed, was equally striking, with jet-black hair and a mustache. They had two children—Samar, two years younger than me, and Omar, a year younger.

Malak and Rasheed were a modern couple, and I over-heard my mother once say to my father, "It's so fortunate Malak finally moved away from Jerusalem and her meddle-some, old-fashioned mother-in-law."

They seemed as fond of dancing as my parents, and after lunch in the living room, my father played music on our stereo, and the grown-ups pushed aside the coffee tables to dance. The music ranged from my parents' favorites like "Mambo Italiano" by Rosemary Clooney, or "Never on Sunday," sung by Connie Francis, to newer music Malak brought along, such as an album by the Egyptian–Italian singer Dalida, who sang in French, Italian, Arabic, and German. Malak knew all the Latin dances my parents did, and they traded partners and even danced with Samar and me. I especially liked dancing the samba, touching our elbows with the fingertips of our opposite hand while rocking our hips back and forth in syncopated steps in an animated circle around the living room.

Other times we drove into Kuwait City to visit Malak and Rasheed. I loved driving from our quiet desert compound into the bustling city where the traffic policemen in their white uniforms and gloves ushered cars in and out of the carousel-like roundabouts. I was fascinated by the newly built, colorful Kuwaiti houses that had begun to spring up along the road as we approached the city. These multilevel homes were painted in vibrant turquoise, pink, green, or red, with large balconies and cement trellises.

"Look, Mommy! Don't you wish we lived in a pretty house like that?" I asked.

"Um-hm," my mother answered, although I could sense she thought they were garish.

Each time we drove into the city, new ones had popped up like iridescent weeds, fanciful, happy, unselfconscious structures. I wished we lived in one of these fruity concoctions instead of in our understated, prefab American house.

ONE AFTERNOON AFTER school, Estelle Arroyo came over and asked to see my mother. Watching the two of them talk quietly from where I sat at the dining room table doing my homework, I could tell something was wrong. Had I done anything to get me into trouble? My mother called me over to them.

"Kathy, have you felt your head itching lately?" she asked.

"Sometimes," I said, feeling it start to itch again.

"Let's have a look." She and Estelle poked through my hair. By then, Margaret had been attending the Arabic school in Shuaiba with me for some months, and that morning her mother had found lice in her hair. Now I was being checked for any as well.

"Uh-oh," my mother said. "Here they are."

"Yep," Estelle agreed.

Because of my hair's light color, the white nits had been harder to spot. Since the teachers didn't routinely check my or Margaret's hair as they did the other girls', assuming our hygienic, modern homes precluded our contracting lice, our hair had become thoroughly infested.

Right away, my mother and Estelle took me out to the patio, sat me on a chair, and brought out the kerosene my father used to light his barbecue. Wetting wads of cotton, they saturated my hair with it to kill the lice.

"It smells! I can't breathe!" I complained, as my mother, using a comb threaded with steel wool, carefully combed through my long hair to remove the stubborn nits. The steel wool made the comb's teeth even tighter, and it was a painstakingly slow and uncomfortable process despite her efforts to be gentle.

"I'm getting dizzy!" I cried, squirming and holding my nose from the piercing smell.

"Kathy, sit still," she said. "This is the only way to get the eggs before they hatch into more lice."

I couldn't believe I had lice! I thought of the girls in my school who had been pulled out of line and isolated in the bathrooms while their hair was drenched in reeking disinfectant, and of how they'd cried in shame and had to leave school for the day. I had felt sorry for them but was confident I'd never have to endure their humiliation. I smelled the disinfectant in the bathrooms for hours afterward. In my unwitting feeling of superiority, I never thought I was as vulnerable as they were. I now saw how lucky I was that I hadn't had to endure this embarrassing experience in school and had only my mother and Mrs. Arroyo to handle my hair. I realized, finally, that I was just like the other Shuaiba girls, neither special nor different. The lice had found me.

twenty

Safia

A FEW MONTHS AFTER WE RETURNED TO KUWAIT, THE FALL after Munib's death, my parents hired a full-time housekeeper. My father had asked his sister Aisha to find a woman from the Mount of Olives who would travel to Kuwait to live with us and take care of the house, in addition to our usual houseboy. Aunt Aisha soon heard from a recently divorced village woman who was looking to support herself away from the village and the husband who had divorced her and taken custody of her five children.

Safia was a plain woman in her early thirties and completely illiterate. When she first arrived in Kuwait, she cried every day for her children. She spoke no English, so my father and I had to translate whatever my mother wanted to say to her, and vice versa. But Safia and I immediately hit it off.

She had been married at the age of fourteen to a young man a year older, and by her late twenties had had nine children, five of them living and four who died as infants. Her abusive in-laws had recently forced their son to divorce her for no reason other than they didn't like her. Under Jordanian family law at the time, in a case of divorce, a father retained custody of any children over the age of seven, regardless of whether the mother was fit to care for them. Her youngest child had just turned seven, so Safia had to give him up to her ex-husband.

Her only means of support was to find work as a housekeeper, but she wanted to move away from the gossip and heartache she'd endured the past two years in the village. Despite her agony at leaving her children behind, and her never having ridden on an airplane, she agreed to travel to Kuwait to work for us.

Safia quickly became attached to me as if I were one of her own; she respected and admired my mother and treated my father like a god. She did everything she was asked to do, including cooking our favorite Arabic dishes—stuffed squash and eggplant, rolled stuffed grape leaves, any number of vegetable and lamb stews. Like Aunt Suad, she was scrupulous about cleaning—vacuuming, mopping, ironing, and polishing the brass tables with Ajax and lemon juice so they shone like mirrors. No job was too great for her to tackle.

She came from a large clan whose various branches lived on the Mount of Olives, yet Safia was one of few village women who did not wear the long embroidered Palestinian women's village *thobe*.

She knew many of the same people I did from my summers in Baba's house. Only from Safia I got a deeper, behind-the-scenes glimpse at the lives of the families living on the Mount of Olives. From her I heard things about the wider world—men beating their wives or other men, wives bucking under the authority of husbands or in-laws—I wouldn't have picked up from my parents.

Whenever I asked her to tell me a fairy tale before I went to bed, she had little imagination for it. But the stories of her life in the village were as colorful as any fictitious tale. There was the scandalous account of a neighbor who secretly rode a horse down to Jericho to elope with a soldier she was in love with. Another neighbor went out one night and met up with a wild hyena—he stiffened in terror and died on the spot. Safia insisted hyenas roamed the Mount of Olives at night, although nobody in my family had mentioned this. Safia also told me of her own children's escapades—how her oldest son, twelve when she had divorced, defied his father, and ran away to visit her one night but was forced to return to his father's home by her mean in-laws. Many of Safia's stories seemed unbelievable because of the improbable and strange way people behaved toward each other. But she insisted they were true.

I never told my mother about Safia's stories. Despite her own penchant for storytelling, I suspected she'd disapprove of Safia's accounts because of the disturbing details of people we might know. Or perhaps she wouldn't have given them much credence. Safia's life was so far removed from my mother's that they might as well have come from different planets. Yet I felt a deep empathy toward Safia—for her bleak married life and the loss of her children—and her stories moved me. I playfully renamed her Sofi, while she, unable to easily pronounce Kathy, called me by my Arab name, Fatima, like some in my Jerusalem family did.

Although I had discarded my imaginary friend, Tima, once wanting to rid myself of the association with my Arab name, I now enjoyed being called Fatima, feeling it connected me to my beloved Jerusalem family. I liked how my aunts enjoyed calling me by the name of their mother, as if saying her name reassured them she wasn't entirely gone from their midst. Being called by the name of the Prophet Mohammad's daughter also made me feel special, anchoring me more firmly to the Arab, Islamic, part of me.

twenty-one

My Mother Departs

FOOD WAS IMPORTANT IN OUR FAMILY. MY MOTHER'S specialty was southern fried chicken or crunchy, cornmeal-dipped fish, accompanied by fluffy buttermilk biscuits. She also made my father's favorite desserts—a pineapple upside-down cake with a caramelized topping of brown sugar or a meringue-topped banana cream pudding. Whenever I came home from school for lunch and saw her back as she stood at the stove frying up chicken, I could barely contain myself, already tasting the crisp skin and buttery meat. I loved biting into her warm biscuits—crusty on the outside and soft and spongy on the inside. I especially liked when she cut them in half the next morning, brushed them with butter, and toasted them so we could spread strawberry jelly on top.

My father was a talented cook too. For dinner parties, he invariably made hummus. I loved going into the kitchen while he was mashing the chickpeas in the bowl with tahini, garlic, and lemon, and I'd wait for him to be done so I could lick the wooden mallet thickly coated with the warm, fragrant peas. He usually made shish kebab to go with it, threading the chunks of meat marinated in allspice, cardamom, cinnamon, and cumin onto skewers between pieces of onions, tomatoes, and green peppers, which he took outside to grill. It always felt like a holiday when he was in the kitchen, smiling and handing me things to taste.

He was also less picky about table manners than my mother. Some Arabic foods were meant to be eaten by hand, especially dips like hummus and silky yogurt *labneh*, using malleable pieces of Arabic pita bread as a utensil. My father also used bread to mop up the sauce on his plate, something my mother never did or allowed me to do, saying it was poor manners.

Once, as the three of us sat down to dinner, my father put a small bowl of olive oil in the center of the table alongside another small bowl of green, powdery za'atar—ground thyme mixed with sesame seeds and salt—a staple for breakfast at Baba's Mount of Olives table. Tearing off a piece of warm pita bread, he dipped it into the bowl of shimmering oil and then into the tart za'atar to coat it before popping it into his mouth. I eagerly tore off a piece of his warm bread to copy him.

"Kathy, put the oil and za'atar onto your own plate and dip the bread into them there," my mother instructed.

I abruptly drew my hand back. "Daddy's doing it."

"I'd like you to spoon it onto your plate," she said, calmly.

"Jean," my father said, "let her dip into the bowl. This is how it's done."

I still recall his reproachful tone with her and the way she became silent, rather than argue her point. But they rarely quarreled.

Although it was understood my father was head of our American household, he frequently deferred to my mother for advice and opinions. My mother, too, although of an independent mind, seemed content to capitulate to my father's customs on occasion, respecting their differences and yet treating them with humor. The incident with the oil and za'atar is the only time I remember the cause of their disagreement, where their innately different upbringings and cultures clashed like cymbals.

The dinner table was usually an enjoyable place for the three of us, a place of recounting the day's activities. After asking about my day at school, my parents would discuss the latest Aminoil gossip. My mother had a peculiar way of relaying this, always careful not to mention any names in front of me. Instead, she would refer to whomever she was talking about as "Doololly," and my father always knew exactly whom she meant, although I suspected she used it as a pseudonym for a number of people. I never met the mysterious Doololly, but whenever my mother used the word, I pictured a frivolous woman in a funny hat, chattering incessantly.

I WASN'T AWARE at the time that Safia's presence in our home had a more vital purpose than merely being an efficient housekeeper. In the late spring of that year, my mother made plans to return to Honolulu by herself to have more tests done with Dr. Terada. We were to join her in the summer when my school was over and my father could take his vacation.

I took in the news of my mother having to leave as easily as she presented it. I had become accustomed to her going into the hospital both in Kuwait and in Honolulu. A few times recently she had suddenly become sick, once even starting to bleed at a dinner party she was attending. She casually mentioned it in one of her tape recordings to her mother, which I overheard, saying she'd been taken to the hospital immediately. I never asked her what the bleeding was from, and she never discussed it with me, perhaps unaware I'd overheard her talking about it.

I also knew at one time before Munib died, she had become pregnant. She had mentioned it in another of her recordings to her mother, laughing as she told her she'd had to raise her own rabbits for the pregnancy tests. I hadn't known the connection between the rabbits we'd kept at home in a box—I'd chosen a white one to keep as a pet and named it Elmer—and my mother's pregnancy tests. She'd simply carried them in the box—all but Elmer—to the hospital one morning when she went for her doctor appointment, and we never saw them again.

The day she told me she'd be leaving for Honolulu, she said she expected me to study hard, even though she wouldn't be present to oversee my homework. She also told me to be extra careful while horseback riding while she was gone. I knew she was mostly excited to see her parents and, of course, Uncle Jimmy and Toni.

Although I knew I'd miss her, I had my usual life with my father and Safia and my school routine with my friends —biking, horseback riding, and going to the beach—until school let out for the summer. Besides, I'd been told when school was over in early June, Safia and I would fly to Jerusalem together where I'd spend the first month of my vacation with my cousins on the Mount of Olives.

MY MOTHER USUALLY wore her shoulder-length hair pulled back in a bushy ponytail or up in a bun. One day, before she was due to leave, I came home from school and found her standing before the bathroom mirror with her hair cropped short behind her ears.

I gasped. "Mommy, where's your hair?"

"Do you like it?" she asked, smiling. "I cut it myself."

I stared at her, not used to her without her thick auburn crown. "I guess so," I said, not yet sure. She seemed too different with this new look. Although I'd seen college pictures of her with a bob and bangs, I couldn't remember her ever having hair this short. It made her face look thinner.

When I went to change out of my school uniform, I caught sight of her glancing at the back of her head with the hand-held mirror. I hadn't made up my mind whether I liked her new hairstyle, but I was impressed that she'd cut her hair by herself. I'd been similarly awestruck when she once described piercing her own earlobes in college with a needle after numbing them with ice, so she could wear pierced earrings. I couldn't imagine the courage or skill she had mustered to do such a thing, and I doubted I could ever manage to pierce my own ears or even cut my own hair.

My mother left Kuwait several weeks later, wearing one of her favorite outfits—a striped olive-green knit skirt and jacket. Before long, we received a letter with pictures of her arrival in Honolulu. Smiling radiantly, as though gazing at a promising future clearly visible before her, she posed alongside my grandparents, Uncle Jimmy, and Pat and Hugh Smith, draped in layers of white-and-pink plumeria leis. They all looked elated to see one another. I was jealous I couldn't be there too.

BY JUNE, WHEN school let out, it was smoldering in Kuwait. The sun bore down from the cloudless sky like a giant heat lamp, searing our arms and legs as we rode our bikes or walked back and forth to each other's homes. It was impossible to play outside for any length of time during the middle of the day. We could only do so if we swam, although we mostly did that early in the morning or in the late afternoon when the sun was less scorching. When Margaret and I were driven back to Mina Abdullah from the Shuaiba school at noon, the heat cascaded in ripples like ocean waves above the black asphalt road, which seemed to be melting under the car's tires.

Soon the *shamals* came, the sandstorms that blew in from the north, and we couldn't go outside at all because the air was so thick with whipping sand. We could barely see in front of us during those blinding storms when it was a challenge to walk from the front door to the car or next door to a neighbor's. Towels had to be placed at the cracks under the doors and at the windows of our house to keep the sand from seeping inside. When it all blew away in a day or two, the humidity would settle over everything like an invisible wet rag. Walking outside on those days was like walking into a bathroom after a hot shower, the air even more infused with the rank, rotten-egg odor of the refinery.

Yet I had come to love the heat, along with the stench from the refinery and the salty scent of the sea at low tide when the fuzzy corals and wet sandbars exposed the hidden life of tiny crabs, snails, and starfish. For all its lackluster appeal on the surface, our desert was rich in its peculiar smells and beach minutiae that I missed during my vacations in the crisp, dry air of the Mount of Olives or the balmy breezes of Honolulu. Whenever I returned to Kuwait with its distinct smells of the sand, sea, and heat, I felt a delicious comfort in the knowledge I was home.

My mother sent us cheerful letters recounting her activities in Honolulu. She wrote of her visits to Uncle Jimmy's beachfront house, her lunches out with her parents, and her trips to the caramel-scented pineapple factory. Along with her chatty accounts came pictures of her dressed in comfortable muumuus as she went on these outings, often with Pat and Hugh Smith and Erik.

My father never discussed my mother's illness with me. He'd simply sigh and refer to her tests and treatments and say he hoped she'd get better soon.

My grandmother was a prolific Polaroid photographer who took pictures of my mother everywhere, even in the hospital wearing her bathrobe and smiling reassuringly for us from the bed where she was having her tests done. Sometimes she'd be wearing a pull-on cap. Although nothing was said about the cap, I guessed it had something to do with her losing some of her hair, but I was afraid to ask. There was another picture of her in a blond, chin-length bob smiling up from the table at a luncheon, her face now visibly gaunt beneath her hopeful grin. It was important to my mother that we see she was active and enjoying herself, even if she had lost weight and had to wear a wig at times.

Yet I wondered if she knew how ripped apart I felt to see her so pale and thin; how a grim shadow would cross my father's face, even when he tried to sound hopeful about the outcome of her treatment.

Later, there was one glamorous picture of my mother

with her auburn hair in a chignon and a caption by Mammaw on the back of the photograph that read, "After Elizabeth Arden." Her hair was swept up as she always wore it when she was going out, so I assumed it had grown back to its usual shoulder length.

My grandmother sent us frequent tape recordings, still our most efficient way of hearing each other's voices, so we could hear my mother telling us in her own words about all the things she was doing. Listening to my mother's uplifting chats assured us she was enjoying herself. The most exciting news was when she told us she'd seen Elvis Presley! She and Mammaw had been driving along one of the winding beach inlets when she'd spotted Elvis and his film crew filming *Blue Hawaii*. I couldn't wait to tell my friends. We worshipped Elvis and loved dancing to his latest hits. My mother had seen him coming out of a helicopter.

Always conscious of keeping me connected to my American roots, my grandmother periodically sent me picture books on American history, as well as novels like *The Adventures of Tom Sawyer* and a book about Harriet Tubman, the escaped slave and abolitionist who led other slaves to freedom through the Underground Railroad. Another one of her gifts was a record collection narrating the stories of famous Native American chiefs like Sitting Bull and Yellow Hand, as well as the Shoshone woman guide, Sacajawea, who accompanied the Lewis and Clark expeditions out West. I would play the stories and songs on my portable phonograph in my bedroom and fall asleep to them at night. Mammaw sometimes sent me an outfit or a muumuu, but her gifts were mainly educational.

While I missed having my mother at home with us, having her in Honolulu meant she was up-to-date on all the newest toys and record albums. Although she was as concerned as my grandmother that I keep up my knowledge of American culture, she also knew I needed fun in my life, especially now while she was far away.

One day, my father brought home a package addressed to me from her. Tearing it open, I found a doll. It was a strange doll, about a foot long with a slender yet buxom woman's figure and tiny hands and feet. It was made of sturdy rubber I could handle and dress up rather than merely display on a shelf like the more fragile collection of dolls from different countries my grandmother had started for me. This doll had coarse blond hair in a fashionable chin-length bob, a tiny nose, slanting blue eyes, and a pouty mouth. She was dressed in a navy-blue airline stewardess's outfit, complete with a tiny Pan American pin on the lapel of her jacket. She was called a Barbie doll. According to my mother, the doll was the current rage with all the girls in the United States. At nearly ten, I felt too old to play with dolls, and yet I liked this one. I'd never had such a sophisticated doll with a grown-up woman's body, and I was the only girl in Mina Abdullah to have a Barbie—all because my mother was in Honolulu.

Dancing comes back into my life in my mid-forties during a fundraiser one night in Washington, DC. I watch a Latin dance performance, after which the two Latin performers invite the guests to dance with them. When the woman asks me to dance with her, I hesitate but soon feel my feet begin to move under me with a will of their own, responding to the rhythm of the drums.

She looks surprised. "Are you Latina?"

I shake my head.

She smiles. "You move like a woman from Colombia."

I have no idea she is paying me a supreme compliment. Among Latins, the Colombians are known for their fast footwork.

"I grew up with this music," I say, suddenly self-conscious but hoping the song will never end.

Then her partner dances with me. He leads me in a sequence of patterns so smoothly that I glide as if through soft butter. I'm barely aware of his arm lifting to turn me. It has been years since I've been led this way, and by a partner who drinks in the music as I do. My hips and feet remember across time.

When the dance ends and the man gives me his business card to contact him for lessons, a door opens. I know I have to go through it. It's by picking up the threads of this music and these dances that I can recover that unbroken time of years ago.

— ⚬§⚬ —

twenty-two

Spin the Bottle

WITH MY MOTHER AWAY, I HAD MORE UNSUPERVISED
time after school. My father had a basic set of rules I had to
uphold when he was at work, such as finishing my homework
and not wandering to the beach or to the stable on my own.
Otherwise, I was free to spend the afternoons with my
friends or go horseback riding with Margaret and her father.
Safia, while in charge of me when my father was at work,
usually gave in to wherever I wanted to go.

By now, more kids had moved to Mina Abdullah. Across
the street from us was Alan Coleman, a British boy my age—
nine—and next door to him was a twelve-year-old girl from
Texas, Judy Scarda. Judy was nearly three years older than
me and had a blond ponytail and freckles. She knew a lot
about everything, especially about Texas. She always wore
cowboy boots, and she had an almost manly authority about
her that inspired our respect. Cynthia and I had played at being tomboys; Judy was a real one. Although she'd physically
developed enough to wear a bra, she made it clear it was an
uncomfortable nuisance, rather than the glamorous accessory
I'd fancied it to be.

Another new family of three boys moved into the house

next to ours. The mother was a petite, kind, Lebanese woman named Eveleen, and the father, Bill, a tall, mustached man with a low, raspy voice, was American. Bobby, the eldest boy, was several months older than me, with his mother's dark brown hair and eyes and his father's low voice. Like me, he was half Arab and half American. But since they'd come directly from the States, none of the boys spoke any Arabic. And there were Derek Monaghan and his sister, Gretta, who were British, and James Graves, the handsome blond on whom I still had a feverish crush.

We were now a troop who walked home from school together or to the commissary to buy candy, went to the beach for a swim—whenever one of the mothers could go with us—went to see movies at the club at night, and danced to the latest pop songs at each other's homes.

At Alan Coleman's birthday party, I was introduced to my first game of spin the bottle. After dancing and playing party games, at someone's request, we all sat in a circle while one of us spun a Coca-Cola bottle. Everyone seemed excited to play this game. The person the bottle pointed at when it stopped had to get up and join the one who had spun it in the kitchen, out of sight, for a kiss. When it was Alan's turn to spin the bottle, it landed on me.

I wasn't attracted to Alan, who was a sweet, goofy boy with a gap between his top front teeth, but I followed him to the kitchen, gave him a dismissive peck on the cheek, and giddily waited for the next person to come in, praying it would be James. I only got to coolly kiss Derek, Bobby, and Alan that afternoon. A few days later, when Judy privately commented on how soft Alan's lips were—letting us know she'd passionately kissed him and all the other boys on the lips—I realized I had missed out on something in those cursory kisses I'd obliged the boys with.

ALTHOUGH ONLY A fifteen-minute drive away, my world in the compound with my American and British friends was starkly different from my Arab life at the Shuaiba school. I didn't dare tell the girls in Shuaiba about our birthday parties, where boys and girls played and danced together—they had no idea of Western dancing or gossiping about boys and parties the way my American girlfriends and I did. They would have been shocked if I'd told them about our games of spin the bottle during which I'd recently kissed half a dozen boys. I worried they'd stop talking to me or tell the teachers.

The Shuaiba girls would have found it appalling for boys and girls to interact with each other so shamelessly. Nor would they have understood if I told them we appeared half naked in bathing suits in the presence of boys. Most of the village girls in my school had little, if any, contact with American or British expats and were mostly untouched by Western mores. The commingling of boys and girls was so frowned upon that our girls' school was timed to let out ten minutes before the boys' school next door so the girls could get home before the boys were dismissed. Those few girls seen lingering in the road once the boys appeared were reprimanded by teachers the next day.

Even the school's teachers, single Arab expatriate women on special work permits, had to adhere to the strict Kuwaiti governmental restrictions put on them whenever they went out as a group to shop or to see a movie. Socializing with men was strictly prohibited.

I slipped in and out of these two worlds, familiar with and

at ease in both, accepting the constraints put on me in the Arab environment as well as the freedoms afforded me in the American compound. In Mina Abdullah, I considered myself to be an American. Among my Shuaiba girlfriends, I proclaimed myself an Arab.

I dared not tell my father of our spin the bottle games either. Alan Coleman's parents regarded them as harmless, but I knew my father would disapprove and might have a talk with Mr. and Mrs. Coleman for condoning such behavior. He might even prevent me from attending any more birthday parties there. Although he let me do much of what I wanted, I sensed he would draw the line when it came to games involving kissing boys.

I wasn't sure how my mother viewed the narrow environment of the Shuaiba school. She never questioned the old-fashioned mores I had to adhere to each day in school and which her husband's female relatives in Jerusalem lived by. She wanted me to continue to learn Arabic, regardless of how the cultural limits put on girls in the village's environment would later affect me. She was generally accepting of cultural differences, so, despite respecting the conservative traditions surrounding us, she might have felt those restrictions didn't apply to her or affect her own life. Had she, however, given any thought to the ways in which the Shuaiba school was impacting me by inhibiting my independence? She never addressed this with me. Instead, she expected me to be self-reliant. Perhaps it didn't occur to her I might one day struggle to find that independence within myself.

Slipping back and forth between my divided identities, previously natural to me, was becoming more complicated as I got older.

Several years later when I was thirteen and a budding teenager, my grandmother remarked on this more conservative, Arab side of me. One afternoon in Honolulu, I had balked at swimming in a neighbor's pool in my underwear when I had forgotten to bring a bathing suit.

"You and Debbie will be alone in the pool, so it doesn't matter if you're swimming in your underwear," Mammaw said.

"But I'm not a kid," I replied, surprised she would suggest such a thing.

"Oh, Kathy," she said, "stop being so Arabic about things."

I was shocked, even hurt, that Mammaw disapproved of my modesty.

My American grandmother didn't seem to understand that the Middle Eastern notion of propriety, something I had to constantly observe, had influenced me in more ways than she might have liked. I'd learned to repress my more rebellious, free nature in order to fit the expectations Arab society held for women. I wanted to belong to the Arab culture, to conform to what I saw as its notion of proper female behavior. I was stunned that Mammaw resented my easy acceptance of my Arab side.

To Mammaw, I was an American. She was concerned I was allowing the restrictive society in which I was growing up to prevent me from having the life experiences she thought necessary for me to grow and mature. It was the sixties. And though it would be a few more years before even American women gained looser gender rules, my grandmother was clearly dismayed that I wasn't questioning the traditional societal limitations put on me.

But by now, I considered myself as much an Arab as an American. I inherently accepted the differing roles of the sexes and even found comfort in the propriety of Arab culture with its more limited expectations of both men and women. Less initiative and daring was expected of Arab women, so it was easier for me to retreat into my shy nature than to thrust myself into the American world of my mother and grandmother.

It was the start of a larger problem, although I couldn't yet see it. The behavior required of me from each of the cultures I belonged to was now beginning to yank me in diametrically opposing directions.

twenty-three

Ramallah

IN THE FIRST MONTHS AFTER MY MOTHER LEFT FOR HONOLULU, I'd sit on the floor in Mina Abdullah browsing through photographs of our years in Tehran and the parties my parents hosted. I saw myself in one, sitting at my mother's feet during one of her bridge luncheons. I had a clear memory of running my hand up and down her long leg to get her attention.

Another picture of my parents and some friends sitting around the swimming pool brought back the earthy smokiness of the canned oysters on toothpicks my mother had set out in small bowls, along with her tangy homemade Roquefort salad dressing on crisp lettuce and the pillow-soft pearls of black Iranian caviar on crackers. These were all things that should have intimidated a picky eater like me. But I'd savored them, associating them with the convivial mood of those fun-filled evenings.

More recent pictures showed my mother in her broad-brimmed straw hat kneeling to dig with her spade in our Mina Abdullah garden to coax the zinnias and snapdragons to bloom in the parched heat. One my father must have taken was of her and me during locust season. The flying hoard of insects had abruptly appeared in Kuwait one summer, descending on my mother's carefully tended flowers in a huge, ravenous cloud and denuding them. She had grabbed the tin lid of a cooking pot and handed me one, so we could rush out to the patio and bang on them to scare off the pests. I smiled, remembering how my Kuwaiti classmates had offered to share their snacks of crunchy, fried locusts with me the next day at lunchtime, a delicacy the Kuwaitis waited each year to enjoy rather than worry about the destruction they inflicted.

I missed my mother's presence and our moments together, just the two of us. I missed walking in the market in Tehran with her and her reading to me in the afternoons in her bed in Mina Abdullah. I missed her cooking, too, wanting to see her make her upside-down cake, watch how she flipped the pan so the pineapple and cherries came out on top rather than the bottom where she'd placed them. I missed helping her dip the fish fillets into the cornmeal before she fried them, as she used to let me. I knew she was alive and well in Honolulu. Yet my memories of our times together slipped through my mind like smoke when I tried to grasp and hold onto them.

WHEN SCHOOL LET out in Kuwait that June, my father saw me and Safia off on a plane to Jerusalem, where I'd spend a month until he could take his summer vacation and we could fly to Honolulu. I loved spending time in Jerusalem. Safia, too, was excited by the prospect of seeing her children after so long.

My oldest uncle, Ahmad, manager of the Arab National Bank in Jerusalem, always stood on the tarmac of Jerusalem's Kalandia airport alongside an airport official to meet our plane.

I saw him from the plane's window as we taxied to a stop, looking distinguished in a dark-brown suit and dark glasses above his thin mustache. Because of his bank position and political connections, Uncle Ahmad had permanent permission to meet the flights of family members or business associates on the runway.

The airport had a flat roof where people stood to wave at arriving or departing passengers, and sometimes some of my cousins were standing up there waving at me as I stepped off the plane. But Uncle Ahmad always stood on the tarmac to greet me.

After hugging me and escorting Safia and me through customs, he took us by taxi straight to the Mount of Olives. We dropped Safia off at her sister's house and then continued to Baba's house, where Aunt Suad stood at the top of the stone steps, waving and calling to me. As I bounded up to hug her and Aunt Aisha standing behind her, Aunt Suad loudly announced to any passersby within earshot that her American niece from Kuwait had just arrived.

Her daughter, Maha, still lived with Aunt Aisha, Uncle Shafiq, and my father's stepmother, Om Hassan. Since Aunt Suad was having trouble tending to two little boys born close in age when she gave birth to Maha, Aunt Aisha had taken in her baby niece to relieve her sister. Maha had continued to live with Aunt Aisha in Baba's house, refusing to return to her parents' home a few years later. She called both her mother and Aunt Aisha "Yamma," or mother, and the living arrangement was agreeable to all.

Two years younger than me, Maha was my main playmate. Her older brother, Talal, who had auburn hair like my mother's, along with his older brother, Adham, lived with their parents in their home a mile away but spent nearly all day during the summer at Baba's house.

Aunt Suad's husband, Ghalib, was a police officer in the Royal Jordanian police force. Light haired and hefty, he often stopped by after work, wearing his beige uniform and police helmet with a silver spike on top in the style of the British Foreign Legion. He usually joined us for dinner and a chat with Uncle Shafiq before he and Aunt Suad took their sons home for the night. Uncle Shafiq now taught at a United Nations refugee school for boys near Ramallah. It was one of several schools for the children of refugee families who had fled their homes in villages across Western Palestine during the 1948 war. My youngest uncle, Basil, worked in Bahrain.

Om Hassan was a quiet woman who wore a muslin scarf tied over her gray braids. Now mostly bedridden, she spent her days propped up with pillows in Aunt Aisha's bedroom where Maha also slept. I was given the spare bed in Uncle Shafiq's room that used to be Uncle Basil's.

First thing each morning, Maha and I ran down to the garden, where she showed me how to pick the paper-thin white jasmine blossoms from the bush. Taking a small cluster of pine needles, we stuck a fragrant blossom on the tip of each needle to form a small bouquet. Once we'd each made one, we raced back up the steps to present them to Om Hassan in her bed. Although she would smile and thank and kiss us both, I could tell our grandmother valued peace and calm. I couldn't help feeling she found my outspoken American attitude unseemly and secretly preferred I be more like Maha, who was by nature a quiet child.

I was excited to tell all my cousins about my upcoming trip to see my American grandparents on a tropical island surrounded by water. Hawaii was far away, and none of them had traveled much beyond Jerusalem. I felt guilty that my family could afford such travel, but I also enjoyed describing details of Honolulu and its different customs, the part of my life they knew nothing about.

"We wear shorts all the time and don't have to wear shoes. It never gets cold there."

"You don't wear shoes?" they asked.

"Never," I said. "We walk around outside barefooted even to stores."

They laughed, puzzled that in Hawaii it was acceptable to walk around outside without shoes.

UNCLE AHMAD, MY father's older brother, lived on a breezy residential street in Ramallah in a white stone house with wide steps that led up to a curved, elegant veranda. His wife, Khadija, also his cousin, was a vivacious redhead with a warm sense of humor, affectionately presiding over her two boys and five girls, some older and some younger than me.

After a week on the Mount of Olives, I'd routinely go to Ramallah to spend a few days with Uncle Ahmad's family. To get there, Aunt Aisha and I took a bus from the Mount of Olives to the Jerusalem terminal, where we boarded another bus to Ramallah. Although a mere eight miles away, the trip seemed to take all morning.

Uncle Ahmad's house had a large garden with several almond and plum trees. Sometimes there was a dog, always cats, and often a few chickens in a coop. A flock of pigeons roosted on the roof, flying away and returning in perfect formation like a squadron of jets. Occasionally, some of them ended up stuffed and baked with spiced rice and meat as one of Aunt Khadija's tantalizing main courses for lunch.

In the early afternoon, my three younger girl cousins and I sat under the plum tree overlooking the street, waiting to buy our afternoon treats of ice-cream pops or *hamleh*, roasted, smoky green chickpeas still in their shells.

My cousins taught me to shake the green fruit off the almond tree branches in the garden, eat the soft, fuzzy outer flesh, and then crack open the inner shells with a rock to eat the watery, still-tender almonds inside that spurted their juice on our tongues. Later in the afternoon, Uncle Ahmad's eldest daughters, Maha and Malak—pretty teenagers nominally in charge of us—would call us in for a more substantial snack of cheese or jam sandwiches they'd prepared.

Each morning, Aunt Khadija busied herself in the kitchen preparing lunch for the ten of us. After breakfast, the dining table in the foyer would be set for her, her husband, and her four oldest children, while her three younger daughters and I sat at a table in the kitchen. With the housekeeper and her two older daughters in the summer to help, Khadija would begin to sauté and simmer, scoop out squash or eggplant to stuff with rice and minced meat, prepare one of her vegetable stews, or roll grape leaves into small, cigarette-shaped cylinders filled with rice and meat.

The aromas of garlic, onion, cardamom, cinnamon, and nutmeg drifted out to the garden where we played. Her specialty and everybody's favorite was *ma'loubeh*—layers of braised lamb and fried eggplant cooked with cumin-scented saffron rice. It was served by turning the entire pot upside down on a tray and then lifting the pot to reveal a large yellow mound of moist rice topped with the meat and eggplant, all garnished with crunchy, sautéed pine nuts and almonds.

While I loved the homey cooking of my other aunts, Khadija's food was a notch above everyone else's. Her impeccable spicing was a skill honed in her youth by her father who, as a young recruit, had trained in the Ottoman army's culinary school.

Upon returning from work, Uncle Ahmad would claim his spot at the head of the dining table, easing the tension of his busy morning at the bank with an icy glass of arak liqueur. After lunch, he and Aunt Khadija would retire to their bedroom for their afternoon nap while we played quietly in the girls' bedroom. When Uncle Ahmad's bedroom door was opened again, we joined him and Khadija on their large bed where they told us jokes and Uncle Ahmad would cuddle and tease his youngest daughters.

"Have you obeyed your mother today?" he'd ask them, raising his eyebrows in mock warning. When they all nodded, he'd grin in approval and give them each a coin to buy a snack. There was an easy, romantic playfulness in the interactions between Uncle Ahmad and Aunt Khadija that intrigued me. Their lightheartedness, whenever he'd flirt with her or take her hand, was so different from the more serious tone of Aunt Aisha's house and even the proper exchanges between my own parents, at least in front of me. Also, taped on the wall of their bedroom was the latest scantily clad Playboy centerfold, often of Brigitte Bardot, that no one thought was inappropriate.

In the afternoons, we sat on the front veranda sipping hot tea and eating slices of watermelon and cantaloupe, while Uncle Ahmad smoked a bubbling *narguile* instead of his usual Marlboros. As a bank manager, he had an active social life, and he and Khadija frequently went out in the evenings to visit friends or business associates. Sometimes they went to a restaurant for dinner and dancing, where they often took their three oldest children. If they were going to a hotel with an outdoor park, they took all of us.

Our favorite place to go was Hotel Audeh—the Ramallah hotel with an outdoor stone patio and dance floor surrounded by pine trees. Other family members visiting from Saudi Arabia or Kuwait for the summer came along. There was smoking and Western-style music, and the women wore shimmery dresses with low-cut necklines, while the men dressed in dapper suits. If there was a live band, we kids ventured onto the dance floor along with the adults.

But mostly, Uncle Ahmad and Aunt Khadija went out alone, leaving us at home in the care of my older cousins. After dinner and cleaning up, we went into the living room, pushed the furniture against the wall, turned on the radio, and danced.

We danced cha-cha, rock and roll, waltz, or anything my older girl cousins taught us from what they'd learned at their Catholic girls' school or from their evenings out with the adults. Dancing was a fixture in Uncle Ahmad's house, and sometimes my older boy cousins could be talked into joining in as our partners, taking instructions from their sisters on how to lead us. Mohammad, the oldest, who was sixteen and a weight lifter, sometimes brought out a metal tray from the kitchen and drummed a lively Arabic beat on it so we girls could belly dance until it was time to go to bed.

The relaxed, modern-day mood among the siblings in Ramallah was noticeably different from the conservative atmosphere of Baba's house. Neither Aunt Aisha nor Aunt Suad listened to Western music, and Aunt Suad, who gaily shimmied to Arabic music when only ladies were present, wouldn't have considered dancing in the arms of a man in public, not even her own husband's. Baba's household on the Mount of Olives was firmly grounded in the traditions of the Islamic East; Uncle Ahmad's more liberal, trendy family emulated a more Western lifestyle. This shift to a more modern outlook in Ramallah was perhaps due to Aunt Khadija's upbringing. Raised in a family of eight girls and three boys in downtown Jerusalem, her father's home had embraced more tolerant ways than had Baba's. I related better to this more Western lifestyle in Ramallah, dancing to familiar Italian and Spanish music. When Aunt Khadija went out at night with Uncle Ahmad, her coiffed red hair and alluring evening dresses reminded me of my mother dressing up to go out. Uncle Ahmad, too, urbane in his pressed suit and white handkerchief peeking out of his outer breast pocket, was plainly comfortable crossing into this Western world for an evening of dancing.

Despite all the lightheartedness, however, Uncle Ahmad and Aunt Khadija had known sorrow not so long ago. One night in Ramallah, Uncle Ahmad pointed out the distant lights on the horizon and told me they were the lights of the Yahud who had taken our land in 1948. It was not said with animosity, rather with a deep, resigned sadness for what had once been.

In 1948, he and Khadija had been newly married and living in Yafa near the sea, where he had his first job at the Arab National Bank branch. When the fighting broke out between the Jewish and Arab forces one morning, a bullet had grazed Aunt Khadija's forehead, narrowly missing her eye. Within days, she and her husband and child made their escape to Jerusalem with only a few items of clothing. Yafa had been one of the coastal towns that was overcome by the Zionist forces and became a part of Israel after the partition. Most of its Arab residents had fled in a mass exodus.

They never returned to Yafa. Aunt Khadija would reminisce about those years of her youth living amid the fragrant citrus orchards Yafa was famous for. She'd brush her hair off her forehead to reveal the still-visible scar above her right eyebrow.

Uncle Ahmad would smile. "My brave warrior."

Neither Palestinians nor Israelis were allowed to cross into each other's territories after the United Nations' borders were created in 1948. No Palestinians living in Israel could visit Jordan. Those living in Jordan were not permitted into Israel to see family members who had stayed behind within the new borders. Nor were Jews allowed into Jordanian-controlled Jerusalem to pray at the Wailing Wall or visit the historic Jewish cemetery on the Mount of Olives. Only once a year, at Christmas, under a special request from the Pope, were Arab Christians living in Israel allowed to cross the border at the Mandelbaum Gate into Jordanian-held Jerusalem to visit Bethlehem.

Although I was vaguely aware of this Arab–Israeli conflict from conversations between my parents and others, seeing the lights in the distance and hearing Uncle Ahmad's wistful tone made me conscious of the toll it had taken on the lives of those I loved.

The threat of our home being taken away had never been an issue in Kuwait. Nor had I heard of this from any of my American relatives. After that night, I became aware of the anguish my Palestinian family felt whenever they talked of '48, the year of the partition that forever changed their lives. It was a look I'd see over the coming years on the faces of other refugees fleeing their homes during war.

I had become aware of the horrors of the Holocaust that year when Cynthia showed me her Italian school history textbook with pictures of concentration camps in Nazi Germany. I had been horrified at the emaciated bodies of the men peering out from behind wire fences and had nightmares of their despairing faces for a long time afterward. I had not connected the torment of the Jews in Europe with the conflict in Palestine. Yet after that night in Ramallah, it was clear that the two were inextricably linked. Despite my safe and comfortable life in Mina Abdullah, events too horrible to imagine were occurring in the world.

twenty-four

Om Hassan

I ENJOYED VISITING RAMALLAH WITH ALL THE COUSINS, sophistication, and excitement. I was equally happy to be back in the quiet of Baba's house on the Mount of Olives. I loved the sound of Aunt Aisha clip-clopping in her wooden clogs each morning as she prepared breakfast, scuttling back and forth from the dining room to the small kitchen with its window overlooking a view of the Mount of Olives slope and the Old City. Uncle Shafiq's bedroom, too, was an oasis of calm, always tidy, with a masculine starkness. There was a serenity about the traditional ways on the Mount of Olives that always made me feel safe.

The village thrived on its morning routine. From Uncle Shafiq's bedroom window alcove, I watched the goings-on outside in the street below. Each dawn, the *athan* call to prayer from the mosque across the street was soon followed by the gong of the church bell from the Russian Orthodox bell tower down the road. The clacking of boots followed as the contingent of Jordanian soldiers, encamped next door to us, started their morning drills. In red-and-white-checkered Bedouin headdresses, the soldiers hoisted and lowered their rifles to the orders shouted out. Once the maneuvers were over and the soldiers had disbanded, a vendor with a wooden tray balanced on his head appeared, calling to customers to buy freshly fried falafel, hard-boiled eggs, and warm rings of sesame-coated *ka'ak* rolls for breakfast.

GRANDMOTHER OM HASSAN, in her late seventies, took ill that summer. My three aunts, Aisha, Suad, and Sameera, lovingly tended to her, fetched her soups, and rubbed her back between the doctor's visits. She'd been a wise and loving stepmother to her husband's young children when she married the newly widowed Baba, and even Aunt Suad, my most temperamental aunt, spoke tenderly of her. When my father talked of Om Hassan, it was always with respect for her gentle sensibleness. Sameera, my youngest aunt, came over daily to minister to her. She was the one most deeply affected by Om Hassan's illness since she'd been raised by her from infancy and had always considered her a mother rather than a stepmother.

Aunt Sameera, sweet-tempered and overly plump from having given birth to nine children, had been married off at fourteen shortly before my father left for America. The reason for her young marriage was said to have been a feud between Baba and a business partner. When the men reconciled, they had sealed their friendship by pledging their children to one another in marriage. Sameera, blonde and pretty, was considered a prize. Although seven years younger than her groom, she'd apparently acquiesced to be wed.

My father, seventeen at the time, had been furious that his little sister had been brokered off like that, especially since her two older sisters were eligible and still unwed. He had stormed out of the house, vowing to stay away unless his father changed his mind. But Baba had been obstinate. He'd given his word to the groom's family and insisted they were honorable people who would treat his daughter well. It was the only time my father had crossed *his* father in that way.

Although I was impressed my father had stood up to his much-admired parent for something he'd considered wrong—and I couldn't imagine him ever making that kind of a decision for me—I also felt Baba had good instincts in making that decision. For Aunt Sameera, as Baba had predicted, was happily married, lucking out with both a loving husband and in-laws who revered her.

Once it became clear Om Hassan's condition was deteriorating, Maha and I were sent away to a friend's house. There were three daughters slightly younger than me in that family whose father, Kamal Sa'eed, had grown up on the Mount of Olives with my father and had also gone to study in America. He, too, had married an American, although his wife, Mary, was of Lebanese descent. Going to Mary's American home always felt closer to my life in Kuwait. She had the latest modern contraptions—a vacuum cleaner, a blender, an electric mixer—and cooked familiar dishes like mashed potatoes and tuna casserole.

That day, Mary did her best to distract Maha and me from the sad events at Baba's house by having us help her bake a chocolate cake with white buttercream frosting like the kind my mother made. It was comforting to speak English, measure out the ingredients for the cake, and use an electric mixer, all things reminding me of home and my mother. Tasting the buttercream was sheer bliss, and I took my time licking the sweetness off the spoon, savoring the memories of doing so with her in our kitchen in Kuwait, consoling my spirit as much as my stomach.

Early that evening, Mary came to where Maha and I were playing with her daughters to tell us the sad news: Om Hassan had died. Maha and I burst into tears. Although we knew Om Hassan was seriously ill, neither of us had imagined she would die. Om Hassan was the only Arab grandmother I had known, and Maha, who had lived with her all her life, couldn't understand that she'd never see her again.

Maha and I stayed at Mary's house over the next three days of the funeral and mourning period, during which my aunts and Uncle Shafiq received streams of condolence visitors. Although Om Hassan had been an unassuming woman, she had been respected in the village for her wisdom and kindness. When Mary finally drove us home to Baba's house, my aunts were dressed in black, and sadness had settled over everyone. Om Hassan's bed was starkly empty, as though a great wind had carried off the warm body that had once lain there.

Later, as I tried to fall asleep, panic gripped me. I missed my father and Mina Abdullah. My mother was thousands of miles away in Honolulu, sick. Om Hassan, with her tranquil, stoic presence, was now buried deep in the ground. I tried to stifle my sobs with the quilt, but I was soon crying uncontrollably. I must have called out to Aunt Aisha because she came into the bedroom and, seeing my terror, sat down on the bed and began to gently rub my back, telling me to repeat with her the first three lines of the Al-Fatiha, the opening verse of the Qur'an. I knew it by heart from the Shuaiba school and through my snuffles recited the lines with her:

In the name of Allah, most Gracious, most Merciful,

Praise be to God, the Cherisher and Sustainer of the worlds,
The Compassionate, the Merciful. . . .

"These words will always make you feel better and protect you from bad dreams," my aunt murmured, as she continued to rub my back.

I kept whispering them with her, calmed by their soothing familiarity. The verses began to lull me away from my fears until I sank into the sheltering oblivion of a dreamless sleep.

DAYS LATER, UNCLE Ahmad escorted me across the tarmac of Jerusalem's airport. Before climbing the steps to the plane, I turned to wave a last time to my aunts, Aisha and Suad, who waved to me from the airport's rooftop terrace. I was always sad to leave them since I wouldn't return until the following summer. This time, I was somewhat buffered from my usual sadness because I was eager to meet my father in Beirut before continuing to Honolulu to see my mother after these many months.

I enjoyed going to Beirut, a lively city with shops filled with toys and clothes not available in Kuwait. We always went shopping and stayed at the Phoenicia Hotel, which stood across from the sea and had a majestic staircase at the entrance and a swimming pool where the swimmers were visible from the bar through enormous glass windows. I liked to watch the swimmers from the hallway outside the bar, their white legs and arms swirling, ballet-like, in slow motion.

We usually stayed in Beirut a few days to visit my father's mother's family. It was a large and lively group of aunts, uncles, and cousins who invited us to their homes for elaborate lunches of small plates of sautéed meats and vegetables and every salad imaginable. Everyone always hugged and kissed us, referring to my father as "Love of my Heart," weeping with joy to see the son of their sister, Fatima, who had left for Jerusalem when she married my grandfather so many years ago and then died so young. This time they would ask about my mother, shaking their heads in sadness to learn she was ill, saying fervent prayers for her recovery.

twenty-five

The Last Summer

I WOKE UP TO A CHILLY, CLOUDY FRANKFURT AIRPORT, TRANSITING on the first leg of our trip from Beirut to Honolulu. Too tired to leave the plane while it was being cleaned and refueled, I pulled the airplane blanket over my head and dozed to the sound of the vacuum cleaners churning down the aisles. We must have also stopped in San Francisco or Los Angeles as another transit point, but I only remember walking off the plane into the warm Honolulu sunshine, swept up in the familiar plumeria-scented Hawaiian breeze, as I ran up to my mother.

She was thinner than when she'd left Kuwait, but the bright muumuu she wore gave her cheeks color as she and Mammaw and Grandy hugged us and adorned us with leis.

The next few days, my parents spent time alone together going on drives and seeing friends. I was relieved to see my mother looking much stronger than she had in some of the recent pictures she'd sent. She talked as jovially as always, her light, southern-tinged voice cascading through the house as she helped Mammaw in the kitchen or called out to me to ask what I'd been doing these past few months and to inquire about her friends in Kuwait.

202 | Kathryn K. Abdul-Baki

I played with the neighborhood kids, and my grandmother drove me to hula classes. Notably absent was Munib. The poignant memories of my baby brother in Mammaw's house last summer before he and my father had left for his surgery in San Francisco flooded me. I imagined him giggling and reaching for the vacuum hose while I vacuumed. I would tear up at the realization that I'd never see him again, that his joyful smile was gone for good. At times, the memory of the awful day a year earlier when my mother had broken the horrible news of his death erupted inside me, drowning me in sorrow.

My grandmother spent much of each morning washing dishes. I could see her at the kitchen window from where I played across the street. She refused to buy a dishwasher, regarding it as a foolish extravagance. When she wasn't washing, she sat on the couch, hunched over a low table and reading. This she did for hours, learning about different cultures or researching a new trip she and Grandy were planning.

In addition to their books, my grandparents had a large collection of records. There were countless Hawaiian ones to which I practiced my hula, and even some Arabic music to which I belly danced in a makeshift costume with a sash tied around my hips. My grandmother also bought me the latest pop albums. I was constantly choreographing shows I performed on my own or with a friend. Although I never saw my grandmother dance, she assured me, with a chuckle, that she and Grandy had enjoyed doing a jaunty dance called the Lindy Hop when they were younger.

In late August, school started in Honolulu. Since my mother's ongoing treatment necessitated our staying on another month before returning to Kuwait, I again attended the Aina Haina school. This year our social studies class focused on Leif Erikson and the Vikings. Images of their horned helmets and plundering voyages fascinated me.

Uncle Jimmy came around whenever he had time to spare from his psychiatric training, sometimes with Toni, but mostly alone. Sometimes he brought his guitar. My mother was admitted into the hospital several more times for tests. This was now a routine part of life, and I started to lose my fears about her stays, knowing each time she went into the hospital she was getting the care to make her better.

One day in early October, my parents abruptly left Honolulu to go to Bethesda, near Washington, DC, where my mother would be admitted to a specialized cancer hospital at the National Institutes of Health. I was to stay a few extra weeks in Honolulu until it was time for me to join them. Nora Hampton, our cousin in the Bay Area, would meet my parents at the airport in San Francisco, where they were transiting for a few hours before continuing to Washington.

My mother was fond of Nora, who was now the fashion editor of the *Oakland Tribune* and always up-to-date on the latest fashion trends. Not wanting to shock her cousin with the weight she'd lost from her illness, my mother jokingly wrote to Nora ahead of time, "Cousin, just you wait until you see me! You're going to be jealous. I'm now so *svelte*."

In early November, my parents sent for me. I left on the flight from Honolulu to San Francisco, as my parents had weeks earlier, for a two-hour transit stop before continuing to Washington. The flight attendant walked me from the plane to the airport gate in San Francisco, where Nora and John effusively hugged me. Nora, as always, called me "my darling child." Then she hustled me off to the ladies' bathroom where, from a large shopping bag, she pulled out several new girls' outfits. Since Honolulu stores carried only summer clothes, my grandmother had written to Nora that I was in dire need of warm clothing for the chilly climate in Bethesda, prompting Nora to pick out an assortment of the latest pre-teen fall fashions.

After I'd tried on a trendy pair of beige ski pants and a sleek white knee-length coat, I skipped out of the bathroom to model them for John. I'd never felt so grown-up and glamorous as I did that day slipping in and out of those fresh outfits in the airport bathroom. Nora, as astute and caring as ever, had wasted no energy or expense to lift my spirits before sending me on the final leg of my solo trip to Washington.

With this enormous gesture of love, she and John put me on the plane to Washington, knowing in their adult wisdom and experience the challenges that lay ahead for me, of which I, in my child's optimism, knew nothing.

Armed with my new fall wardrobe, a blessed obliviousness continued to bolster me, despite my growing awareness of the gravity of my mother's illness. Whether I'd chosen this innocence or whether it was innate, I regarded the world as a predictable place run in an orderly fashion. Although I'd lost my brother, which had confirmed my early childhood existential fears of loss, I instinctively felt that what lay ahead could only be positive and happy.

BETHESDA WAS SODDEN and overcast. My father and I stayed in a motel near the hospital, and my mother stayed with us part of the time. I wasn't used to so many dreary, rainy days, the windshield wipers brushing nonstop at the shower of water pounding the car's glass. The bleakness of the weather reflected the ominous reality of the hospital, especially now without the lustrous Hawaiian sunshine.

The clouds seemed to be bleeding rain. I thought of that word my mother had used—the *hemorrhage* she'd referred to several times. The word had stuck in my head during the past year, and I supposed it had something to do with her pregnancy, her losing the baby, and her subsequent illness. I envisioned the sky now hemorrhaging rain, and I wanted to ask my father what all her bleeding meant. Yet I was uncomfortable asking him, afraid it would be too painful for him on those solemn morning drives to the hospital in Bethesda to see her.

The hospital sat on the vast green lawn of the National Institutes of Health. The complex had numerous large buildings and walkways, and I soon established a routine of riding the elevator up to the floor my mother was on and spending time watching television in the spacious visitors' lounge or going down the hall to the vending machines to buy candy or a Coke. I made friends with the other children in the lounge, and with one girl in particular, my own age, who was also sick with cancer but well enough to play with us. She was petite, and her hair was sparse and very short, just like my mother's was now. I felt sad knowing she was so sick, although I dared not think of what lay ahead for her—or what might lie ahead for my mother.

I was also homesick for Mina Abdullah and my friends, for the sun and our beach, and for Safia, who would have returned from Jerusalem to Kuwait to ready the house for us. School, too, had already started in September, and I dreaded the amount of work I'd have to make up. Although I knew my mother needed to be in Bethesda, the pull of my life and friends back in Kuwait made me impatient to get back there as soon as possible. For now, going back and forth to the vending machines and the visitors' lounge with the other children made the hospital visits somewhat less dismal.

ONE DAY, A slim older man with graying hair strode down the hospital corridor alongside my father and leaned down to give me an affectionate hug.

"Hi," he said in a soft, southern voice, smiling as he fondly appraised me and took me in his arms. This was my Uncle Leo Ashburn, my father told me.

I'd heard of my Tennessee Uncle Leo and his wife, Zora, with whom my mother regularly corresponded. I was astonished, however, to learn later that night that Leo was not my mother's uncle but her birth father from whom she'd been adopted by Mammaw and Grandy when she was a baby.

As my father and I ate TV dinners in our small furnished apartment, he explained to me how my mother's birth name had been Marilyn Jean *Ashburn*. Pedigo was her mother's maiden name. My mother's birth mother, Martha Arlena Pedigo—Lena—was Leo's first wife and Grandy's younger sister.

As a young mother, Lena, my grandmother, had contracted tuberculosis, a dangerous disease at the time, and had been sent to recuperate in a sanatorium. It was during the Depression and Lena realized she wouldn't survive her illness. Feeling Leo wouldn't be able to work while caring for their two small children, she urged him to allow her older brother, James, a dentist near Nashville, and her younger sister, Nell, who lived on a nearby farm with her husband, to each take one of their children to raise. James and his wife, Helen—my Mammaw and Grandy—had no children of their own yet, and were eager to care for Lena's infant daughter, Jean. Nell and her husband, Thurman, also childless, wanted to care for Lena's four-year-old son, Jimmy. Agonized to have to give up either of his children but realizing he had little chance of providing them with a stable home while working and trying to care for them, Leo had finally agreed to his wife's wishes. He allowed the children to live with—and later be adopted by—his wife's siblings.

I understood now why my birth grandfather had hugged me with such warmth that morning. Although I was shocked to hear about my actual relationship to him, it suddenly became clear to me why my mother had talked so lovingly of Uncle Leo and Aunt Zora, his second wife. Leo also had my mother's sparkly gaze and cheerful smile. Although his name was familiar to me from the Christmas cards and the gifts he and Zora regularly sent us each year in Kuwait, this was my first recollection of meeting him and of being told he was my grandfather. I was further surprised to learn that he and Zora had four nearly grown children—three boys and a girl whom we'd seen in pictures enclosed within the Christmas cards. Those young people were my uncles and aunt.

It was all so confusing! My mother's Tennessee family was proving to be as complex as my father's Jerusalem one with all his half-brothers and half-cousins.

A few weeks later, my father and I prepared to return to Kuwait. My father had been absent too long from his work, and I had to resume school. My mother appeared stronger than she'd been in Honolulu and seemed capable of handling her hospital stay until Mammaw and Grandy arrived the next day from Honolulu to stay with her until she finished her treatments and followed us to Kuwait. I was sad to leave my mother in Bethesda, even with Mammaw and Grandy to care for her. But I was also tired of days of overcast weather and of the hospital where the dull walls and the smell of disinfectant were a constant reminder of her illness. Her smile as she waved goodbye to us from the hospital corridor assured me she'd be joining us back in Kuwait very soon. I was thrilled I could finally return to our normal life, to our warm desert home, and to my friends.

The dancer stretches her long, slim leg behind her as she leads a male student in international rumba. As he approaches her, she backs away, each step languorous, tantalizing. When he comes close to her again, she spins away, her hand still in his. Then she swings back to him, tempting, teasing.

I stand transfixed. She is part gazelle, part cheetah—sensual but dangerous. On the prowl. Her dancing articulates so many things I've always felt—the need to express my sexuality, my womanhood, in a bold yet restrained way, proud and yet grounded. Every move she makes has the strength and subtlety of a well-trained gymnast. It is my first experience watching up close a woman of her caliber dancing. She is beautiful, mystical. Unearthly.

Nancy Ramirez is an American-born Puerto Rican woman with copper skin, jet-black hair, and the slim, muscled body of a marathon runner. When she finishes teaching, I approach her.

"Are you available for lessons?" I ask.

Nancy becomes my first international Latin teacher, leading me on a path I'd been dreaming of since my first dance steps as a child.

— ⚭ —

twenty-six

The Beatles and Dottie

EACH TIME WE RETURNED FROM OUR LONG SUMMER VACATION, so many things had changed in Mina Abdullah. Often newly hired employees from the United States, mostly petroleum engineers, had arrived, bringing their families with them, which meant I'd have new friends. Sometimes it also meant my old friends had moved away, either back to the States or wherever their fathers' next jobs took them.

I was accustomed to Cynthia being gone to her Italian girls' boarding school in Beirut. Being a teenager in boarding school gave her an edge. Over the past year, whenever she returned to Mina Abdullah for the Christmas and Easter holidays, she existed on a different plane, as though she'd finally reached a level of sophistication we had aspired to when we emulated the teenage Donnie Dinkle.

Gretta Monaghan, who was British and the older sister of Derek, a sandy-haired, freckled boy my age, had also left for boarding school in England. Derek was one of the boys I'd kissed in spin the bottle at Alan Coleman's birthday. He lacked the charisma of my current crush, James Graves. But with his sister now in England, the rest of us envied Derek for having direct access, through Gretta, to all the latest British fads, rock stars, and celebrity gossip.

During the Christmas, Easter, and summer holidays when Cynthia and Gretta returned to Mina Abdullah, they brought back the latest dance crazes with them. The twist was out of fashion now. Newer dances like the jerk, the shake, and the mashed potato were taking over. Having learned them at school in Beirut and England, Cynthia and Gretta taught them to the rest of us—how to shimmy our hips from side to side as we stood in place and how to make patterns with our arms, pretending to hold our noses and go underwater or drive a car. My favorite song was "Take Five," a jazz number by the Dave Brubeck Quartet that Cynthia and I played over and over. She and I spent hours in my room as she taught me to emulate the smooth movement of her hips to the jazz tempo.

Gretta mesmerized us with her accounts of "dreamy" Prince Charles back in London, who was now the romantic obsession of every British schoolgirl. Although I found the young prince awkward looking, Gretta insisted he was "groovy." She also brought back the latest British pop records by Cliff Richard and Donovan, dismissing our old music flames—Ricky Nelson and Elvis—as obsolete. On one of her vacations, Gretta brought back an album by a new British band she said was now London's biggest rage—the Beatles.

The Beatles was a funny-sounding name and an even odder-looking group of young men with cherubic faces and mops of dark hair that flopped over their eyes. They were nothing like the suave, masculine Ricky or Elvis of the shiny, slicked-back hair. I didn't know what to make of the Beatles at first, but once Gretta played their music on her portable record player—"Love, Love Me Do," and "She Loves You, Yeah, Yeah, Yeah"—and, along with Cynthia, started to dance the new dances, the rest of us were hooked. Derek's bangs flopped over his eyes as he moved his head from side to side, as instructed by his sister, in imitation of the Beatles, and we all gyrated to the new sound.

IN DECEMBER, MY father and I set up our usual Christmas decorations along with our artificial Christmas tree. It almost felt as though my mother were with us. Although she wasn't there to prepare her brandied fruitcake and her elaborate southern Christmas dinner, the tree had a sea of gifts underneath it for me that she and my father had shipped before they left Honolulu, so I'd have plenty to open on Christmas Day.

Luckily, I'd returned to Mina Abdullah in time to participate in our school Christmas play. Our teacher, Mrs. Tremmel, planned a reenactment of the birth of Jesus, which we would perform on the patio of the club. I was to be the angel Gabriel, who announced the forthcoming birth. Judy Scarda, as the oldest girl, was given the role of Mary. Although I was jealous, since James Graves played Joseph and would be leading Judy by the hand for much of the play, I had the more dramatic costume—a floor-length white gown set off by stage lights—to make the dramatic proclamation about the arrival of the new king.

I attended the various Christmas parties held in our neighbors' homes, and my father and I played Christmas carols on our stereo. Since Safia didn't know how to make turkey, stuffing, or sweet potatoes, my father and I were invited to Cynthia Dawson's house for Christmas Day lunch.

As the chief executive of Aminoil, with many entertainment obligations, Mr. Dawson employed a Lebanese chef and several Indian waiters. The Dawsons' chef made all of Mrs. Dawson's American Christmas recipes as well as a few French dishes.

"The food is really good," I said to Mrs. Dawson, taking a bite of something orange and fluffy that tasted like sweet potatoes but was different from my mother's, which had a rich, syrupy sauce.

"Thank you, honey," Mrs. Dawson said.

Despite the delicious food, I was never at ease sitting at the Dawsons' formal dining table where the waiters carried silver platters and stood beside us as we served ourselves with heavy silver serving spoons and forks. Clumsily, I tried to serve without spilling. The cutlery also confused me. I had two forks and picked up the smaller one to eat the turkey with.

"That's the salad fork," Cynthia whispered to me. I quickly switched forks.

"It'll be so nice when Jean is back with us next Christmas," Mrs. Dawson said, smiling at my father and then at me.

I nodded. I glanced at my father, who was eating silently. I missed my mother's breakfast cinnamon rolls she made each Christmas morning and the homey feel of just the three of us gathering around our tree to open gifts. Despite the Dawsons' kindness, the formality of their table made it hard for me to relax.

Finally, Cynthia and I were excused from the table. We ran back to her room, and before Roger could catch up with us, we locked him out, put on her newest Beatles records, and danced.

IN MOST WAYS my life was idyllic and peaceful. The protected compound of Mina Abdullah gave us the freedom to come and go safely with the sand and sea as our playground. Living among the other expats' small nuclear families, we became each other's extended families. Our parents socialized and depended on each other much more than if we had lived in a larger town or city in the United States, and they all cared for each other's children. Most of the expat mothers in the compound were homemakers, having accompanied their employed husbands. Only a few of the women, like our teacher, Mrs. Tremmel, were also working wives.

One of our neighbors, an American named Dorothy Volkman—Dottie—was a vibrant woman with a stunning smile and red hair styled in a pixie cut. She and her husband, Joe, one of the American engineers, lived in our old house, which she'd filled with festive South American antiques and souvenirs bought during their years living in Venezuela. Although older than either of my parents, Dottie always seemed unburdened and full of energy and was always meticulously dressed and coiffed. Having once trained as a professional dancer, she was a standout dancer at parties and particularly enjoyed dancing with my father, one of the best male dancers in Mina Abdullah. Joe, a mustached, pipe-smoking man, was content to stay out of the limelight and watch his wife beguile everyone else.

It was Dottie who first opened my eyes to the allure of formal dancing. Before my mother had left for Honolulu, Dottie decided the girls in the compound could use some dance instruction and invited us over once a week for lessons. Judy Scarda, ever the tomboy, refused to be lured into taking the lessons. But Margaret and I and a few younger girls leapt at the opportunity.

Dottie started us with ballet and then moved on to tap dancing and some rudimentary flamenco steps. She even taught us to play castanets as well as the fast, stomping footwork of the Mexican hat dance. I'd never seen anyone move as gracefully as Dottie did when she put on a performance for us. Her fingers curled slowly through the air as though through thick caramel, her neck arching like a swan's, her head bending slightly to follow the movement of her arms. She was as pliant as a rubber band, and when she kicked her leg, her foot shot up higher than her shoulder. I dreamed of dancing that beautifully someday, of being watched and admired the way she was.

Dottie was also a talented party planner. The previous year, when my mother was preparing to leave for Honolulu, Dottie arranged my tenth birthday party in her home and suggested a Western theme. She came up with games such as "pin the gun on the cowboy" and "pass the cowboy hat" and made a colorful piñata filled with candy and prizes. She also baked and decorated a large chocolate cake in the shape of a cowboy boot.

With all my recent travels to Jerusalem, Hawaii, and Bethesda, as well as dealing with my mother's illness, time had passed quickly for me. The new year 1963 rolled in, and in February I'd turn eleven. With my mother still away, Dottie offered once again to organize a birthday party for me. With memories of last year's party still vivid, I wanted my eleventh birthday to be as much fun. I asked her if we could have a pirate-themed party this time. She agreed, and we devised games of "pin the sword on the pirate" and "pass the pirate treasure." In January, I gave my friends special handmade pirate party invitations.

But a week before my birthday, I rode my bike up to Judy one afternoon and said, "Don't bother to come to my birthday party."

Judy stared at me. Without asking for an explanation for my flippant announcement, she replied in her calm, Texas way, "Okay."

I still don't know why I said it like that. Perhaps I'd wanted to draw a reaction from her, curiosity or even annoyance that I would say something so mean for no reason. Perhaps I wanted sympathy or to create some drama to go along with my own confused and frightened feelings tearing at me—raw feelings so hard to fathom as to be almost unreal.

As Judy continued to patiently watch me, I broke down and told her the rest: I wouldn't be having a birthday party at all because my father and I were traveling to the States to see my mother the next day. We'd just received news that my mother would not be returning soon, as we'd hoped. She had gotten sicker.

twenty-seven

I Turned and Left

BETHESDA IN FEBRUARY WAS EVEN COLDER AND BLEAKER THAN it had been in November. The first time my father and I went to see my mother in the hospital, my grandmother met us in the waiting room. Mammaw went down the hall ahead of us to let my mother know we'd arrived. She paused in the doorway a second and called out in an upbeat and tender voice I'd never heard her use with my mother before, as though she were speaking to a child. "Jean, look who's here!"

As my father and I stepped into the doorway, my mother strained to sit up, aided by the nurse. She was thinner than I had ever seen her, and she was now completely bald, with a slight trickle of blood at her mouth. I felt I'd suddenly been dropped into a freezer, unable to utter anything but a small, feeble greeting.

She seemed a shell of her former self, so wispy and light that I was almost afraid to touch her. Nothing could have prepared me for how weak she was, how frail and helpless. She'd been nowhere near as sick when we left in November. In the three months since then, we'd exchanged a few tape recordings. In one, she had enthusiastically described buying a chocolate ice cream cone from an ice cream parlor in Bethesda, making us laugh as she talked of how much she'd enjoyed licking every bit of it.

"And I licked, and I licked, and I licked," she'd said, chuckling, as I listened to her describe the sensation of the cool chocolate on her tongue. I'd so wished I'd been there to lick one too.

Then, last month, she sent us a card and had signed her name in a childlike scrawl. Her impeccable, slanted handwriting, always confidently dashing across the page, had changed so much I hardly recognized it. I'd chosen to believe it was a temporary disability that would go away.

I tried not to show my horror at her condition now or to talk about it with anyone, sensing my grandmother wouldn't allow it and discussing it with my father would distress him. But I frequently overheard a word said with hopefulness by the adults—*methotrexate*—the new drug my mother was being given. It was showing promising signs for her improvement.

I resumed my hospital routine of several months earlier. I watched television in the waiting room, went up and down the hall and elevator to the vending machines, or played board games with the other children I met who were visiting sick family members. There were the periodic trips down the hall to my mother's room, but she mostly slept. Other times, I had to sit and do some of my Calvert schoolwork.

On days when she was stronger, my mother asked me about school.

"What are you studying now, honey?" she'd say, turning her gaze to me.

I'd shrug. "Stuff."

"Are you keeping up with both your Arabic school and your Calvert work?"

"Yes."

"Can I see some of your work?"

I'd fidget impatiently and retrieve my pages of math sums or social studies notes from my Calvert notebook. She'd glance at them carefully and nod.

I didn't want to talk about my homework in her hospital room, when I could be in the waiting room playing with the other children or watching television. I longed for her to be herself again, to see her wearing her pedal pushers or dresses instead of the bland hospital gowns, to watch her fix her hair, stand at the stove frying chicken, or take a spade to the flower beds. I wanted her to touch her tongue and dab my cheek with her damp finger to wipe away a smudge; I yearned for the scent of cigarettes and lipstick from her purse. I just wanted to talk to my mother about *her*, about when she'd get better, about *whether* she'd get better. Yet I said nothing.

One day, when my grandmother and I sat in my mother's room, a young man Mammaw referred to as a pastor dropped in. "Well, Miss Jean, how are you today?" he asked with a broad smile.

"Just dandy," she said softly, and they exchanged a few pleasantries.

It seemed strange he would come by. My mother had never shown an interest in church and neither had Mammaw. I remembered going into the Greek Orthodox churches in Jerusalem a few times with my mother and Uncle Shafiq while we were sightseeing. I remembered the solemn priests, their long beards streaming down their chests as they swung pungent incense canisters on chains and chanted methodically in Arabic and Greek. Otherwise, we'd never gone to church, not even in Honolulu.

This genial pastor looked nothing like the priests I'd seen

in Jerusalem, whose solemn countenances appeared to give their prayers added significance. Although my mother seemed pleased to see him, I doubted whether this pastor's casual demeanor carried much real weight with God. I also worried his coming might mean my mother needed his prayers and was not getting better as we all hoped.

Some days, my father sat at her bedside, talking quietly or wiping her brow with a washcloth. She'd smile at him, and he'd smile back. I wondered what they talked about. Were they making plans for when she came back to Kuwait? I never asked my father about their private conversations.

The skies in Bethesda remained perpetually gray. My father and I stayed in a furnished apartment in the same building as my grandparents, and he and I took solace each morning having breakfast in a nearby diner before heading off to the hospital—soothing meals of bacon and eggs, warm buttered toast, and pancakes. The aromas of fresh coffee and smoky, frying bacon from the kitchen drifted over the counter and wrapped around me, lingering in my nose and hair, fortifying me before releasing us into the cold outside.

One night, after I'd gone to bed in the bedroom in my grandparents' apartment, I overheard Grandy talking on the telephone in the sitting room with a family member in Tennessee.

"We don't know," I heard him say in a gloomy tone. "Maybe tonight."

I listened in disbelief, lifting my head off the pillow. Was he referring to my mother? To her *dying?*

His words made her condition suddenly far more real than I'd dared to imagine. How could it be that she might die? *Tonight?*

I started to cry, then to sob loudly. My father must have been at the hospital because at some point, it was my grandmother's voice I heard calling out sharply, "Now, Kathy, hush up!"

Maybe she'd come in earlier to comfort me, but Mammaw's snapping at me came like a slap. How was I supposed to react? And why weren't she and Grandy crying? I wanted her to come in and hug and kiss me, to soothe me as Aunt Aisha had after Om Hassan died. But nobody came into the room.

I began to recite the Fatiha, the way Aunt Aisha had shown me to banish my fears and bad dreams. I repeated the Arabic verses to myself between sobs, desperately wanting them to take away my pain.

In the name of Allah, most Gracious, most Merciful,

Praise be to God, the Cherisher and Sustainer of the worlds,

The Compassionate, the Merciful. . . .

I may have stopped crying for fear of further irritating my grandmother or because I was comforted by repeating the familiar lines. Instead of taking me in her arms, my grandmother had expressed anger at my grief. I knew Mammaw was anguished to watch her happy, vibrant daughter wither away. What I didn't understand then was that her inability to comfort me was due to her own despair at her powerlessness to bring her daughter back to health— and her utter helplessness to take away my pain.

But the distress at the possibility my mother might die that very night bore into me like a stake.

SOME DAYS LATER, my mother appeared to be doing better, so, reluctantly, my father made plans for our return to Kuwait. We'd been in Bethesda three weeks, and my mother had been urging him to take me home. She would be fine with Mammaw and Grandy, she assured him. But I was missing too much school, and he was missing too much work.

We visited the hospital once more to say goodbye. When I went to hug my mother, something inside me told me I would never do so again. This sudden fear that she was going to slip away from me forever was overpowered by an equally strong disbelief that this could happen. I told myself I was being overly dramatic. She was indeed getting better, just as she said. A part of me wanted to hug her tight and curl up beside her in bed because it might be for the last time, and yet another part of me pulled back, protecting me from the inevitable horror of losing her for good. I also knew no matter how much I wanted to stay beside her, I had no control over anything. We had to leave.

The shock that she could die, just as Munib had, was so great that a numbness cloaked me in instant denial and dread. On some level, in some horrible, childish selfishness, I wanted to get the misery over with, to no longer be in limbo about whether she'd live.

I hungered to hear her say she loved me. I wanted to tell her I loved her, but I was too confused, and it wasn't something we ever said to each other in quite those words. Instead, I stoically held her in an odd, cold way, as though I were watching someone else hugging her. Then I turned my back and left.

twenty-eight

Easter Basket

I FELT SAD AND GUILTY FOR HAVING ABANDONED MY MOTHER, especially since I had been adrift in Bethesda and wanted to come home. Deep down, I knew her condition was bleak, yet not having to face it—and her—daily in the hospital enabled me to forget her illness for a while. It was a relief to be back in dry, sunny Kuwait with Safia and my friends. The routine soon set in as if I hadn't been away these past weeks, and Dottie and I began to reorganize my pirate birthday party.

The short winters in Kuwait were welcome reprieves from the heat of the rest of the year. Even when it got cold enough that we had to wear coats and mittens, it felt good. It rarely rained, but when it did, the rain came down hard and fast. The sand greedily lapped up the water as soon as it touched the ground, except where the sand was mixed with clay or dirt; there it wasn't immediately absorbed, leaving the mud to dry in large, flat chips. Swaths of these mud chips, like curly pieces of chocolate, spread between our yard and the beach, and my friends and I ran across them, delighting in the feel and sound of them crunching like glass under our shoes.

Our winter Shuaiba school uniforms were made of a

woolen material with sleeves that scratched my skin, even with my long-sleeved undershirt, and we wore long pants under our uniforms for warmth. The moisture from the nearby beach, however, made our classrooms damp and cold. The teachers brought in space heaters, which took a bite out of the chill, but we were constantly rubbing our hands together and blowing on them to warm them. On those days, I couldn't wait to go for our midmorning cup of warm lentil soup, and even more when it was time to return to Mina Abdullah to my English class in the comfort of the centrally heated classroom.

One afternoon, I went into my father's bedroom where he was stretched out on his bed taking his customary half-hour nap before returning to the office. My neighbor Bobby had just gotten a female boxer puppy he named Sandy, which I'd stopped by to play with on my way home from school. I thought the boxer curious-looking with her square face and bobbed tail. Still, I was envious of the way Bobby and his brothers played with the energetic puppy, throwing sticks for her to chase and dragging a rope in front of her that she would pounce on. The puppy would affectionately throw herself on Bobby, who lovingly rolled on the ground with his arms around her. We had Sabha, of course, but a horse wasn't a pet I could cuddle and train, like Bobby hugged and trained his boxer. I wanted a real pet.

I lay down on the bed next to my father and asked, "Daddy, what do you want most in the world?"

With his eyes closed, he drowsily replied, "I want your mother to get well."

I saw the hollow look of pain cross his face, as it did whenever he talked of Munib or of how much he wanted my mother to be home again.

"Me too," I replied, somewhat put off by his answer, which was a distraction from the subject I wanted to talk about. My mother's getting well was almost a given now that we were away from the hospital. I kept telling myself she would be back in a matter of months to resume her life with us the way it used to be. Although I had, on some unconscious level, already said goodbye to her, I expected her to return.

"But, what's the *second* thing you want most?" I asked.

Without a moment's hesitation, my father said, "I don't want anything else. I just want Mommy to get well."

Roused from his nap now and understanding I had something on my mind, he asked me what it was *I* wanted most of all.

I immediately replied, "I want a dog!"

He smiled slightly and nodded.

MARCH PASSED UNEVENTFULLY. There was the endless amount of schoolwork I'd missed during our trip to Bethesda, so my afternoons were filled with catching up with work for both of my schools. Although my teachers understood the reasons for my absence, they insisted my missed work be turned in as punctually as possible. My father helped me when he could, and my schoolteachers tutored me. But I had fallen behind, and it took many afternoons to make up the work.

What remains clear about that month was the lead-up to Easter, when I went with my father on his Fahaheel food shopping trips. The Fahaheel market, twenty minutes away, had numerous outdoor produce stalls with a variety of fresh fruits and vegetables in crates imported from Lebanon, Jordan, Syria, and India. The road was also lined on both sides with stores carrying imported household goods. The Indian shop-keepers, the main merchants, sold brassware from India and Iran, side tables and chests inlaid with copper and mother-of-pearl, tinseled fabrics, kitchenware, books, stationery, paints and crayons, and an assortment of LP records. While my father shopped for groceries, I went next door to the Indian store to check whether they had any new Beatles albums.

In the spring, the stores also carried imported cellophane-wrapped Easter baskets for the expat Christian community. Like my expat friends, I always had an Easter basket in which my mother and I placed artificial grass and boiled eggs we'd decorated. Additional chocolate eggs and treats would be added later that night by the Easter Bunny. Although I knew the Easter Bunny was my parents, I still enjoyed playing out the ritual with her each spring.

I'd always yearned for one of the elaborate, ready-made baskets sold in the stores that my mother said had too much candy. This year, with her away, I asked my father to buy me one. He told me he'd keep it in mind, but it was too early to buy an Easter basket. I pointed out the one I had my eye on in the Fahaheel store—it had a tall chocolate bunny and lots of little chocolate eggs and was wrapped in purple cellophane.

The evening before Easter, my father came into my room as I lay in bed reading. He looked overly tired.

"Kathy, I have to leave early tomorrow morning for Bethesda. Mommy isn't doing well again."

When I looked up at him, his face had drained of color. "Am I going with you?"

He sighed. "Not this time. You can't miss any more school."

Relieved, I asked, "How long will you be away?"

"Not long. You'll be spending a few nights at the Daw-sons' house."

This idea excited me. Cynthia had just come home from her Beirut boarding school for the Easter holiday.

My father touched my head. "I'll be back soon," he said. He hugged me and kissed me good night.

I hugged him back. I was already anticipating the next few nights at Cynthia's and the fun we'd have. We'd started to enjoy cooking simple things, and she'd show me her new records. I turned out the light, eager to start my Easter vacation.

As soon as I woke up on Easter morning, I remembered my father saying he'd be leaving very early to catch his flight to London and then on to Washington. I ran into his bedroom, but he was gone. I wandered into the dining room. I was sure with all his concern about traveling, he'd forgotten about the Easter basket he'd promised me.

Then, where the sun shone through the window onto the dining table, I saw the purple cellophane–wrapped basket, exactly like the one I'd pointed out to him. It had several large chocolate Easter bunnies and small chocolate eggs and jelly beans scattered on the straw grass. He'd remembered!

I had started to unwrap it when Safia emerged from the kitchen. My father had told her I was to go to the Dawsons' house this morning. I was happy. Cynthia and I could spend even more time together listening to her new records, and she could teach me more of the latest dance steps she'd learned at school. She'd promised to teach me a dance called the Watusi. Cynthia also had the new Donovan album, one that hadn't yet reached Kuwait. I couldn't wait to hear it. I quickly packed my pajamas and a clean set of clothes, picked up my Easter basket, and ran next door.

twenty-nine

The Longest Night

THAT EVENING, I HAD DINNER IN THE DAWSONS' DINING ROOM served by the white-jacketed waiters. After Cynthia and I had been excused from the table, Mr. Dawson came into Cynthia's bedroom where we had just settled onto the floor to listen to her new records. He gently asked me to accompany him into their living room.

The Dawsons had two large separate sitting areas where they held official Aminoil functions. He led me to the blue floral-print couch in the less formal of the two rooms that opened onto the patio and beach in front. We never sat in the sitting rooms, since the bedroom quarters were large enough for our activities, so when Mr. Dawson asked me to sit down on the couch beside him, my heart began to pound.

"Kathy," he said, softly, looking into my eyes with a pained, caring expression, "honey, your daddy called me this afternoon from Bethesda to tell me that your mommy . . . went on up to heaven."

I still hear his sad voice as it bore this crushing avalanche. It took me some seconds to register what he'd said before I screamed in disbelief.

"No! That's not true!"

I ran back to Cynthia's bedroom where her mother, Ray, was coming out of her own bedroom, her eyes and nose puffy and red from crying. She took me in her arms and held me close, stroking my back to calm me as I continued to scream, sob, and shout into the air until I was hoarse.

Cynthia was crying too. Even Mr. Dawson, who joined us in Cynthia's bedroom, wiped his eyes as he patted me on the back. As the shattering news sank in, I began to cry out for my mother.

Finally, I managed to ask, "When is my daddy coming back?"

Mr. Dawson took a deep breath. "He'll be back next week, honey. After your mother's funeral."

I cried through the night. Disbelief and anguish bore into me whenever I stirred awake in the spare bed in Cynthia's room and became aware again of my mother's death. Utter despair made me curl up tight, praying for some miraculous force to haul me out of this terrible dream. Early the next morning, I woke and started to cry all over again at my awful new reality.

After breakfast, I wanted to go home to Safia. Cynthia went with me.

"Sofi, my mother died," I said in Arabic.

Safia's nostrils flared, and her eyes reddened the way they did whenever she spoke of her children. She had loved and admired my mother. I hugged her and laid my head on her full bosom, as I often did when I needed comforting.

Then Cynthia and I went to the home of another neighbor who was also my mother's friend, and we told her—like angels proclaiming sacred news. I wanted to tell as many people as possible, to unload my sorrow onto anyone else who would help me bear it. I wanted all my mother's friends to hug me and cry with me.

Years later, I learned from Safia that my father had received the news of my mother's death the night he left. I'd later fill in the missing pieces as well as pieces I didn't even know were missing. When he left for the airport early Easter morning to take that lonely flight to London, he knew he'd never see his wife alive again. Safia told me when he'd received the phone call from my grandmother, he sat slumped on the sofa in the living room for a long time before finally getting up to pack his suitcase to leave on a dawn flight to London. He had told Safia the news but made her promise to wait for Mr. Dawson to break it to me the next day at his home, where he and Ray could comfort me.

I understand now my father had been too grief-stricken to confront my distress along with his own. I never asked him why he hadn't told me himself or why he hadn't taken me to my mother's funeral. Perhaps he and my grandmother—perhaps even my mother—had thought it would be too traumatic for me. My mother had known she didn't have much longer to live, and she didn't want us there when she died.

Cousin Nora would one day tell me, "Jean was so tired from being sick, she just turned her back on the world. Sweet Jean."

I pictured my mother lying on her bed in the afternoons in Kuwait, covering her head with a pillow as she often did to shut out the noise of the air conditioner and other stray sounds so she could nap. Then I pictured her turning onto her side in that sterile hospital bed in Bethesda, alone, a pillow over her ear as she quietly drifted off. Never to return.

Years later, when I asked Uncle Jimmy why my mother had sent us away rather than spend her last weeks of life with us, he explained that at the end, she had even sent her father away, despite his objections.

"She just wanted to be with her mommy," he said softly, in his knowing psychiatrist's voice.

Her mommy. Mammaw. Her rock. *Our* rock. My mother had trusted her iron-willed mother not to break down and thus help her to bear her own journey. It had been her wish that we leave, and my father had fulfilled it, even though he'd desperately wanted to stay.

My mother wanted to shield me as much as possible from her impending death. But her not expressing her feelings to me would haunt me for many years. Like torn threads that lead nowhere, my questions would never be answered. At least, not by her.

Jean Ashburn Pedigo Karjawally died of uterine cancer on April 13, 1963, the day before Easter Sunday. She was thirty-one. In an incomprehensible twist of fate, the cure for her type of cancer, choriocarcinoma, would be found that year.

I'd never get to have teenage battles with my mother; never watch her grow senile and forget my name, become cranky with dementia, or simply, uneventfully, grow old.

She is forever, in my mind and heart, frozen in youth.

Ten years later, my firstborn daughter would be born on the evening before Easter Sunday, the same day my mother died. The holiday, which for years had been cloaked in sadness for me, became a joyful time of celebrating my daughter's birth.

WHEN I WAS thirty-one, I tried to kill myself. I had everything to live for—a husband who loved me, children I adored. But the well of emptiness inside me sprang up and told me life was meaningless, *my* life was meaningless. I was taken to the hospital and a day later returned home, sad and ashamed for having attempted such a thing. The attending doctor who checked on me in the hospital, an older man who appeared settled and content in his life, asked me whether I had envisioned my children at my funeral, imagined their feelings, when I had taken all those pills to end my life.

I shook my head. I hadn't. Selfishly, I hadn't envisioned anything but ending my own pain and inability to face life one more day with the deep feeling of worthlessness inside me, a feeling of complete despair. I had been abandoned by the universe.

A therapist later suggested that at thirty-one, I was the age my mother was when she had died. I'd always wanted to be like her. Perhaps, in wanting to die, I was being pulled by some powerful force to follow in her footsteps. And yet . . . she had fought so hard to *live.*

thirty

Tell Them Not to Forget Me

THE NEXT DAY, I WENT HOME BY MYSELF. I WENT INTO my parents' room and opened my mother's dresser drawer. There was a pair of red nylon pajamas she often wore. They were soft and cool, with a bit of lace on the sleeves, the pants loose and short, like pedal pushers. I touched them, took them out, and tried them on. I rubbed my hand over the nylon, my fingers searching for the feel of her. I started to cry. I folded them and put them back. I imagined the tinkling of her charm bracelet and the floral scent of her perfume as she walked down the hall to the bathroom to fix her hair and makeup before returning to her bedroom to slip on her evening dress. I could almost catch a whiff of my father's Old Spice and hear him humming his favorite Harry Belafonte song.

I opened my mother's closet and gazed at her clothes, at her custom-made high heels from Hong Kong she'd barely had a chance to wear. They were lined up on the floor—lime green, purple, red—faithfully dusted each week by Safia. Her dresses and suits hung silently suspended as if waiting for her

234 | Kathryn K. Abdul-Baki

to rescue them from the hangers and give them life. I still expected her to come home and wear her paisley-print turquoise dress with the V-neck she'd sewn for herself in Tehran, the one that brought out the blue of her eyes.

I inhaled the undisturbed air of the closet, conjuring up her scent, pulling whatever memories I had of her closer around me. I attempted to retrieve some sensory sensation of being touched or kissed by her, but I had none. Only a vast emptiness stared back at me. I cried. Safia, who had come into the room, cried with me.

My prayers, those few I had recited, doubting my mother would really need them, had never been answered. Neither had my father's. I knew he had prayed even more fervently than me for her recovery. *Why had God no mercy*, I raged to myself, *leaving a husband and a child alone in the world? Was he testing us, the way he'd tested Abraham when he told him to sacrifice his son?* When I ranted to Safia about the heartless, selfish God who hadn't listened to our pleas to make my mother well, she looked at me in horror and covered her mouth with her fingers.

"*Haraam, haraam!*" she gasped. ("It's forbidden!") She asked Allah to forgive me for speaking so blasphemously.

WHEN MY FATHER returned, there was a deafening finality about the funeral having taken place, which was unbearable. With tears in his eyes, he told me how, together with my grandparents, Uncle Jimmy, and a few Tennessee relatives and Washington friends, he had buried my mother in a cemetery in Bethesda under a beautiful tree. She had wanted to be buried in her favorite gold-colored pantsuit.

Now that my father had witnessed her burial, there could be no fanciful imagining that somewhere my mother was still alive and would one day return to us to slip on her straw hat and work in her beloved garden. I had to readjust to the pain of reality that ripped through me, just as it had after Munib's burial.

My father also told me that shortly before she died, my mother had asked Mammaw to tell us not to be too sad about her death. "But tell them not to forget me."

I listened in disbelief to this request. It was so unlike my mother to bare her feelings this way, even if only to her own mother—to ask that her husband and child not forget her. Not one to be sentimental, my mother had taken almost everything, good or bad, in stride. She had been sunny and optimistic, but I couldn't remember her openly talking about love, affection, or even sadness. She'd never appeared to give emotions much weight, didn't seem to hold grudges. She was friendly and cheerful but not gushy and much too busy doing the many things she loved to ruminate on the past. In this way she was like her strong-willed, southern mother. My grandmother always said focusing on the past or on what we could do nothing about was foolish. My mother was more likely to shrug off things with a chuckle, unlike my father and his Arab sisters and brothers who were effusive when it came to their passions, loves, dislikes, angers, and longings.

Yet my mother had finally revealed her true vulnerability— and her fear and love for us—in her poignant final request. At the time, I found it hard to believe she'd actually spoken those words. *Tell them not to forget me.* But my father broke down in tears when he told me, so I assumed she *had* said them. My grandmother wouldn't have lied to him.

In looking back, I am moved by my mother's evident fear—so out of character for her—that we would be continuing our lives without her, that she would become but a hazy memory.

Sadly, this was partly becoming true in the weeks and months after her death. For all the times my mother must have expressed her love for me with a hug or a kiss, I couldn't remember them. I couldn't come up with a single concrete image like I had of my father burying his face in my neck in the mornings with kisses. All the times we'd sat together in her bed in the afternoons while she made up elaborate stories for me, read me *Charlotte's Web*, or helped me with my schoolwork, and those nights when she and my father had moistened my chest with heated cloths and Vicks to release the congestion from a cold, all seemed missing one detail— her loving embrace. Despite all the evidence of her love, I couldn't conjure up a concrete memory of her squeezing me in her arms simply out of the sheer joy of being my mother.

Her absence filled me in those months following her death as I pored over photographs of us together. In one, she is twenty-one, kneeling on the grass somewhere in Virginia, her full, yellow summer skirt spread around her. Her arm is outstretched, and she holds a cigarette between her fingers. She watches me, smiling, as I toddle across the lawn. *Did she kiss me when she tucked me in at night?* Closing my eyes, I'd try to retrieve some image of being kissed by her, but I couldn't. Only a sad emptiness where a soothing memory should have been. The most revealing sign of the fear she must have felt at leaving us was to be found in those words she'd spoken to her mother in the final days of her life—words, I now thought sadly, she should have spoken to me and my father: "Tell them not to be too sad but tell them not to forget me."

Forget her? Did she really think we could ever forget her? How could we *go on* without her? How could *I* go on? Was I expected to flounder and manage once she was gone, just as she'd expected me to cope amid the countless relatives when I first met them in Jerusalem, or adapt in Arabic school without knowing the language when I'd first started? Why hadn't she reassured *me* how much she loved me and how much she wanted me to remember her? She had never expressed those feelings when I was with her in the hospital, choosing instead to ask me about my boring schoolwork. *Maybe*, I thought bitterly, *that was the American way.* No room for sentimentality or foolishness.

Those words of love and fear at leaving my father and me she had chosen to speak only to Mammaw, the mother who had sheltered and nurtured her when she was a motherless baby. I could only conclude she'd wanted to protect her grief-stricken husband and terrified daughter from the inevitable, wanted to shield us from her own sorrow. Our last memories of her, she had insisted, would be of a brave, smiling wife and mother, hell-bent on recovery.

SOON AFTER MY father returned, Aunt Aisha came from Jerusalem to stay with us in Mina Abdullah to give us some family support. Her arrival was wonderful for him and me, as well as for Safia.

Aunt Aisha, at thirty-six, was two years older than my father. She was loving, kind, and dependable, as well as respectful of our more Western lifestyle in Mina Abdullah, so different from her own. I'd always loved her for her warmth and because she didn't treat me like a child. She'd also loved my mother dearly. This added touch of womanhood filling the house was comforting as she threw herself into helping Safia with the cooking and tending to my father and me.

Although Aunt Aisha was attractive, with dark, velvety eyes and hair the same jet-black as my father's, she'd never married, saying no man had ever caught her fancy. She was also more serious than her younger sister, Suad, and hated drawing attention to herself. Where Aunt Suad didn't care about offending someone if she thought she was right, Aunt Aisha was measured in her speech and avoided confrontations. Where Suad loved singing and dancing, often lamenting she could have been a famous singer or actress if only her father had allowed it, Aisha had always been the no-nonsense older daughter. Although she'd only attended school until the seventh grade, she often read magazine articles or the newspaper.

She talked admiringly of my mother, of her expert tailoring, her joy of gardening, and her generosity whenever she visited the family in Jerusalem. If my mother had worried my father and I might forget her, my Jerusalem family would not only never forget her; they'd come to idolize her.

Aunt Aisha often repeated to me, "No man ever brought a more perfect woman into our family than Khalil did when he married Jean."

I soon discovered, though, that with Aunt Aisha in the house, my freedom to come and go as I wished was abruptly curtailed. With only Safia around, I could easily escape to play with my friends. But, unwilling to upset my father in any way at this time of his grief, my aunt was intent on upholding his rules.

My father's rules weren't many, but he wasn't in favor of me running off with my friends on a whim, especially if those friends included boys. Aunt Aisha monitored where I went, so I had to get her permission whenever I left the house and assure her I'd only be going across the street to Alan's house or next door to Bobby's for an hour or so, with their mother's supervision. Like Safia, Aunt Aisha spoke no English, and since most of our neighbors were British or American, it made her uncomfortable to have to go out looking for me if my father asked her where I was when he got home from work.

Luckily, in other ways, my aunt was uncritical and treated me as an equal. She'd ask me to curl her hair, for instance, and always approved of any hairstyle I fashioned for her, something my mother had never let me do for her. She also let me use makeup at home—pat my face with her face powder and put on her red lipstick—and she let me drink coffee diluted with milk, as she did on the Mount of Olives.

What Aunt Aisha did superbly, of course, was sewing. With my mother's sewing machine, she made me a half dozen new summer dresses in fabrics she and I picked out from the stores in Fahaheel and Ahmadi. She could replicate any style I chose from a magazine, and she never questioned my choices or told me a certain style was inappropriate for my age. She enjoyed watching me blossom into a preteen.

With the sewing machine humming again and the house buzzing with female activity, the pain of missing my mother was, at least for the time being, somewhat blunted.

thirty-one

Family Refuge

IN THOSE FIRST HOLLOW AND DISORIENTING MONTHS AFTER my mother's death, my father drove us into Kuwait City more often to visit his cousin Malak and her husband, Rasheed. These family visits filled with joking and camaraderie bolstered him, and I enjoyed seeing him smiling and buoyant. My father and Malak were the same age and had grown up together in Jerusalem. Malak, with her irreverent sense of humor, was always fun to be around.

My father particularly liked Malak's cooking. We'd gather around her table for her signature dish of braised lamb necks over a bed of savory cinnamon-and-cardamom-flavored rice. Lamb necks were considered a delicacy, and Malak baked them long and slow so the meat melted off the bone at the touch of a fork.

The cousins also came to spend more Fridays at our house. After returning from swimming and having lunch, the adults drank tea and Turkish coffee as the men played backgammon or watched soccer games on TV. Samar, Malak's nine-year-old daughter, who was long-limbed like her mother, with a tawny complexion and waist-length black hair, would be asked to dance. She always obliged, swaying her arms like Cleopatra and thrusting her hips to the Arabic beat, finishing off with a breathtaking backbend she'd learned in her gymnastics class in school.

By comparison, I felt self-conscious and awkward around her, especially when it came to belly dancing. Now that I was older, I'd lost some of my earlier spontaneity. I was no longer comfortable being a solo performer, especially around Samar, who had watched many more Arabic films featuring agile Egyptian belly dancers than I had. It was only when my father put on the Spanish or Italian music that I felt comfortable joining in with the grown-ups to dance the cha-cha or rumba.

My father always got around to playing Harry Belafonte, and we all rocked to "Will His Love Be Like His Rum?" But it was when the "Banana Boat Song" came on, and my father started to sway his hips and sing "Day-O" along with Harry, smiling down at me as he took my hand to join him, that my world suddenly shifted. It was almost as if my mother were back with us in this very room, dancing. With each beat of the music, her presence grew stronger, filling my lungs with joy, until all my heartache—*our* heartache—became no more than an illusion.

LATER THAT SPRING, my father took a short trip on his own to Spain. He said he wanted to take a break from work. But I suspected he also needed a break from his responsibilities—including caring for me—and some cheering up from the past heartbreaking months dealing with my mother's illness and death. Also, I was in school and couldn't go with him. I asked him to bring me back a Spanish flamenco dress, something formfitting with a long, ruffled train that I could wear to show off the flamenco dance steps I'd learned from Dottie.

When he returned two weeks later, describing the magic of Barcelona and Madrid, he proudly showed me the outfit he'd bought me. I barely contained my dismay. The bulky, knee-length wool skirt and square bonnet he said was an authentic girl's outfit from Catalonia looked nothing like the sensuous, multitiered Spanish dancer's skirt I'd envisioned. Not wanting to hurt his feelings after he'd put such thought into choosing my gift, I tried on the heavy skirt and tied the bonnet under my chin. Fortunately, he'd also bought me a pair of red flamenco dance shoes with thick high heels that fit perfectly. I strapped those on and drowned my disappointment at the ungainly outfit in a round of stomping to the Mexican hat dance.

In addition to his executive work in Aminoil, my father had recently been given a lighthearted assignment of arranging social evenings for the senior expat employees at the club. He enjoyed overseeing these club productions—they took him back to a happier time when my mother was alive—and he was always on the lookout for inventive ways to provide entertainment. His experience at the American Officers' Club in Tehran, with its frequent dance evenings, had given him a few ideas. He began to organize happy hours in Mina Abdullah, followed by dinner and dance parties themed for the occasion, such as Halloween or Christmas. With the new club's large indoor space and wide patio, music could be played both inside the party room and outside when the weather was pleasant.

My father sometimes took me along with him to the adult dance parties at the club where I danced with him and with several of his friends. There was a live band—four Aminoil

Iraqi petroleum engineers who moonlighted as musicians—that played and sang current hits in different languages: the Italian love songs "Al di là" and "Volare," the Spanish "Ojos Verdes" and "Cuando Calienta el Sol," as well as a variety of Frank Sinatra and Connie Francis hits. The band always ended the evening with a rousing rendition of the popular "La Bamba," its exuberant tempo spurring everyone onto the dance floor.

In addition to charming the expat adults, the band totally mesmerized me. I was finally seeing for myself this exciting world of grown-ups, who all seemed so much younger and more carefree on those dance evenings than they were in their day-time roles as hardworking executives or conscientious mothers. Dancing to a live band was even more exciting than dancing with the boys at our birthday parties. These handsome young Iraqi crooners inflamed my heart in a new and strange way.

At eleven, I was discovering the hypnotic effect of young men singing romantic songs. I had grown taller this past year, my head reaching my father's chin, and was on the brink of both the mystery and thrill of a new world opening up to me, of infinite years ahead to go dancing with a passionate and agile partner. Although I couldn't yet understand it, the seeds were planted for my lifelong attraction to men who danced, men who, in effect, were like my father. Some mysterious force would surge through me, draw me to the man who moved to the rhythm the way he did. Perhaps I was growing up too soon, fantasizing about the future, and living adult life to a small degree rather than enjoying each moment of my childhood. But on those magical nights at the grown-up parties, I, too, was reliving my parents' exuberant evenings of the past. Losing myself in the magnetic cadence of the music and dancing, I felt totally happy again.

ONE MORNING SEVERAL months after my mother died, my
father told me to go to the storage room behind the kitchen
because there was something there for me. I ran outside, eager
to discover the surprise. When I opened the storage room
door, a small, caramel-colored ball with floppy ears roused
and shook itself, then ambled toward me out of the dark
room. I couldn't believe my eyes! I knelt down and hugged the
fuzzy, round puppy. He was a German shepherd mix, and he
nudged his cold nose against my arms and started to lick my
face. My father had remembered how much I wanted a dog.

Cynthia had just returned from boarding school, and
when she saw my new puppy, she smiled and said, "He's your
pal. A real pal." And so, I named him Pal.

In the days and months to come, Pal became my constant
companion, gazing at me with his liquid brown eyes, lounging
near me when I read, and snoozing at my feet under the dining
table during meals. Safia instinctively recoiled whenever he
wandered toward her, claiming dogs were "unclean," yet she
put out extra scraps of meat and raw bones for him to gnaw
on and made sure his water bowl was always replenished in
the heat. Pal, in turn, endeared himself to her with his affectionate gazes, learning to placate her by not sniffing or licking
her legs.

thirty-two

Hani's Wedding

IN SUMMER, AUNT AISHA, SAFIA, AND I FLEW TO JERUSALEM together. Due to my mother's illness, my father had taken too much time off work to take a long vacation, so our summer trip to see my grandparents in Honolulu would be postponed until the following year.

Everyone in Jerusalem treated me with special kindness. For me, it was a time to adjust to being motherless among my aunts and uncles who bolstered me with affection and love. Even my cousins were overly solicitous, aware that I'd experienced a tragedy. Although they may have envied what must have seemed like my coddled life traveling back and forth to Kuwait, Beirut, the United States, and Hawaii, they knew I was suffering.

Aunt Suad's daughter, Maha, now nine, and I still raced down to the garden each morning to make our jasmine bouquets, but without our grandmother to present them to, they didn't have the significance they once had. We jumped on the rope swing Uncle Shafiq hung for us, and after he'd drawn water up from the well, we helped him water the flowers in the garden. Then we all went in for our breakfast of fresh hummus and falafel bought from the boy making his morning rounds with his tray. In the afternoons, we dressed to go to the city to visit relatives or to see a movie.

In the early sixties, there was still no television at Aunt Aisha's house, so it was a treat to ride the bus with Uncle Shafiq in the early afternoons from the Mount of Olives to Jerusalem to go to the cinema. He always got us seats in the upper tier of the theater, the family section, rather than on the ground floor, which was reserved for single men and said to be frequented by coarse hoodlums. Uncle Shafiq was our favorite uncle. A soft-spoken man with gentle eyes and wavy brown hair brushed back from his forehead, he still taught school, was unmarried, and had infinite patience to talk to us about any subject we raised, especially history.

The movies were either American with Arabic subtitles or Egyptian. Sometimes there was a double feature, with one of each. If there was a cowboy film, Maha's brothers, Talal and Adham, came along. If we went to an Egyptian movie, my aunts would go with us. Aunt Suad was especially keen to see the latest Egyptian films and knew all the personal stories, scandalous and tragic, of the famous actors.

The bus route from the Mount of Olives to Jerusalem was short, originating at our bus stop in front of the Russian church and first crossing to the adjoining hill of Mount Scopus to let off passengers at the German Augusta Victoria Hospital complex. The palatial hospital had been built in 1914 by the Empress Augusta Victoria Foundation to serve the German Protestant community, then living in Ottoman Palestine.

A few feet from the opulent structure was an encampment of Jordanian soldiers guarding a line of barbed wire and sandbags beyond which the bus wasn't allowed to go. The sandbags and wire marked the official border between Jordan and Israel, a stretch of no-man's-land, Uncle Shafiq told me, now overseen by the United Nations. *No-man's-land.* The term sounded ominous. He pointed to a similar Israeli army post through a clump of pine trees that guarded the other side of the sandbags and wire, where Israeli territory started. I searched for a glimpse of the Israeli soldiers patrolling the other side of the sharp wire, but the trees obscured any clear view of what lay beyond. When I asked Uncle Shafiq what would happen if someone from either side tried to cross this no-man's-land, he told me they'd likely be captured by the soldiers or shot. This feeling of impending death at the sight of the soldiers and sandbags, despite the fanciful Augusta Victoria Hospital alongside it, always made me anxious until the bus was safely back on the road down to Jerusalem.

SAFIA CAME TO visit us daily from where she stayed with her sister, bringing us reports of the exploits of her two oldest sons, now teenagers, who regularly sneaked away to see her. One afternoon, when Safia, Aunt Suad, Maha, and I were walking along the street on the Mount of Olives, Safia pulled me aside and pointed to a little girl of about nine, with ruddy cheeks and brown pigtails, playing with some other girls in the street.

"That's Noora," she whispered, looking anxious.

Noora, her only daughter, whom she wasn't allowed to see. Safia often talked about Noora. When she turned seven, she'd been taken away from her to live with her father and new stepmother, who purportedly beat her. I could tell the girl recognized Safia from her furtive gaze in our direction, although she quickly turned away, pretending not to know her.

Aunt Suad, never one to be cowed by anyone or anything, immediately called to Noora, "Don't be afraid, girl, come and see your mother!"

But Noora scampered away down an alley, and we never got to talk to her. Safia started to weep. I hugged her, my heart aching.

"May you all burn in hell!" Aunt Suad cursed under her breath at Safia's heartless in-laws. "Don't worry," she reassured Safia. "She'll soon be grown and will defy her father and come see you."

Safia continued to cry, and I held her hand. I knew I'd never have allowed anyone to tear me away from my mother, were she still alive. Safia's grief had grasped the air of that afternoon like claws, drawing the breath out of all of us.

SAFIA'S FAMILY BRANCHED into many other families of the Mount of Olives, so that nearly all the villagers seemed to be distant cousins of hers. Weddings were frequently held in the summer, so relatives returning from working in Kuwait and Saudi Arabia the rest of the year could attend. Since Safia was related to many of the brides and grooms through intermarriage, she was invited to attend these weddings. Not wanting to run into members of her ex-husband's family, she often declined.

Aunt Suad, known for the vitality she put into any gathering, was invited to these celebrations as well, and she made sure to attend as many as she could. She lived in a house within a cluster of other villagers' homes and socialized constantly with her neighbors, attending all weddings and birth festivities.

Although our family was considered city folk from Jerusalem rather than homegrown Mount of Olives' villagers, Aunt Suad was fondly accepted by the villagers as one of them. I was always curious to listen to the stories the village women told Aunt Suad over coffee in her foyer whenever Maha and I visited. The women's stories, often involving disobedient daughters-in-law or men beating their wives or other men, titillated me because they revealed aspects of the behavior between men and women I wouldn't otherwise have seen.

During that particular summer, a handsome young male relative of Safia's named Hani was getting married. I'd seen Hani once when he delivered something to Aunt Aisha. He had dusky skin, smooth black hair that curled below his shirt collar, and a flirtatious glance. I was excited when Maha and I were given permission to attend the women's bridal party along with Safia and Aunt Suad. The ladies-only evening party would last until ten o'clock, at which time Hani would arrive with members of his family to fetch his bride to her new home.

When we arrived at the bride's family home, the party had already started.

"Oh, my, would you look at the bride," Aunt Suad said with a chuckle.

A slight, skinny girl, the bride sat on a pedestal as stiff as a doll, a white gown fluffed about her, her face heavily made up. Her hair was pulled back in a tight bun under a sparkling tiara and a short white veil. A diamond necklace covered her throat, and diamond earrings dangled from her ears. Although I'd been told she was sixteen, I was shocked to find she looked no older than me.

Although Maha and I often fashioned little wedding veils and played at being brides ourselves, the idea of actual mar-

riage at this age was unimaginable to me. Aunt Suad had previously said the bride had finished tenth grade but wouldn't
be going back to school now that she was getting married. I
wondered how the bride felt about this.

The relatives and guests sat in chairs lining the walls of
the room. Most of the women wore embroidered village
thobes and the traditional white village scarves on their heads,
and all sported shiny gold jewelry for the occasion. Once we
were seated and had been offered glasses of lemonade and
semolina *ma'amool* cookies, Aunt Suad gamely joined in the
singing of traditional wedding songs. Some guests, mostly the
older women, got up and danced the slow-swaying village
dances while the solemn-eyed bride watched, occasionally
whispering something to a woman sitting next to her.

At one point, the bride got up and left the room. She returned a few minutes later dressed in a floor-length yellow
chiffon gown and resumed her place on the pedestal as the
women admired the new dress. She soon left the room again
and returned wearing a red evening gown, to the admiring
nods of the women. She did this several more times over the
next hour, each time modeling a dress of a different color, until
we'd finally seen her entire wedding trousseau, bought for her
by her groom. Eventually, she reappeared in her white gown
and joined the other dancing women in the center of the
room, swaying her body shyly. I was surprised by her demure
behavior. Was she bashful to be the center of all the attention,
or was she anxious?

I thought of Mammaw and what she'd think of this wedding celebration of a girl not much older than me who was
being married off without having finished school. I was sure
she'd disapprove. My own idea of being sixteen was to be like

ebullient Donnie Dinkle, going steady and wearing a boyfriend's ring, happy to be living the teenage life. Even my teenage cousins in Ramallah, who enjoyed dressing up and going out with their parents at night, resumed their carefree school lives the next day. This girl, about to be thrust into a world of adult responsibilities, looked apprehensive.

It didn't take long for the wedding guests to start clamoring for Aunt Suad to dance.

She protested, "No, really, I'm too tired."

But the women continued to urge her until she finally rose from her chair. Unshackled by the restraints she felt around her sedate sisters at home, among the village women my aunt began to playfully thrust her hips and shake her shoulders. She moved each part of her body with the control of a professional dancer, her arms serpentine, her chest rising and dropping to the drumbeat, her hips trembling in a rapid shimmy. Unlike the bride, my aunt wasn't shy. Egged on by the enthusiastic clapping of the wedding guests, she flirted with the other women, closing her eyes as if lost in the music, living out her dream of being a dancer. The music and clapping seemed to inhabit her body as fiercely as Harry Belafonte's songs did my father's when he swayed his hips to the Caribbean percussion. She kept beckoning for Maha and me to join her in the center of the room, but we vigorously shook our heads, gluing ourselves firmly to our chairs. While I admired my aunt's bold exuberance, I was mortified by the idea of being the center of attention amid a throng of complete strangers.

Finally, wedding favors of candied almonds were passed around, signaling the end of the party. To my disappointment, Aunt Suad and Safia rose to leave before the groom and his male entourage arrived.

"Can't we stay longer?" I begged. I wanted to see Hani again and watch him and the bride be carried on chairs above the men's shoulders in the festive way of celebrating bridal couples.

"No, no, we have to go," Aunt Suad said, hustling us out of the room.

I never did learn the bride's name, but I was told she and Hani were cousins and thus knew each other.

"Why didn't the bride look happy?" I asked as we walked home. "She didn't smile much or look like she was having a good time."

"Who knows?" Aunt Suad said with a shrug, still basking in the euphoria of all the dancing she'd just done. "She's just a silly girl."

But Safia looked aghast at the idea a bride would appear enthused at her wedding.

"A bride shouldn't look eager to see her new husband," she said.

"Even if she likes him?" I asked.

"Even so."

"Why not?"

"That would be shameful," Safia replied. "A bride should be discreet."

I thought about that. "Well, does she like him?" I asked.

"Of course she does," Safia said. "She *wanted* to marry him."

Her reassurance that the bride was only acting reserved somewhat eased my confusion. Still, the young woman's behavior was nothing like I imagined a bride's to be on her wedding day. It certainly wasn't what Hollywood movies I'd seen portrayed, with all the starry-eyed kissing my friends and I called "mush" and turned away from. Secretly, though, I suspected it was how I'd one day act with a romantic partner.

Didn't Arabs have those same feelings of romance? Didn't they look forward to being kissed by someone they were in love with? Hani was good-looking, and I could imagine him being romantic. I had no notion, then, of virginity, or the value placed on it in Arab culture. Or that guarding it was a girl's foremost priority until she was wed.

I didn't dare ask Safia or Aunt Suad how the bride was going to sleep in the same bed with someone she barely knew, whether they would kiss or do that thing called inter-course. Nobody talked about it, at least not in front of Maha and me. But it was clear some of the women at the party were thinking about it from their exchanged winks and smiles at some of the lyrics in the wedding songs.

I never saw the bride again, although over the next few years, Hani would come sauntering down the road in front of Baba's house. When I asked Safia about her, she said the bride now had several small children to care for and was too busy to go gallivanting about. I continued to ask Safia about her, asking her whether she was happy. Safia only shrugged, as if happiness wasn't a particular priority for a woman once she was married.

What became of the young bride? How many children did she have? Was Hani a good husband, or did he become one of those abusive men complained about to my aunts by some of the village women? As I remember the shy, diffident girl, oddly indifferent to the festivities at her wedding, I like to imagine she's known moments of passion and joy in her life.

thirty-three

Portentous Summer

AS USUAL, ON MY TRIPS TO JERUSALEM, I WENT TO SPEND A week at Uncle Ahmad's house in Ramallah. Each morning my younger girl cousins and I watched my oldest cousin, Mohammad, tall and dark like his father, lift weights in his sleeveless undershirt to build his already sizable muscles. He had little to do with us since he was already in high school. His sisters, Maha and Malak, also in high school, made sure we younger girls made our beds, got dressed, and had breakfast. My younger male cousin Maher, two years older than me, would sometimes join us to play Monopoly or cards. But he generally preferred to hang around his older brother and shoot BB guns or else tend to his elaborate stamp collection, which his younger sisters were allowed to look at and admire but never touch.

I had a strange relationship with Maher. He was lean, with dark eyes and hair and a flaring scowl on his handsome face. Ever since I could remember, our families had joked we would marry each other, as first cousins often do in Arab Muslim families. This caused a subtle tension between us, a confusing attraction and yet a pushing away. Neither of us was ever sure how to relate to the other.

One day, the household was abuzz because the president

of the Arab National Bank—of which Uncle Ahmad was the Jerusalem branch manager—a certain Mohammad Bek, was visiting from his home in Beirut. He would be coming by that afternoon for tea. This was especially exciting for Maher, since the president's teenage son was coming with his father. The young man was said to also have a large stamp collection, so Maher was eager to compare notes on stamps with him. Coincidentally, my father was also making a stop in Jerusalem for a few days on his way from Kuwait to Beirut for business and would stop by Ramallah for lunch. It had been a month since I'd seen my father, and I missed him and was eager for his visit.

It was good to see my father, though briefly, and Aunt Khadija made him a pot of stuffed grape leaves that were now in season. After lunch, as the family waited for the bank president and his son to arrive, Maher warned his younger sisters that the young man was *his* guest and we could not be lurking nearby, bothering them. Maher was already thirteen and his guest several years older. We weren't interested in whatever the young man and Maher were going to do anyway, which would undoubtedly involve endless poring over stamps. My three cousins and I made plans to go to the *muntazah* (park) in downtown Ramallah, where there were swings, an ice cream parlor, and vendors selling roasted corn on the cob.

Ramallah was much smaller than Jerusalem, so we were allowed to walk to town unsupervised and window-shop. In Kuwait, shopping was limited to our camp commissary or the Fahaheel and Ahmadi markets, which I could go to only with my father. Walking to Ramallah independently with my cousins was an adventure.

After browsing the shop windows, we bought our usual

snacks of ice cream and roasted corn, strolled around the park, and, when it grew late, headed back home.

Rounding the corner to Uncle Ahmad's street, we saw two figures walking toward us, the only other people on the road. It was Maher and his much-anticipated guest, the son of the bank president.

As we drew nearer, we girls wickedly elbowed each other, remembering how Maher had sternly warned us not to intrude on his visit with his guest. Evidently, the young men hadn't spent much time exploring the stamp collection. The two boys kept walking without acknowledging us, and we dared not annoy Maher by calling out to him.

But as we passed them, I stole a glance at Maher's guest. For an instant, the young man happened to look our way too. To my surprise, his eyes met mine with a knowing twinkle that instantly drew me in, as though we were meeting again after a very long time. For what was no more than seconds, I had two startling but distinct feelings. The first was that I'd known this stranger in some previous life. The second was—I'd one day marry him.

I was immediately confused. I'd never had this acute déjà vu about anyone else before. I'd never heard of reincarnation, either, but was surprised to feel this familiarity about someone I knew nothing about except he'd assembled a huge stamp collection.

At the same moment, that second unanticipated feeling seemed much more than some little-girl fantasy. I knew in the core of my being—a fleeting, incomprehensible, yet concrete awareness—this young man would one day be my husband.

The next afternoon, my cousins and I went to the airport with Uncle Ahmad to say goodbye to my father, who was traveling on to Beirut. My cousins and I ran upstairs to the terminal's rooftop to wave goodbye to him when he walked to the plane.

As the passengers began to cross the tarmac, we spotted my father and called out loudly. When he turned around and waved to us, we saw he was walking beside another man— the bank president who had visited Uncle Ahmad yesterday— and his son, who were apparently flying home to Beirut on the same flight.

I felt giddy at the sight of the young man. I hadn't mentioned my feelings of the previous day to anyone, and I was beginning to think they'd been an absurd fantasy triggered by the household's excitement about his father's visit. Still, the feelings baffled me. On some level, I wasn't sure how to understand my strong sense of having known the young stranger before. And yet I couldn't help imagining a budding romance developing between him and me, even though I knew we weren't likely to ever see each other again.

THE LAST FEW weeks of vacation passed, and the time came for Safia and me to return to Kuwait. Aunt Aisha promised to join us several months later in the spring. For now, she had to take care of Uncle Shafiq and Maha and her many sewing jobs on the Mount of Olives. It was the usual bittersweet parting— sadness at leaving my aunts, cousins, and Uncle Shafiq, and yet I was eager to get back to Kuwait and to my friends and my beloved dog, Pal. I needed to anchor myself to Mina Abdullah and my familiar surroundings after two months of being a guest in Jerusalem.

Despite my love for the picturesque slope of jade olive

trees near Aunt Aisha's house, I also yearned for the immense, flat sheet of beige sand to appear from the plane's window, once we'd flown beyond the rounded hills of Jerusalem and Jordan. I remembered how barren and forbidding the Kuwait desert had looked the first time I'd glimpsed it with my parents when I'd searched in vain for the small sandbox my father had promised me.

Now, as soon as the desert grew visible below us, I couldn't wait to land and feel the familiar hot breeze on my face. For all its barrenness, I'd developed an abiding love for the stark landscape and the infinity of the flat horizon. This felt like home more than anywhere else I'd been, no matter how beautiful.

Safia wept on the plane as usual, already missing her children. She'd only seen her two older boys when they were able to sneak away from their father's house to visit her. She hadn't seen her two younger sons or Noora again. Now she'd be separated from them for another full year. Yet I knew Safia was also just as ready as I to resume our routine in Mina Abdullah. She was happiest when she ran the household and was free of the Mount of Olives' village gossip as well as the torment of knowing her children were nearby but forbidden to see her.

It took only a few days to sink back into our life in Mina Abdullah. My father had funny stories to tell me about Pal chasing stray cats while I was away and Sabha galloping across the beach with Jalal astride her. My father's male friends continued to drop by most nights after dinner for a cup of Turkish coffee and games of backgammon. I resumed going to my friends' birthday parties and occasionally to the adult dance parties with him.

Despite all this sameness to our lives, however, for my

father and me life *had* changed in profound ways. It was finally becoming clear my mother was truly gone. It was to be only he and I from now on, with Safia to run the house. As long as my mother was alive, even when she'd been in the hospital in Honolulu or Bethesda, I'd felt a solid connection to certain people—her American women friends who constantly asked about her—and to my place in the world as her child. With that cord now severed and despite my father's doting love, I felt adrift. Although I rarely talked about it, the shock of my mother's death was still numbing, preventing me from expressing my drowning sorrow. It carved torrential gullies into the deepest part of me.

Having Safia with us was one of the things that saved me that year. My parents couldn't have known when they hired her just *how* important it would become to have engaged a permanent caretaker from the Mount of Olives who knew my family. Safia and I spoke a shared language in more ways than one—the language of the Arab culture and the Palestinian community, and now, the shared language of grief.

When Safia first came to live with us, crying because she missed her children, I'd tried to comfort her by assuring her they would soon grow up and be able to see her of their own accord. The world, in my child's view, worked in a certain order, and it made sense to me that the wrong inflicted on Safia would one day be righted—justice would prevail.

Now that my own world had disintegrated, a world that had not followed a logical or just plan at all, she did the same for me. Whenever I brought up my mother, Safia understood my grief and cried with me. Her empathy bolstered me, and I spoke freely with her as I never could with my father, not wanting to cause him sadness.

I'd often felt a childish superiority to my mother with my knowledge of Arabic, although I knew full well that it was due to her that I'd learned to speak it so proficiently. She'd never learned more than a necessary few words to get by, but she'd insisted I master it. I was now grateful for her decision to enroll me in the Shuaiba school. Were it not for her foresight, I'd never have learned the language, which was now such a vital link to the Arab part of me that was all I had after her death.

SADLY, MARGARET ARROYO moved to England that year. Her family had abruptly left Kuwait during my last trip to visit my mother in Bethesda because her father had been transferred. Another strong tie was now gone since Margaret's mother, Estelle, had been my mother's good friend.

I missed Margaret, and I missed little blond Robby, who had followed us around, so full of laughter and energy. Most of all, I missed horseback riding with Margaret and her father, rides that had become an integral part of my life on those afternoons after school, lifting me from the gloom engulfing me after Munib's death. Both their horses were now gone, leaving Sabha alone again in the pen, snorting and sniffing the air as though longing for her previous stablemates. Only Jalal and Mohammad were her companions now. My father was hardly inclined to ride her anymore, and I wasn't allowed to ride alone.

thirty-four

Flying Dutchman

SOME MONTHS LATER, OUR EXTENDED FAMILY IN JERUSALEM—
the well-meaning cousins concerned about my father's newly
bereaved status—began considering the various single women
in the family who would make him a suitable marital match.
A twenty-year-old cousin, not quite ten years older than me,
was flown to Kuwait, ostensibly for a visit. A pleasant young
woman I knew from my summers in Jerusalem, she came to
Mina Abdullah with the cousins one weekend. I thought she
was visiting us because she'd never been to Kuwait.

After everyone left, Aunt Aisha complained to Safia that
her busybody Jerusalem relatives were flaunting the young
woman as a prospective bride before her grieving brother
who had no intention of remarrying.

I was shocked that my father's relatives would try to
match him up with someone so soon after my mother's death,
and with a young woman not much older than I was. Didn't
they realize he wasn't interested in remarrying, especially to
such an inexperienced young woman? Although Arab, my
father was American, too, and he didn't have much in com-
mon with a woman who'd never been out of Jerusalem. Was

she seriously considering marrying a widower fifteen years older, a man who already had an eleven-year-old daughter?

Yet apparently, my father was now considered a desirable prospect among the women in the family. Although his female cousins had always complimented my mother's beauty and intelligence, they were not about to let a man as attractive and successful as their Khalil slip away to a stranger again. Certainly, his American wife had been lovely, they said, but now that she was gone, sadly, there were women in the family who would make him a perfect wife. There were even red-heads like his American wife, if that's what he liked.

To my relief, my father made it clear he was not interested in remarriage. When he learned young women were being set up for him to meet, he sent firm word from Kuwait, through his sisters, that he was not looking for a wife.

And there were other women suddenly interested in him. A British woman named Sheila began to stop by our house in the evenings to chat with him. I liked Sheila. She was cheerful, with platinum-blond hair, a pert nose, and a dainty black mole above her mouth. With her perfect figure and glossy hair, she was considered a bombshell in Aminoil. She lived with her British husband and five-year-old son in the Shuaiba compound, where her husband worked at the jetty on the Aminoil oil tankers. Since he was gone several nights a week for work, Sheila, apparently lonely, came to ask my father for advice about her husband's job.

Although I enjoyed Sheila's company, I often got sleepy and wanted to go to bed before she left. Once she brought her little boy, who had her same light-blond hair, to go swimming with my father and me. She was a good swimmer and taught me to dive, showing me how to hold my palms together and point my head downward as my father lifted me on his shoulders out of the water. When she came in the evenings, though, she came alone.

Sheila's visits became more frequent until they were practically every night. She'd sit on our sofa and wait for my father if he was working late at the office, and I resented having to entertain her until he got home. As soon as I had finished supper, the doorbell rang, and Safia and I would roll our eyes, knowing it was probably Sheila. I suspected she had a crush on my father, and I worried it might be mutual. The thought that he might be even remotely attracted to another woman was disturbing.

One day, I asked him why Sheila came to our house so often.

He looked surprised. "Does she bother you?"

"Well, sometimes you're not home, and I need to do my homework," I said, using the pretense of her taking up my time.

"If you don't want her to come, I'll tell her not to," he said simply.

Sheila never came back to the house. I still saw her whenever I accompanied my father to the club parties, and she was always polite to me. I felt guilty she'd been banished from our home—regardless of her motives—because I'd voiced my discomfort. My father never mentioned her again.

My father was doing his best to continue his life without my mother. He occasionally cried, and he talked about her a lot. The house was still so full of her. Her baby picture along with mine sat on a living room shelf; her closets and drawers held her clothes. The kitchen shelves had her colorful cookbooks, and in the cupboard sat the heavy cast-iron skillet she used to fry chicken and make her cornbread and gravy. The Persian rugs were the ones she and my father had picked out in Tehran, as were the two large brass trays that Safia kept gleaming. There was the carved wooden chest she'd bought from the Indian store in Fahaheel where she stored the embroidered tablecloths she'd bought in Hong Kong. Even the garden showed the results of her labors: the snapdragons, petunias, and zinnias she'd planted continued to sprout as though yearning for her attention.

Most comforting of all to me in those early months after my mother's death was when my father opened the portable safe so I could look at her jewelry. I'd pick up her rings, necklaces, and bracelets. My favorite was her clunky gold charm bracelet because the charms reminded me of our vacations where she'd collected each one. It was one of the first things she'd put on when she got dressed to go out. The jingling of the gold charms as she styled her hair had always hinted at the fun she and my father were about to have, and her light laughter still swirled around me as the bracelet clinked when I slid it onto my wrist. The cold metal oddly embodied her so I could almost smell her perfume, skin, and lipstick.

I WAS IN fifth grade and having difficulty keeping up with my work at both the Arabic and Calvert schools. Leaving Shuaiba every day at noon to catch two hours of English work in Mina Abdullah meant I missed out on my science and Arabic grammar classes there. I was similarly lagging in my Calvert work. Although my teachers at both schools continued to sympathize and give me extra coaching, they were frustrated at always needing to make allowances for me because I wasn't able to put in the required work at each school. For the first time, I was also feeling the pressure of my bicultural life tugging at me—was I Arab or American? Muslim or Christian?

Although I was more American in my outlook because of my mother's overwhelming influence at home—my father and I ate bacon with our eggs for breakfast despite the Muslim shunning of pork, and Christmas was my favorite holiday—I felt an abiding loyalty to my Kuwaiti school friends and love for my Muslim family in Jerusalem. Yet the struggle to do well in both schools overwhelmed me. My English classroom, where each of us worked independently at our own grade level and curriculum, was less restrictive than my Shuaiba one. And, despite Mrs. Tremmel's strict demeanor, she was less stern than the teachers at Shuaiba. Finally, I asked my father the previously unthinkable.

"Daddy, can I quit Shuaiba school?"

He stared at me, astonished. "Quit Arabic school?"

"Mrs. Tremmel is always mad because I'm behind in my Calvert work. And my Shuaiba teachers get angry when I miss their classes to leave early. I can do so much better if I concentrate on my English work."

I saw the pain in his eyes at the thought of my abandoning my Shuaiba school. "Mommy wanted you to keep up your Arabic," he insisted.

"I know she did," I said. "But it's too hard to do both. I feel like an outsider in Mina Abdullah and an outsider in Shuaiba. *Please* let me quit Arabic school."

I'd blurted it out and couldn't stop now. After a few months of my relentless begging, my father gave in.

Although it was hard to think of leaving my Arab classmates and the school I'd known since first grade—I would miss Abu Omar's soup each midmorning, the games at recess with the other girls, and especially my gentle, smart friend Aisha Rashid—I was relieved not to have to deal with two schools anymore. There'd be no more uniforms, no more lining up to sing the national anthem, recite the Fatiha, or have our nails and hair inspected. It would be an end to five years of my previous regimented school life. From now on, I could walk across the sand to the Mina Abdullah school with the other expat Mina Abdullah kids, and I could wear jeans or even shorts if it was hot. I felt such an overwhelming weight lifted off me that I couldn't stop smiling.

TO CHEER US both up that summer, my father bought a boat. He'd been talking about it for some time and finally found one he liked for sale—a double-hulled red catamaran. He named it *Flying Dutchman*. He also bought a set of water skis for me. The only other person in Mina Abdullah to have a boat was Mr. Dawson, Cynthia's father, and his was a small single-engine outboard he used for fishing. It couldn't pull anyone on skis. The *Flying Dutchman* was in a different league.

The boat was an instant hit with our friends and cousins on the weekends as they took turns riding with us. Some weekday afternoons, my father and I rocketed alone across the water, often with me on skis riding the boat's frothy wake. We also went on fishing expeditions, starting out in the cool of dawn, when the sky vibrated with the first spurts of orange light and the sun emerged low over the azure water. As the morning wore on, we dropped anchor over several sandbars a mile offshore, where the shallow water was a clear, light aqua.

Sometimes we only caught several foot-long baby sharks my father released back into the water, but other mornings we caught large *hamour,* sea bass that Safia cleaned for dinner. Our fishing expeditions became an escape for both of us. My father enjoyed manning the boat and all the details of preparing the tackle, which forced him to focus on something other than his grief. For me, the exhilaration of soaring across the water was a frisson of joy, the way galloping across the sand on horseback with Margaret and Carlos Arroyo once was.

Before long it was early spring, and Aunt Aisha arrived from Jerusalem again. Safia and I were always glad when she came because the wives of my father's Arab friends came to visit her, and the house came alive with female chatter. As usual, she set up my mother's sewing machine, mended my father's clothes, and sewed me new dresses.

Modest and simple in her tastes, Aunt Aisha was a devoted sister and aunt, determined to steer us through this difficult time as lovingly and helpfully as she could. A vehement guardian of all things related to my mother, she shed tears, along with Safia and me, whenever she recounted the good times she'd had with my mother on our visits to Jerusalem. Although Aunt Aisha loved all her brothers, she had a special place in her heart for my father, since he was her only brother from the same mother, Fatima, and they had been motherless together so young. She never contradicted anything he said or failed to carry out his wishes.

My father had always had a quick temper. With my mother no longer around to soften it with her humor, he'd started to lash out more at the rest of us, whether it was for lunch not being served on time or a poor grade I'd received in school. Although Aunt Aisha got irked by his occasional criticizing her or Safia for something they'd forgotten to do, she bore it without complaining. Family, to her, couldn't be broken by an occasional harsh word, and womanhood was the glue that held a family together. She would calmly put aside her irritation at her brother's fuming until the tide calmed and he became his usual, upbeat self. And my father knew he could count on his sister to always be there for him, despite his outbursts.

thirty-five

Be a Writer

MRS. TREMMEL, OUR CLASSROOM TEACHER, ALONG WITH Dottie Volkman, instilled in me the love of performing. She put on several school plays in Mina Abdullah each year, in addition to the annual Christmas play. The first she trained us to perform was *The Nutcracker.* Using an abbreviated Tchaikovsky score from the original ballet, she choreographed simple steps for each of us to portray the dolls that came to life in the classic Christmas ballet. I was given the role of the Arabian dancer and was to slink genie-like across the stage to haunting Arabian music. Even though Tchaikovsky's music wasn't Arab at all, I didn't mind; my dazzling costume consisted of flashy gold harem pants, a gold blouse, and a filmy veil I wrapped around my face.

At Christmas, since Judy had moved back to Texas, I was, at last, given the role of Mary in the Nativity play. I was excited, especially since my next-door neighbor, Bobby—my new crush now that James Graves had also left Mina Abdullah—was to be Joseph. I suspected Bobby also secretly liked me, so I wasn't too upset when, at the end of each rehearsal in front of his friends, he would grimace and drop my hand, which he was required to hold through much of the play.

In the spring, Mrs. Tremmel had us rehearsing for *Peter Pan.*

Because of my red hair, I was given the role of Peter, while the role of the dark villain, Captain Hook, went to Bobby. I had fun practicing Peter's cheeky, almost flirtatious, crowing call to annoy Captain Hook.

The notion of taking up an acting career popped into my head after all our play rehearsals, and one afternoon I wanted to get my father's opinion. As he rested on the recliner in the living room after lunch before returning to his office, I knelt beside his chair and asked him what I should be when I grew up.

Attempting to catch a short nap, my father said, sleepily, "Be a writer, Kathy. Study journalism like your mother did."

His answer took me by surprise. I wasn't sure what a journalist did. I had no idea my mother had even studied journalism. I'd never known what her occupation had been aside from being my mother and my father's wife. I remembered she'd worked for the American army in Tehran, but I didn't know what she'd done there.

Although I'd rarely seen her without a book or a newspaper when she was lying in bed before her afternoon nap, the fact that she was a writer was a revelation. Later, I learned she'd published a story in *Seventeen* magazine at the age of eighteen. It was a story about the heartbreak of a young Tennessee girl when her beloved hometown was slated to be buried under the new Tennessee Water Authority's dam, a subject of some controversy at the time. (It was, to my knowledge, the only piece of fiction she'd published, although from reading her letters to her mother, there appear to have been other unpublished efforts.)

My father had said something else that stamped itself into my consciousness: "Be a writer because you can do it at home while you're raising your children."

I had vaguely envisioned a future for myself with a husband

and children of my own, so what my father said made sense to me. I now realize he was trying to steer me in a practical direction to serve me well in the future—a future he assumed would include marriage and a family. In his view, a woman could best serve her own needs, as well as her family's, by pursuing a career at home.

My mother had primarily been a homemaker, as had my grandmother, despite her advanced degree in English literature. Even Aunt Aisha sewed for her clients at home. All my Jerusalem aunts were homemakers, as were most of the women we knew in Kuwait. I knew my father wanted me to have a good education, and had I shown an interest in medicine, engineering, or teaching—professions done outside the home— he would have supported my choice.

Perhaps he assumed I'd inherited my mother's love of words—she'd constantly corresponded with her mother and other relatives and friends. Or he might simply have been tired after his morning at the office and wanted to give me a ready answer, so I'd leave him to doze for the next half hour. Whatever his reasoning, the idea of my becoming a writer stuck. I imagined the stories I'd create, maybe even write for magazines like *Time* or *Newsweek,* which he routinely read on his recliner.

After that afternoon, I told my friends I would be a writer and never considered becoming anything *but* a writer. Perhaps a part of me wanted to bring my mother back. By choosing her skill, one she hadn't been able to fulfill for very long, I could embody her in some way and have her back with us by simply *becoming* her.

Perhaps, by suggesting I follow in her path, it's what my father was hoping for too.

⟿

ONE EVENING, MY father, Aunt Aisha, and I drove into Kuwait City for dinner with Cousin Malak. These evenings with family were becoming more essential to him, and he enjoyed the company of Malak's thoughtful husband, Rasheed.

I enjoyed visiting Malak and being part of the lively crowd. It felt good to see my father laughing and engaged with his cousins. By the end of the evening, I was so tired I lay across the back seat of the car and fell asleep for the hour it took to drive back to Mina Abdullah from Kuwait City. As I dozed, I overheard my father and Aunt Aisha talking about a man who had recently died of a heart attack in the Ambassador Hotel in Jerusalem. He appeared to have been someone important.

My father and Aunt Aisha sounded shocked and sad. The man's name was Mohammad Bek.

Their words roused me. Although I'd never met Mohammad Bek, I clearly remembered he was the bank president who had visited Uncle Ahmad in Ramallah this past summer. I also remembered his son walking in the road with my cousin Maher that afternoon—the young man with the large stamp collection. I still recalled the fleeting moment when our eyes had met in that bewildering sense of recognition, followed by the absurd notion I'd one day marry him.

I now felt a heavy, overwhelming gloom. I wasn't the only one to have lost a parent. *He* was grieving too. I felt a renewed connection to the young man who was now suffering a loss similar to mine.

thirty-six

Boarding School

IN THE SPRING OF 1964, I WAS TWELVE AND FINISHING SIXTH grade of the Calvert course, when several British and American friends began to talk of going away to boarding school. Derek was excited to join his sister, Gretta, in London; Bobby was eager to start eighth grade as a boarder at the American Community School in Beirut, the prestigious ACS, where Cynthia now went. Cynthia had moved from her Italian girls' school to the coed American ACS and loved it. Whenever she returned to Mina Abdullah on her school breaks, she glowingly described the parties, the boys, and shopping at the chic Beirut stores with her girlfriends.

Hearing about all this made me want to leave our compound too. The thought of staying on in Mina Abdullah where I'd be the oldest student in our little school while all my friends started school abroad became intolerable.

When I suggested to my father that I go away to boarding school, he thought the idea absurd.

"Why do you want to leave?" he asked. "I heard that a new American school is opening next year in Kuwait City. It will include a high school."

"But I want to go to Beirut," I said, "like my friends."

"If you go to the new school downtown, you can be driven there each day instead of flying two hours to Beirut where you'll be gone for months at a time."

"But, I want to be a *boarder*, Daddy."

He looked at me and smiled sadly. "If you leave, I'll be all alone with only Pal and Safia to keep me company."

Despite my strong sense of guilt at the thought of leaving my father, especially since my mother's absence weighed so heavily on him, I couldn't bear staying behind in what we all now regarded as the baby school. My friends were embarking on a thrilling new life away from home. I remembered blithe Donnie Dinkle and her boyfriend, Kelly, and how their boarding school life in Switzerland had seemed so dazzling. I'd waited forever to join their ranks.

I'd been anticipating the day when I'd become a teenager and get to dress and act like Donnie. But I'd also recently begun to suspect that American teenage ways—dating, going steady, speeding off with a boy in an MG—were things my father was not going to allow me to do.

When he reluctantly considered my going away, he asked his Arab friends whose daughters attended boarding schools in Beirut which schools they recommended. Several of them sent their daughters to a British girls' school—the Lebanese Evangelical School for Girls, or LESG—that was considered the best English girls' school in Beirut. For my father, this was an acceptable choice. My dream of boarding at the coed American school with my friends—a school he was certain had lax rules regarding students' behavior and safety—wasn't going to be an option.

I angrily complained, "I want to be with Cynthia and share in *her* life. Even Bobby is going to ACS!"

But my father was adamant. "You can attend the British girls' school, or you can stay in Mina Abdullah. Subject closed."

Since I couldn't accept the idea of staying behind while everyone else went away, in time the British boarding school in Beirut began to have a certain appeal, though I bristled at attending an all-girls school again.

DURING THAT YEAR, my father started acting strangely.

He became even more concerned about where I went and what I did with my friends. He made it clear he disapproved of boys knocking at our door to invite me to go outside or to go swimming, even though it was only Bobby, Derek, or Alan. He'd glance at me with a skeptical raise of his eyebrow, as if what I was about to say bore no resemblance to the truth.

"What do those boys want?"

I'd shrug. "Just to go swimming."

"Who's going with you?"

"Somebody's mother."

He'd glare at me a while longer, sometimes without saying a word. But his disapproving scowl often succeeded in changing my mind about joining my friends and dissuaded most of the boys from coming over if they saw his car parked in the driveway.

Those boys were the same group of kids I'd practically grown up with—and in our isolated compound, they were among my only choices for friends—but my father had come to regard them as young men and me as a young woman, vulnerable to their devilish, young men's ways. In a return to his Middle Eastern roots and values, he disapproved of the permissive way American and British parents allowed their children too many liberties, such as having kissing games at birthday parties. So, it was only after he went back to work in the afternoons that I could sneak off to swim with my friends rather than sit at home and do my homework, which is what he expected me to do.

Safia, or Aunt Aisha when she was visiting, would try to enforce my father's wishes that I stay inside when my friends came calling. But I was usually able to persuade them I was only going for a short swim, the beach was right in front of the house, and they could even come and check on me. Besides, a parent was always there to watch us, I assured them. I would get home in plenty of time to finish my homework.

Unfortunately, the boys quickly caught on that my father had become strict about my activities and Aunt Aisha had the job of monitoring me. They even referred to her sarcastically as "Aunti," which they said with a slight sneer, laughing at the thought of her policing me whenever she came to call me to go back home before my father returned from the office. I often laughed right along with them, also referring to her as "Aunti" in front of them. But I adored her and would never have dreamed of doing anything to hurt her feelings or to get her into trouble with my father, so I'd irritably trudge home. Eventually, the boys stopped asking me to join them.

My father, despite his assertions of love for me and his affectionate hugs and kisses and fond reminiscences of the good times he and my mother and I had shared, suddenly became my jailer. At first, I sulked quietly, unhappy to be left out of the fun my friends were enjoying.

"Why can't I play with my friends like I used to?" I asked angrily.

He refused to give me a logical reason, leaving me to

fume alone in my room. Even my not speaking to him for several hours didn't cause him to waver.

While my mother had been alive, my father had always been Kal, comfortably going along with the Western conventions of our expatriate community in Mina Abdullah, relying on my mother to take charge of the household and of me. Despite having many Arab friends, he'd prided himself on being an American and spoke admiringly of America's progressive ways. I remember him and my mother discussing issues—they'd sometimes disagreed about ways of handling things, having come from two very different cultures—but life ran smoothly at home. Now my mother had been dead for a year. Her influence over the household had receded, as had the liberal American part of my father. With his American wife no longer around to temper my father's old-fashioned mores, I now had to face an unforeseen new battle on my own.

Although my mother had been particular about making sure I did my homework and minded my manners, she'd never seemed concerned with adhering to the restrictive social mores of Arab society. To her, it was perfectly natural that I play with boys, attend my friends' birthday parties, and occasionally spend the night at a girlfriend's house. Even our main celebrations had been Christmas, Thanksgiving, Easter, and the Fourth of July, like those of our American and British friends. The Islamic festivals of the two Eids had been more minor celebrations, largely revolving around platters of rice and lamb.

In Kuwait, Westerners were generally free, within moderation, to do as they wished. People were expected to behave discreetly; public drunkenness, lewd behavior, and grown women wearing shorts in public spaces were not allowed under threat of deportation. Yet Western women and non-Kuwaiti Arab women were not required to cover their hair or dress in the black abayas that most Kuwaiti women wore over their clothes when in public. All women were free to shop in the markets and mingle with men in businesses. The new generation of urban Kuwaiti women, especially those of the middle and upper classes, had increasingly more social freedom; women could drive cars and run their own businesses.

My father, though, often seemed oblivious to these new freedoms women were gaining. Without my mother and left with the job of raising a young girl on his own, he fell back on the only thing he knew and felt comfortable with, the traditions and mores he himself had grown up with a generation earlier. Where my mother had fostered my independence to an almost frustrating degree, my father was now concerned about protecting my virtue and reputation—and *his* reputation as my father.

While still concerned that I do well in school and plan for a future career, he cared more that, as a girl approaching womanhood, I do what was proper within an Arab context. He questioned me more closely about my friends' birthday parties—who would be going, what games were played, and the like. He began repeating the phrase "Act like a lady," which he never had before.

SINCE I NO longer attended the Shuaiba school, I'd lost touch with my Arab girlfriends. I learned from a former classmate whose father worked in Aminoil that my brilliant friend Aisha Rashid had been taken out of school by her father and was now engaged to marry an "old man." Aisha married? And to an old man? I cried. Aisha was only in sixth grade and was the smartest of us all. How could her own father do this to her? School was free, so it wouldn't have cost him anything for her to complete her studies. Why hadn't the teachers intervened and convinced him to let their star pupil remain in school a few more years?

While I knew my father wasn't about to do something so backward as marry me off, I was increasingly vexed by his curtailing my freedom just because I was a girl. On the one hand, he wanted me to be like my mother; he always praised her intelligence, spunk, and refusal to take minor problems too seriously. He clearly admired her boldness, especially her fearless decision to marry him without bothering to consult her family. But he showed no signs of allowing me a measure of that independence or letting me make my own decisions as she had. I began to suspect I'd never have the liberty to do as I wished. I sensed that, to him, my being viewed as an American within the Arab community was akin to being regarded as inferior—something tainted, secondhand—something *used*. Guarding my honor as a young Arab woman was becoming paramount to him.

"But Mommy was American," I'd say.

"She was different," he'd answer, insinuating she had been more chaste than the average American woman.

What he meant, I knew, was that he didn't *want* to know what her life had been like or which men she had dated before him. Although he knew better, he considered himself her first man. If I dared to suggest to him that she might have gone out with other boys in high school or college before she'd met him, he'd cast me an incredulous glance, as if the idea were absurd.

"She wanted me to go out and do things," I argued. "She said I should be more adventurous. But you're not letting me."

"Your mother would have wanted you to act like a lady," he replied.

"She never said that to me," I countered.

"If she were here, she would have."

"Well," I said, challenging him, "you told me you were a rebel. Why do *I* have to follow so many rules?"

"I was a rebel," he admitted. "But I'm a man. It's different."

I knew there was no point to arguing this. My being a girl had come to mean one thing to him: locking me up in a cage to preserve his reputation as my father.

I felt more isolated, which made me even more determined that by next year I'd be far away from his control at boarding school in Beirut, even if it meant going to a dreaded all-girls school.

ALTHOUGH MY MOTHER had explained sexual reproduction to me when I was seven, shortly before revealing she was pregnant with Munib, she'd considered me too young to enlighten me further on intricate female matters such as puberty and menstruation. At almost twelve, I had begun to grow pubic hair, and my breasts felt tender, so I wrote to my grandmother and asked her to send me a few training bras that I remembered my friends talking about. My father, too, could see I was physically changing. Since Aunt Aisha wouldn't be arriving from Jerusalem until the spring for her usual months-long stay, he arranged for Ray Dawson, Cynthia's mother, to explain certain "female things" to me.

I was eager to go to the Dawsons' house on the appointed

afternoon after school, to learn these female secrets my father had hinted about. Ray sat at her sewing machine in her bedroom as she mended some clothes, and casually explained I might start experiencing some unfamiliar physical symptoms such as stomach cramping and "vaginal spotting" because I'd soon start to get my "period" once a month. I was dumbfounded. I'd never heard these terms before. I mentioned my mother had bled when she was sick and had referred to it as hemorrhaging, but Ray assured me the kind of bleeding she was talking about was something normal and healthy for a woman. She even showed me the sanitary pads she and Cynthia put in their underwear to absorb the blood.

I never knew Cynthia got her periods. She'd never talked about any bleeding with me. This was an entirely new aspect of growing up for me. I left the Dawsons' house with an odd feeling of having been kept ignorant about many aspects of maturing. I'd seen no evidence of any woman ever bleeding periodically, not even my mother, and none of my Arab aunts or Safia had mentioned it. But I now understood what those large cotton pads in my mother's bathroom drawer had been for. Was this something meant to be hidden? Did all women, even glamorous movie stars, get periods and have to deal with messy bleeding down there? The thought was disgusting.

I went home and told Safia what Mrs. Dawson had told me. Only then did Safia admit she also menstruated. I was surprised, never having seen any evidence of this. I surmised this monthly bleeding was an ordeal that needed to be handled in secret, completely hidden from the outside world. Yet despite this evidence of shame and embarrassment associated with it, I looked forward to the day when my stomach started to cramp and I got my period. Just as I impatiently waited to get the training bras my grandmother promised to send me. It was one more step in my growing up and discovering what it meant to become a woman. Most of all, it would signal the start of my becoming independent.

INDEPENDENCE FOR WOMEN continues to be a universal struggle, even among the new generations. Decades later, my American-born teenage daughter one day demanded in exasperation that I make up my mind whether she was Arab or American. If she was allowed to go to parties with her friends, why couldn't she date? Her American friends' curfews were later than hers. It was too confusing for her to be raised as both an Arab and an American. While she was expected to perform in an American environment, outdated notions of female propriety she sensed in our family held her back. In a burst of teenage rebellion, she demanded I confront my values and consider that she, unlike me, was being raised in the United States with fewer ties to the Middle East than I still carried within me. Although we had a liberal household, I realized I had come to expect that she would hold onto a worldview no longer compatible with her generation. Consciously and unconsciously, I was pressing my father's cultural values onto her.

My expectation that she would carry on a lifestyle alien to her was unreasonable, she protested. I had no answer for her. But eventually I understood. She was right. Whatever tenets had been drummed into me as a child growing up in the Middle East were not relevant in her American environment. I had to reconsider my rules, just as I'd wanted my father to do with me. Only I hadn't known how hard to push. My daughter did, and I eventually gave in.

thirty-seven

Planning for Europe

MY GRANDMOTHER, DETERMINED TO KEEP MY FATHER AND ME safely in her sphere, became my steadfast link to America. She constantly wrote to us, typing several times a week on her signature thin blue aerogram fold-up letters. She'd relay the events in Honolulu, which always included news of the latest blooming flowers in Grandy's garden and the news of my neighborhood friends.

I hadn't seen Mammaw since the winter in Bethesda over a year earlier when my father and I went to visit my mother for the last time. I have no memory of her addressing my mother's death in her correspondence or talking to me on the telephone, which we could now do long-distance in emergencies. I do remember her letters continued to faithfully arrive and bring me comfort.

I was saddened, though, to read Uncle Jimmy and Aunt Toni had gotten divorced. Uncle Jimmy now lived in Philadelphia, where he was doing his residency in psychiatry at the University of Pennsylvania. I hadn't seen him since my last trip to Honolulu. When I told my father of my sadness at Uncle Jimmy's news, he shrugged and said it had been expected, as if there were a host of details he had been aware of all along that

I had not. Still, I began to wonder why people had to get divorced, how they could leave someone they clearly loved. I was thankful my mother and father had continued to love each other, even though we'd lost her.

My grandmother, meanwhile, had organized a month-long summer trip to Europe for her, my grandfather, Uncle Jimmy, my father, and me. When I heard this, I was so happy I barely slept for the next few days. I'd only been to Europe as transit stops on our way to Bethesda or on our journeys home from Honolulu. There was so much about Europe I'd read about that I wanted to see firsthand. Although I was disappointed we wouldn't be going to England—land of King Arthur, Robin Hood, and more importantly, Cliff Richard, Donovan, and the Beatles—my grandmother's itinerary did include Scandinavia, home of the Vikings.

We were all to meet in Oslo to travel by boat through the Norwegian fjords before flying to Stockholm. There, we'd embark on another boat trip through the locks in Sweden and visit the nearby island of Göteborg, after which we'd take a tour of Denmark by bus from the northern tip of the country down to Copenhagen. A cruise down the Rhine River through Germany would end in Basel, Switzerland.

My father would be with us only the week it took to go through Norway and part of Sweden, since he had to return to Kuwait for work. Uncle Jimmy would stay on several more weeks through the end of the Rhine River cruise and then return to Philadelphia for *his* work. I would continue to Switzerland with my grandparents, and once my grandfather left for Honolulu, my grandmother and I would travel to Kuwait, where she would help me prepare to leave for boarding school in Beirut.

The amount of planning for such a complex trip, taking into account everyone's differing schedules, would have confounded anyone but Mammaw. She thrived on figuring out the logistics of getting us all to so many different places, and she carefully coordinated our various itineraries from her planning perch in Honolulu. She had a knack for visualizing where we'd go and booked everything to take place during July and August so that by September I'd be back in Kuwait to get ready for school.

It was an extraordinary undertaking, for she wanted us to be together to heal from the devastating loss of my mother the previous year. It must have also been a soothing balm for her to feel she was introducing me to new places, which my mother surely would have wanted. For my grandmother had lost a daughter she adored, a young woman who had not only shared her keen intellect but had also been her loving friend. Although my mother's free-spirited nature had been diametrically different from Mammaw's methodical, disciplined one, over time they'd grown as close as any mother and daughter possibly could.

I sometimes wondered whether my mother and I would have ever grown that close, with our obvious differences in temperament and outlook—her American coolness against my Middle Eastern emotions. For despite resenting my father's overprotective, Arab ways, I still tended to be more like him, more volatile and sensitive. In that way, he and I always shared a subtle understanding and acceptance of each other, something I'd not had with my more easygoing Western mother. I never questioned whether he loved me. His love was transparent. I could tell he adored me even when he was angry with me.

⟳

ONCE SCHOOL WAS out for the summer, Safia, Aunt Aisha, and I flew to Jerusalem where I'd spend a month before continuing on to Beirut to meet my father and start our European journey.

On the Mount of Olives, it was the usual routine with Maha and her two brothers. There were afternoon outings to Jerusalem with Uncle Shafiq, strolls in the Old City where, now that Maha and I were both older—she was nine and I was twelve—he'd explain the significance of the various landmarks, as he'd done with my mother and her parents years earlier. Besides visits to the historic mosques and churches, he'd lead us on walks along the high ramparts of the Old City's ancient walls.

That summer, Safia decided to embroider me my own village dress, a *thobe* like the Mount of Olives women wore. She bought a soft, cream-colored fabric known as Rosa and took me to be measured by the village seamstress, who specialized in tailoring women's thobes to be embroidered.

With vibrant, scarlet thread, Safia embroidered the bodice in tiny cross-stitch in the shape of grapevines, flowers, and birds. She stitched the birds' eyes and wings in bright blue. When the entire bodice was covered, without a hint of the mesh guide showing underneath, she embroidered the long skirt in the same pattern of vines, birds, and flowers. She adorned thick red rows going from my waist down to my toes, three inches wide and four inches apart. Occasionally, she brought the thobe to Aunt Aisha's in the mornings and worked on it, plunging the needle into the cloth and pulling it back out as she created each new leaf, bird's wing, or grape.

It took Safia the entire summer to fill in all the segments. I'd sit next to her and watch her fingers repeat the hypnotic motions, but I'd quickly grow restless and pick up a book or go outside to the garden with Maha. I'd never seen Safia sew more than a button on a shirt or mend a torn dress of mine in Kuwait, so I gasped when she finally laid out the magnificent, finished garment. Only now did I fully appreciate the painstaking labor required to make each village woman's thobe, and the extent of Safia's love for me that had spurred her to do it.

To complete the outfit, she bought me a silver-and-blue satin sash to tie at my waist. When I tried on the embroidered robe and shiny sash, I felt I truly belonged to the village. My Arab self was newly anchored again, and although we were from Jerusalem, the Mount of Olives was now ingrained as deeply in me as Kuwait.

AUNT SUAD WAS particularly cheery that summer. Her husband, Ghaleb, the policeman, had returned from an extended absence and was painting the interior of their house. This seemed almost a celebratory event, as though Aunt Suad were a bride and Ghaleb was preparing a new home for her. Maha and I went over to watch him paint, and as we sat admiring his work, Aunt Suad served us her special rich, hot cocoa. Nobody made cocoa as delicious as she did, stirring heaping spoons of the dark powder into the boiling water in the Turkish coffee pot, adding sugar and letting it bubble and thicken until it resembled dark tar. She then poured it into glasses for us to slurp as we watched the yellowed walls of her sitting room transform into a beautiful, shiny aqua under Uncle Ghaleb's deft brushstrokes.

Bustling between her cocoa wizardry and blissfully su-
pervising her husband's painting, Aunt Suad had a different
sparkle in her eye from the usual frenzied one she had when
she cleaned. This glint was softer, as though she was rediscovering her love for her husband. For that afternoon, Ghaleb
was the genial, handsome policeman Aunt Suad had fallen in
love with, the attentive husband and father, affectionately
joking with his sons and daughter as he dipped his huge
paintbrush into his bucket and sloshed the walls until they
looked as lush as the sea in midmorning sunlight. I loved seeing
the excitement shining in my aunt's eyes and marveled that
the simple act of her husband repairing their home could have
this magical effect and cause her to feel this good.

We couldn't have known that three years later, shortly
after he sent Aunt Suad and their sons to Baba's house to
safety at the outbreak of the June 1967 Arab–Israeli war,
Ghaleb would be shot dead in the cross fire between the Israeli
and Jordanian forces as he lay asleep in his bed. His body was
discovered days later once the shelling stopped.

I WAS TO meet my father in Beirut in a few weeks to visit my
new school before we continued to Europe. I was bursting
with excitement to see the school and to get all the supplies
enumerated in the acceptance letter—uniforms, bedding, toiletries, and identification numbers to be sewn into my
clothes, sheets, and towels.

I couldn't wait to embark on my new life as a boarder, to
be the girl my mother would have been proud of, someone
open and eager for new undertakings and adventures. Although
I wouldn't turn thirteen until February, becoming a boarder

heralded my teenage years. The two went together—boarding school and a new teenage life. Although I was leaving everyone and everything I loved behind in Mina Abdullah—my father, Pal, Safia, the beach, and my younger friends who weren't yet going away to school—nothing weighed too heavily on my mind compared to all that gloriously beckoned from Beirut.

At the end of my month in Jerusalem, Uncle Ahmad took me through customs one morning and walked me across the tarmac to the plane. I waved to Aunt Aisha and Uncle Shafiq standing on the airport terminal's rooftop, the sunlight behind them beaming down at us.

It would be one of the last times I departed from Kalandia airport. Three years later, after the 1967 war, Israel would annex East Jerusalem and the West Bank, closing the Kalandia airport to commercial flights from Arab countries. From then on, I could only get to Jerusalem by crossing the Allenby Bridge into Jericho from Jordan after being granted special permits from Jordan and Israel. It would become an arduous, day-long trip made with hundreds of others journeying to visit family or to get home, undergoing exhaustive and humiliating body and baggage searches in Israeli customs in Jericho, now Israeli territory.

I glide backward, stretching each leg, my toes lightly caressing the floor. My face nestles against my partner's cheek, my eyes almost closed. We are wrapped in an embrace, our chests pressed together, as we move in a passionate walk to the melody spun by the violin, piano, and bandoneon. Argentine tango. I blindly trust my leader, since I cannot see where I'm going, and he keeps me on a safe path, away from the other dancers. Laser-focused on each other, and on our wordless dance conversation, each step I take is a response to a suggestion—an invitation—from him.

We dance with "one heart and four legs," as the Argentines say. This intimate embrace, our "connection," is the heart of tango. It's what draws me to this dance—the ultimate partner dance.

Like other Latin dances, Argentine tango was brought to the New World by European immigrants and African slaves. In time, the Italian-flavored European music dominated, eclipsing the rhythmic African influence. Unlike the lighthearted Afro-Cuban island dances, tango music is poignant; although the Spanish lyrics are romantic, they are often sad.

Stepping in complete unison with my partner, I lose myself in its exquisite melancholy.

—— ⁓⁕⁓ ——

thirty-eight

A Surprise Meeting

I WAS MET BY MY FATHER AT THE BEIRUT AIRPORT AN HOUR later. He took me by taxi to the Phoenicia Hotel, promising I could swim the next day in the hotel's inviting oval pool, where the swimmers were visible from the bar through the large windows behind the bartender.

In 1964, Beirut was a thriving city of stately European apartment buildings, Arab-inspired architecture with elegant archways, and an active business district. Stylish shops and outdoor cafés lined the streets, and beaches were minutes away from green, pine-covered mountains. All the wondrous things Cynthia talked about when she came home on holidays were, at last, within reach. I couldn't wait to experience it all for myself in my new school in October.

This was also my first real leisure trip alone with my father, and I acted as mature as I could to make him proud to have me as his traveling companion for our two days in Beirut. Although I knew there would be the visits to his mother's family for lunch to see his aunts and cousins, there would also be time for us to go shopping and swimming in the hotel's crystalline pool. I'd outgrown my bathing suit, but my father said we'd buy a new one the next morning.

We had an appointment to meet the headmistress of my new school that very afternoon. My dream of becoming a boarder was finally coming true. But when the taxi pulled up to the school gate, my heart clenched at the sight of the long, pebbled walkway flanked by imposing, yellowed stone buildings. It looked old enough to have been the sinister Lowood Institution in Charlotte Brontë's *Jane Eyre*! With classes out for the summer and no students around, it appeared especially cold and forbidding. As soon as I stepped out of the car, I regretted having agreed to attend an all-girls school again. I wanted to tell my father I'd changed my mind about boarding school and wished, instead, to spend the next year in my cozy Mina Abdullah school, whether or not my friends were there.

Once inside the gate, however, a girl my age with light-brown hair and a saucy smile came up to us.

"You're the new girl," she said. "I'll take you to Miss St. John." Although she was clearly Arab from her accent, she spoke perfect English, and I was somewhat put at ease by her enthusiasm and cheerful face.

Miss St. John, pronounced "Sinjin," was the tallest and thinnest woman I'd ever seen. She had a high-pitched voice and piercing British accent, and she wore a long skirt and an austere, dark blouse. Her dark hair hung limply below her chin, where her cheeks caved in, giving her a despondent air. Once again, I caught my breath. What had I gotten myself into?

But when she reached out to shake my hand, her tone was surprisingly warm.

"Welcome," she said, a kind look on her face. "You're going to be a wonderful addition to our school. We have only one other American, a lovely girl like you."

After handing my father some papers to fill out, Miss St. John led us on a tour of the school. Upstairs were the long dormitories with six to eight beds in each and large shuttered windows filtering in the afternoon light. Down the hall was an enormous bathroom with sinks, toilets, and showers.

She took us back down a flight of worn stone steps to the main floor and dining hall where boarders and some day students came for lunch and where boarders also had breakfast and dinner. There was an outdoor recreational area with basketball nets for playing netball and for folk-dancing lessons, and a large, chapel-like auditorium where students and teachers gathered each morning to hear announcements and—it being an evangelical school—say prayers and sing Bible hymns. If my father had any reservations about my getting a strong daily dose of evangelical religion, they were evidently overshadowed by the school having a clear structure providing the safe, all-female environment he wanted for his soon-to-be teenage daughter.

We were led up another flight of stairs to an adjoining building, where there was a large kitchen with rows of sinks, counter space, stoves, and ovens.

"This is where you'll have home economics classes," Miss St. John said brightly. "Your teacher, Miss Enderbee, is from Australia. She's enormously amusing."

Finally, she took us to a slightly musty-smelling library with a vast selection of books and inviting sofas with upholstered skirts.

"Girls love to come here to read or do homework during study periods," she said.

Although the school buildings still felt antiquated compared to my modern Mina Abdullah school and even my

Shuaiba school, there was an appealing old-fashioned charm about them that made them seem less ominous than when we first arrived. I looked forward to meeting my dorm mates when I returned in early October and to embark on my new independent life.

"What do you think?" my father asked, once Miss St. John had escorted us back to the main gate.

"The cooking and folk-dancing classes sound fun," I said. "I think I'll make friends."

"I know you will," he said.

Glancing at him, I was surprised to see an unmistakable look of sadness cross his face. It was that look of profound loss I'd seen after Munib's and then my mother's deaths. Seeing the school firmly reinforced that we would be apart from each other for the first time. We'd lose the life we'd grown accustomed to these past few years in Mina Abdullah. I sensed he was already grieving yet another part of his life that would be gone.

His sadness tugged at me. I knew I'd miss him just as much once I started school and couldn't see him for months at a time. But I was too overcome with excitement at witnessing firsthand what my new life would be like to dwell on what I knew deep down would be a difficult separation. I remembered how he had described his eagerness to leave for America at seventeen, and his father's sadness at losing him—and later his own regret at the ten years they'd been separated before his father's death. Yet at that moment, like all young people on the verge of a new beginning, I felt pure elation to be embarking on my new path.

AFTER OUR SCHOOL meeting, my father told me we were invited to dinner at the home of friends of Uncle Ahmad's, a nice family he had just come to know.

"Do we have to?" I said, surprised and disappointed at having to start my long-anticipated vacation by sharing our special time together with new people.

"You'll enjoy meeting them," he replied with a smile. "There are seven children in the family, and they're all friendly and interesting. There are even two kids your age. Unfortunately, their father recently died."

He seemed eager to go. Setting aside my frustration, I put on my new blue dress with the bateau collar Aunt Aisha had made me, and he and I took a taxi to the family's apartment for dinner.

In the car, I had a brief intuition of who we were going to visit. The family lived in Beirut, and they knew Uncle Ahmad. The father had tragically died last year. The pieces fit. I remembered the banker's son a year ago in Ramallah and my strong, instant connection to him. But before I could ask my father whether the family we were visiting was that of the deceased bank president, the taxi pulled up to an apartment building, and my father opened the car door for me.

Several young women greeted us when we arrived at the apartment.

"Bonsoir," they said in French, smiling at us.

The five sisters resembled each other; all were petite and had the same olive skin, dark eyes, and dark hair pulled back into some form of ponytail. They all wore dark skirts and blouses, a sign they were still in mourning for their late father.

They spoke in Egyptian-accented Arabic with my father—they'd previously lived in Cairo—and with me a mix of Arabic and a little English. Among themselves they spoke French. Despite the family being dressed for mourning, there was a lighthearted air about the siblings' banter as they joked with one another and with my father.

My father and I were ushered into the living room. A young man of about sixteen got up from where he'd been sitting on the sofa watching TV. He, too, smiled and shook hands with us. His name was Ahmad, and he was the only one not dressed in black, but in a pair of gray plaid pants and a gray shirt. He had black hair and brown eyes and the same sincere demeanor and twinkle in his eye as he'd had when I'd seen him the year before in Ramallah.

I felt myself blush at seeing him again, remembering my brief notion, then, that he'd one day become my husband. Those thoughts now seemed silly. He was obviously very mature, especially when, prompted by my father, he began discussing politics with him. I could see he inhabited a totally different, more adult world than mine. To my relief, he showed no sign of remembering me.

The lady of the house came to greet us. She, too, was a petite woman with a pleasant smile and short, graying curly hair. Unlike her children who spoke to each other in French, the language in which they were educated, their mother spoke only Arabic.

"Don't worry," she said to me with a good-natured wink. "I still understand perfectly what they're saying." I found myself liking her immediately.

Just as my father had said, there were two kids my age, an outgoing boy with blondish hair and a quiet girl with a curly brown ponytail. The elegantly set table in the dining room was spread with platters of food.

After dinner, I was pleased when my father invited the two kids close to my age—the light-haired boy, Mahmoud, who was a jokester, and his sister Hala—to join me at the hotel for a swim the next day. Mahmoud acted differently from his more composed older brother, and I eagerly anticipated some fun pool time with him and his sister.

"I don't have a bathing suit," I reminded my father.

The eldest of the sisters, Gamila, a striking young woman whose hair was done up in an elaborate chignon, overheard me.

"Would you like me to take you into town tomorrow to buy one?"

WHEN MY FATHER dropped me off at the family's apartment the next morning, the mother met us at the door and kissed me warmly on both cheeks. She led me to the sitting room and told me Gamila would join me shortly.

There was no sign of the young man, but the sisters greeted me as cheerfully as they had the night before, each one kissing me on both cheeks as though we were old friends. They all still looked alike to me, and I had trouble telling them apart since they all dressed in navy blue or black.

We waited a long while for Gamila. Her sisters and mother brought me a cold drink and offered me chocolates.

"It takes Gamila *forever* to fix her chignon and paint on her eyeliner," one of them said, rolling her eyes.

Gamila finally came to the sitting room. Her hair was once again fixed in the many-layered chignon of the night before, and the black eyeliner on her upper lids meticulously came to an upward flick at the outer edge of each eye, like the depictions of pharaohs in ancient Egyptian art. She was quite pretty. Her slanted eyes and full lips reminded me of pictures of the Italian movie star Sophia Loren.

A TAXI DROPPED us in the heart of the noisy, traffic-congested downtown. We walked down bustling lanes jammed with carts of fresh fruit and vegetables. The stores here were even more elaborate than those in Ramallah, with modishly dressed mannequins in the windows. Although the cart vendors called out loudly in Arabic, the stores were distinctly European, with everything written in French.

At a shop selling lingerie and bathing suits, Gamila told the female vendor, in French, that we needed a bathing suit in my size. The vendor brought out several stylish women's bathing suits, and I immediately felt intimidated. It was my first time shopping for an adult swimsuit with a padded bra rather than the flowered, cotton, young-girl ones my grandmother usually sent me from Honolulu. Although it was exciting to try them on, I felt like an impostor as I showed each one to Gamila. She, though, seemed to think the suits were fine for my age and helped me choose one with a deep cutout back pulled together by a string tie that made me feel very daring. It felt good to go shopping with a woman who treated me like an adult.

After she paid for it, Gamila took me to a nearby bakery where she bought us each a small tart filled with cream and slices of fresh strawberries on top she called *tartes aux fraises.*

"Aren't they delicious?" she said. We ate them hungrily in

the taxi on our way back to the hotel where my father waited for me at the entrance.

Later that afternoon, Gamila's funny younger brother and his sister arrived at our hotel. All three of us took the elevator down to the swimming pool level and plunged into the water. Throughout the afternoon, we dove into the pool, swimming toward the windows and waving to the people sitting at the bar sipping their drinks. I was enjoying my new friends so much I regretted having to leave the next morning for Oslo to meet with my grandparents and Uncle Jimmy for our trip through Europe.

LATER THAT NIGHT in our hotel room, my father sat across from me and started a conversation that must have been one of the most difficult of his life.

"You know how much I loved your mother," he began.

I nodded, wondering why he was bringing this up now. The topic of my mother's death was still hard to talk about and inevitably cast a sadness over us both whenever we talked about it.

"Without Mommy, life has been very lonely for us," he continued, quietly, a slight quiver in his voice.

I nodded again, but an uneasy feeling began deep in the pit of my stomach; my instincts told me he was about to say something I didn't want to hear.

"Well," he said, gently, "people are telling me I should get married again—to expand my family—"

A wave of nausea washed over me. Before he could say another word, I butted in, "No!"

He paused. "Mommy wanted—"

"No!" I shouted in shock and disbelief.

My father, who had made fun of the Jerusalem cousins sent to Kuwait as possible marriage material. Marry again? What was wrong with him? How could he think of loving anyone besides my mother? How could anyone else possibly ever take her place in his heart or in mine? And what about me? What would happen to me if he remarried?

My worst nightmare had been of having a stepmother like Safia's daughter, Noora, had, a mean woman who beat her. I couldn't believe my father was thinking to "expand his family," hinting he wanted other children. Wasn't I enough? I realized fear of his one day remarrying had haunted me ever since my mother's death. I'd never said anything about my fears, but I worried each time an attractive woman visited.

I started to cry.

"Kathy, nobody can ever replace your mother," he said, reaching out to me. I pushed him away. "Honey. . . ." he started, but I put my hands over my ears, shutting out his words.

"I'm sorry," he said, finally. "I won't mention it again."

I reluctantly allowed him to take me in his arms.

I don't remember what else we said to each other before we went to bed, only that it took me a while to stop crying after he assured me he would put the thought of remarriage out of his mind. Although I didn't like seeing him looking so sad, I never wanted him to suggest it again.

The next morning, we left Beirut on a flight bound for Norway. When we arrived in cloudy, chilly Oslo, all I wanted was to get to my grandparents' hotel room and fall into the safety of my grandmother's strong, loving arms. Mammaw was the only one who could understand and protect me from my terror of losing my father to another woman.

thirty-nine

My Grandmother's Gift

I BARELY RECOGNIZED MY GRANDMOTHER IN HER GRAY traveling skirt and jacket. I'd seen pictures of her wearing dresses in Tennessee, and she had worn slacks in the cold month we'd been together in Bethesda, but I'd gotten used to her in colorful Hawaiian muumuus, which was more her style. On our first outing in Oslo the next day in the rain, I tried not to giggle when she donned a broad-brimmed hat that reminded me of Dr. Seuss's Cat in the Hat.

Not surprisingly, Mammaw had lined up several educational things for us to do in our few days in Oslo before our four-day trip through the fjords, the Norwegian waterways that protruded like fingers inland from the sea. We went to a museum to see the remains of the fearsome Viking dragon ships—surprisingly small for the legendary Viking pillaging—and to another museum to see the *Kon-Tiki* raft that modern-day Norwegian explorer Thor Heyerdahl and his crew had voyaged on across the Pacific fifteen years earlier. Although the fragile-looking raft fascinated my grandmother, I was more interested in the replica of the menacing giant whale shark suspended below the craft as it had lingered on their voyage. At lunchtime I had my first taste of the tantalizing smorgasbord—a buffet of open-faced Scandinavian sandwiches of sliced meats, cheese, and pickles on dense, dark bread—that awaited us at the hotel.

The fjord cruise was the first time I'd spent a night on a boat. The calm lakes and the towns of toylike wooden houses were serene, but the food served on the boat was terrible, nothing like the delicious smorgasbord of Oslo. After a few nights of dismal meals, we began to load up, instead, on fruit, crackers, and Norwegian cheeses whenever we docked. My grandfather also discovered the local cherry brandy, Cherry Heering, that he liberally stocked up on and drank with his meal each evening.

Uncle Jimmy had brought along his guitar, and he played and sang for any passengers around. He could even play Harry Belafonte's "Jamaica Farewell," which my father and I sang along to. After my grandparents and I retired to our cabins each night, he and my father would sit out on the deck of the boat and serenade the young Norwegian women who, despite Uncle Jimmy's frequent off-key singing, apparently found both men charming. Finally, we disembarked in Bergen, and from there we all flew to Stockholm.

As I sat next to my grandmother on the flight to Stockholm, chatting and laughing about the ship's dreadful food and Uncle Jimmy's off-key singing, she said, "I wish Kal and Jimmy would get married again. They both look so foolish on their own. They need to get on with their lives."

I stared at her. I didn't know whether my father had broached the subject of his remarriage with Mammaw, but her comment stunned me.

"Why?" I blurted out.

"Jean wanted Kal to remarry," she said. "She wanted a companion for him and a mother for you."

"I don't need a mother," I replied, angrily. "I have Safia and Aunt Aisha. And *you*."

I couldn't believe my mother's own mother wanted her son-in-law to remarry and "get on with his life," as she put it. A life that would not include her daughter and would take him away from *me* once he had a new wife, and—even more unimaginable—perhaps other children to love and care for. Hadn't my mother's dying wish been that we not forget her? How could my father embark on a new life with someone else and still remember and love her? I'd never expected my grandmother to condone this move on his part.

Mammaw continued. "Just think how alone he'll be in a few years when you grow up and go away to college, and later on, when you get married."

It wasn't a long conversation, but she'd made her point. My father should marry and start a new life with a new companion. I wouldn't be with him forever. While I understood my grandmother didn't want my father to spend his life alone and my mother might have, unselfishly, suggested in the weeks before her death that he remarry, I just couldn't imagine a new person barging into our life and taking her place. I felt lost and utterly betrayed by the one person I was sure would stand by me. It was as if the earth had split open beneath me. I barely remembered the rest of the short plane ride.

The next few overcast days in Stockholm were even more clouded by my distress at what Mammaw had said. Although she was, as my mother had been, more practical than emotional about things, I was devastated she'd be the one to encourage my father to marry again. His own sisters were still fiercely loyal to my mother, ridiculing any attempts by other family members to introduce him to marriageable cousins. Besides, he was thirty-five, which seemed too old to remarry. A step-mother for me? My stomach turned. He would never do that! Not to my mother or to me. I imagined Safia's horror at the suggestion of another woman replacing my mother in our house and bossing her around.

And yet, was my grandmother intimating I was being selfish to want to deny him his own future happiness once I was grown? I *did* want to see my father totally happy again, see the joy in his eyes when he visited friends or cousins, or when we danced or listened to calypso music. I hadn't seen that part of him in a long while. There was always an under-current of sadness behind his smile.

He hadn't mentioned remarrying again after that night in the hotel in Beirut, but since my plane conversation with Mammaw, the subject hung heavily in the air as I realized how lonely he must be. A different loneliness from mine, but still, an emptiness I couldn't fill. I'd never thought of my father spending the rest of his life on his own, never envisioned his life after I grew up and moved away to pursue *my* life. I'd tended to think of us as a unit. He and I—forever.

I certainly didn't want to be the cause of his misery, now or in the future. I also suspected my grandmother, without overtly saying so, was hinting that my father would need a nudge from me if he were to consider remarriage. So long as I was adamantly opposed to the idea, he might give it up. I re-membered how Sheila had stopped coming by our house in the evenings after I'd told him she bothered me. So, despite my own feelings of confusion and dread, I felt I had to give him the encouragement he needed.

MY FATHER WAS due to leave us in Stockholm, and I would continue the trip alone with my grandparents and Uncle Jimmy. On the night before he left, as he packed his suitcase in our hotel room, I opened the subject.

"Mammaw said you should remarry."

He looked up at me.

"I now agree with her," I said.

He looked surprised, perhaps wondering what had caused my change of heart.

"One day I'll have to start my own life," I went on. "I can only do that if I know you have someone to love and spend time with."

Although I could hardly believe I'd uttered those words, now that they were out, I knew I couldn't take them back.

My father was silent for a few moments. Then, he said, "Mommy told me I should remarry. She didn't want either of us to spend the rest of our lives alone. I didn't want to hear her even suggest I have a life with someone other than her, but she insisted I not remain single. She said it would be best for you, too, to have a mother."

I was silent. I tried to imagine a third person in our lives. I conjured up the faces of all the women I knew in Kuwait, but I couldn't imagine living with any of them. Finally, I asked my father whether he had someone in mind.

After a pause, he said, "I gave it *some* thought, but when you looked so unhappy . . ."

My curiosity was piqued. "I'm okay with it now," I said. "Who were you thinking of asking to marry you?"

Marry you.

The words tumbled out of my mouth but sounded surreal.

Again he paused, then said, "How about one of the Hilmis?"

He was referring to the family we'd visited the previous week in Beirut, the widow and her seven children.

"Mrs. Hilmi?" I asked, flabbergasted.

He chuckled. "No, no. Mrs. Hilmi is practically as old as my mother."

"Who then?" I was confused. Although Mrs. Hilmi's hair was threaded with gray and I knew she was older than my father was, her daughters seemed barely out of their teens. None looked old enough or mature enough to take on my mother's role.

"Well," he said, "what about Gamila?"

"Gamila?" I stared at him.

Sure, Gamila had been friendly, and shopping with her had been fun. But she was very young. Although I'd since learned she'd graduated from college, she still seemed too inexperienced a partner for my father.

"She's twenty-five," he said. "I know she's ten years younger than I am, but she's very mature. And very good-hearted."

Gamila? I thought of her fancy chignon and meticulously painted eyes. While Gamila didn't fit into the evil stepmother mold, I could only imagine her as an older sister. Not a *stepmother.* The word clanged in my head.

I couldn't help wondering, suddenly, whether Gamila had known on the day she took me shopping that she was being considered as a stepmother for me. Had my father tricked me into liking her before letting on his intention to marry her? As though reading my mind, he was quick to tell me he wasn't even sure whether she would accept his offer of marriage.

"I haven't asked her yet because I wanted to see how you

felt about it," he said. "When you rejected the idea, I put it aside. I don't know whether she'll accept my proposal. She could refuse."

It hadn't occurred to me Gamila might refuse my father's offer, although marriage to an older man she barely knew might not be what a woman her age had in mind—especially a man with a soon-to-be teenage daughter, a man who was still grieving for his beloved wife.

"Would she say no?" I asked him, half hoping his answer would be yes.

He shrugged. "I'll have to find out."

"When will you—find out?"

"When I get back to Beirut," he said. "But it may not be right away because she might need time to think about it. I'll let you know as soon as she tells me."

The thought of somebody else now sharing our house, the dining table, and even my father's bed was unfathomable, as was the idea of my possibly having new siblings later on. I couldn't envision it. Part of me, too, was resentful of Gamila's youth and vigor. My mother had been so sick and fragile when I last saw her. I felt I'd be betraying her by welcoming a young, healthy, beautiful woman into our lives.

Also, if my father married an Arab woman, how would that impact me? I'd been brought up in an American household. Could a woman like Gamila fit in? I began to see myself veering off course from being my mother's American daughter, as though the Western part of me—her legacy—would become illegitimate.

And something else made me shudder.

"What if I change my mind and don't like Gamila after you get married? Will I have to leave home? Leave you?"

"Leave *me*?" my father said, looking incredulous. "Honey, that will never, *ever* happen."

He wrapped his arms around me, and we held each other a long time.

I WENT TO bed with my universe upended. I hardly slept, my mind racing in dizzying circles. Yet, strangely enough, I also found myself starting to wonder what it would be like to become part of a large, gregarious family like Gamila's. I'd enjoyed the afternoon I'd spent with her sister and brother in the hotel pool, and her sisters were all jovial and smart. Two of them were in law school. Her mother had been caring, and the older of her brothers, for whom I still felt an odd connection, was attractive with his warm, brown eyes. None of them were objectionable, so why would Gamila be? And since she'd recently lost her own father, she might be more sensitive to my feelings of resentment that she was intruding into my life and memories of my mother. Although I was frightened of what lay ahead, I began to feel a kernel of hope.

And there was something else sprouting inside me—some mounting feeling that in accepting my father's new life, I was also growing into the kind of person my mother would admire, someone who bravely took on the unknown and welcomed a new path for both my father and me. This would have been her way, the confident American way, of handling the situation.

Before I went to bed, my father hugged me again and said, "It'll be hard for me to contact you for the next two weeks because you'll be on the move until you reach Basel. But I promise you'll have a letter waiting for you at your hotel in Basel, telling you Gamila's answer."

forty

The Letter

WITH MY FATHER GONE, I HAD UNCLE JIMMY MOSTLY TO myself. To my delight, he taught me chords on his guitar and was always game for a long walk with me to explore whatever town we stopped at on our boat trip through the canal locks in Sweden. His jovial company helped ease the pain of missing my father and distracted me from worrying about what he'd write in his letter.

Since we mostly went on these walks alone, to give me something to do, Uncle Jimmy put me in charge of navigating, relying on me to use street maps to take us wherever we wanted to go. This was a new skill for me since I'd never needed a map in Kuwait. Although the responsibility was exciting at first, I soon found navigating frustrating. I couldn't always understand the maps, and Uncle Jimmy refused to help me. Instead, he waited calmly as I impatiently studied the squiggly lines to find a route that made sense.

I was surprised by Uncle Jimmy's attitude. On one level, I understood this to be a culture clash. He expected me to forge ahead and figure things out on my own, as though he were not with me. As though I were in America. This was so contrary to how my Arab uncles would have acted.

"My uncles in Jerusalem wouldn't do this to me," I grumbled. "They'd be happy to help."

"Oh?" he said, raising his eyebrows in mock surprise, as though this were a strange justification for my not wanting to use my head to solve something on my own.

"We help each other. That's the *Arab* way of doing things."

He smiled and continued to wait patiently.

When I complained to my grandmother about his odd behavior in not helping me out with the maps, she ignored me, refusing to get involved in this squabble between her American son and Arab granddaughter. It seemed my grandmother and Uncle Jimmy were trying to get me to stand alone like a single tree, to be self-reliant. It was the American way. Yet I yearned to be part of the surrounding forest, enmeshed in and protected by my family group, as was my Arab family's way.

From Sweden, we embarked on the bus tour through the Danish countryside. While sitting next to a friendly, dark-haired American woman we'd met, I was unexpectedly overcome by the nearly forgotten, yet familiar, scent of my mother—a faintly lemony whiff of the woman's skin or perhaps her perfume. It was as if my mother were sitting next to me in the flesh.

As I breathed in, I grew faint with longing, trying not to draw attention to myself by inhaling too deeply. Occasionally, I glanced at the woman, as if she might have magically turned into my redheaded mother. I fought the need to lean up against her, rest my head on her shoulder, reach my arm around her to cuddle her. I simply sat and sniffed in quietly, deeply, hoping she wouldn't notice. When we explored the various towns, I was impatient to get back onto the bus and find an excuse to sit next to the woman again so I could bask in the nostalgic aroma. How I missed my mother! I missed her love and companionship—now practically forgotten—her smile, her joyful laugh. Most of all, I missed being able to touch her and smell her.

Soon, we arrived in Copenhagen, where I'd been eager to ride the roller coasters at Tivoli Gardens. Uncle Jimmy rode on all of them with me.

I was sad he had to leave us in Basel.

WHEN WE FINALLY reached our hotel in Basel, a cozy sitting room with plush pink chairs greeted us. My grandmother inquired at the front desk about any mail we had received, and after a slight search, the concierge produced a white envelope addressed to me in my father's handwriting.

Holding my breath, I ripped the envelope open.

Having only weeks ago been horrified by the idea he would remarry, the possibility Gamila might refuse my father's offer had obsessed me ever since he left. I'd replayed over and over the day she and I had shopped together and how pleasant she had been. What if she refused him, and he eventually proposed to someone else I didn't like as much?

I glanced at the paper, my heart pounding until I dared to skim the words at the top.

"Dearest Kathy," he wrote. "Gamila accepted."

I read it again, to make sure. "Gamila accepted."

My grandmother, who'd known I'd been anxious about the letter, stood by, carefully watching me.

"Oh, Kathy," she said softly, watching the grin spread across my face. It was a tender tone I didn't often hear from her, in contrast to her usual brisk manner.

It must have been an equally bittersweet moment for

her. Was she feeling she was now losing her daughter for good and maybe me, her granddaughter, as a result of my father's remarriage? Was she worried that a woman from such a different culture than her own might influence me in ways she couldn't foresee? Might possibly estrange me from her over time?

Whatever her feelings, my grandmother smiled warmly at me. "Why, that's just wonderful."

In that moment, staring at the letter, I suddenly felt an incredible force surrounding me, lifting me onto a new journey as a young woman, unafraid to face the unknown.

My father had been a loving and devoted husband to my mother and an incredible father to me. But it was time for him to start living for himself, to rebuild his life, as my grandmother had said. He had been my Harry Belafonte, filling my life with music and dancing that had brought us so much joy in both good times and bad. Now he had to leave and seek his own fortune, just as Harry had. And I had to stand back, to be that girl on the shore in Kingston Town, fearlessly waving him on his way.

epilogue

THE BACHATA ENDS, AND ABRAHAM RELEASES ME. WE HUG, acknowledging we'd enjoyed dancing together and would meet and dance again sometime soon.

Perhaps it's a sublime curse to have grown up with a father who danced so well. I understand this blissful dance interlude with Abraham is brought on by my hunger for that fleeting time of my childhood. Those short years, like perfect glass before they were shattered by titanic losses.

I take a deep breath. I've been gone twenty minutes from the other dance room where I left my group, and now my friends and my husband will wonder where I am. I turn away from Abraham and all that dancing with him has reawakened. *Will I tell anyone about my dancing with him or about my brief journey back in time?* I smile. Maybe I'll keep this extraordinary voyage into the past to myself.

As I walk away to rejoin my group, letting go of my past, my mind moves back to the scene at the hospital a few months earlier.

AT THE AGE of eighty-eight, after decades of smoking, bypass surgery, and a recent heart attack, my father had developed end-stage heart failure. Lying in his bed at the hospital, he no longer responded to us or opened his eyes. His doctors said there was nothing more to be done. He would continue to sleep and eventually succumb to kidney failure—a result of heart failure. He wouldn't suffer, they assured us. With care and medication, he'd simply and gently fade away. We so wanted that for him. Certainly, his serene demeanor as he dozed belied any discomfort or illness, as though he were taking a brief nap and would soon wake up.

I was almost expecting him to do so, as I used to be whenever he'd catnap in Kuwait after lunch, naps I'd often interrupt to ask him something of seemingly infinite importance. I sighed now, remembering the anxious and impatient child I'd been, unable to appreciate his need for a brief midday rest from his busy workday.

Glancing at him in this hospital room, love and grief pouring from me, I wished he could hear me tell him just one more time how much I loved him, how grateful and lucky I was for the years of his love and guidance in my life. I wanted him to know I regretted not being a wiser and more tolerant daughter at times, rather than battling him on inconsequential matters. But he was no longer conscious of my words. I could only hold his hand, imagine him humming, "Day-o . . . da-a-a-o," as he swayed to Harry Belafonte's lilting calypso beat.. I could almost hear him sing "Jamaica Farewell," smell the cinnamon and carnation of his Old Spice cologne, catch him smile and wink at me as he prepared to go out for a night of dinner and dancing, leaving the past and us behind. And I had no choice but to stand on the shore in Kingston Town and wave him on his way.

WE'D GATHERED AROUND my father in the hospital that day, my husband standing next to me, my two younger sisters sitting on his bed. For Gamila, my stepmother, had given my father two more girls, sisters for me. And I had, indeed, married the elder of her two brothers, Ahmad, seven years after my father married her.

I often wondered about my intuition at eleven when I first saw the young man who would become my husband. I wondered whether it had been true foresight that he and I were destined to be together, as I'd strongly felt then, or whether from that moment I'd subconsciously guided myself into an eventual romantic relationship with him.

He told me he first fell in love with me when I was fifteen, and he saw me dancing. It was in Beirut. I remember wearing a purple woolen dress when he entered the room where I danced with his sisters. He didn't remember the dress, only the dancing. I also remember the look of pleased surprise in his eye, perhaps the same recognition I'd felt when I first saw him in Ramallah and knew we'd one day be together. He still has that twinkle in his gaze that had so struck me that day.

We married and came to the United States during college to continue our studies, intending to return to Beirut once we were done. The ensuing civil war in Lebanon prevented us from going back, however, and my husband had instead embarked on a banking career in New York where we remained for several years. As the war in Lebanon dragged on, we realized the United States must become our new home and finally settled permanently. We now lived in Virginia, near Washington, DC. My father and his family lived in nearby Maryland. They had come several decades ago from Lebanon—where we had moved after Kuwait—to escape the civil war there.

My sisters lovingly tended to our father in the hospital

that morning, tucking his blanket around him, placing a portable computer playing his favorite songs on the bed beside him. Gamila sat on a chair, glancing at the monitors and diligently writing down her husband's vital signs to show to the doctors when they made their rounds. Never relying solely on the nurses' charts, she'd kept her own during the month she lived with my father in his hospital room. She was immaculately dressed, her hair, now white, still in an elaborate chignon, her eyeliner sweeping across her lids like an Egyptian pharaoh queen. She knew my father liked well-dressed women, and she wanted to please him in their last days together, even if he was not aware of her presence.

She fretted he could no longer eat, sure that nutrition would bring back his vigor and prolong his life. I understood her distress. He'd so enjoyed savoring a good meal. I could see him dunking a piece of warm pita bread in olive oil and green za'atar at the dinner table in Kuwait, see him smile at me in the kitchen as he handed me the mallet dripping with warm, garlicky hummus he'd just made.

The February day in the hospital was my birthday. I'd been married for forty-five years and had three married children and two grandchildren. Yet, faced with losing my father, I felt as helpless and abandoned as a child. I was in denial about his health, as we all were, not fully accepting the end was near.

A few months earlier when he was still working in his office, I often met him for lunch at a nearby restaurant. We'd reminisce about so much of what he and I shared in the past when it was just the two of us. So much heartbreak and yet so much joy and laughter. Our bond remained solid.

In those last months, he'd talked a great deal about my

mother, Jean, of the amazing kismet that led them to meet in the Middle Eastern deli in Washington where he'd worked evenings. He spoke of their youthful years in Tehran and Kuwait, of her passion for adventure, of her support as he built his career, and of her encouragement to accept new challenges wherever his job led him. She'd been the dauntless wind beneath his wings, fostering his ambition and drive. He, in turn, had admired her creativity and intellect. I heard Harry singing as my father took his young Tennessee wife in his arms and twirled her around our living room in Tehran, while she smiled at him, proud of herself for having absconded with such a talented and fun-loving man.

I've often wondered what my mother would have become had she survived her illness. Whether she would have pursued her writing or been content with the role of wife and mother she'd also clearly enjoyed.

Over the years, as I raised three children in the United States, I learned to embrace a more Western outlook, accepting that my children's lives would require them to integrate into American culture. Yet my father, while continuing to appreciate America's many freedoms and opportunities, had clung stubbornly to his Eastern roots. It was a trait that often became a source of tension between us.

Perhaps, having married Gamila, he'd grown closer to the Arab part of himself in the latter part of his life. He had abandoned the Middle East twice, in his youth by choice, in search of education and opportunity, and later when forced to flee from war. He ached for his homeland with its genial, uncomplicated way of life, and he yearned to go back. Yet he was unable to give up the new life he'd worked hard to create here in America.

For him, the opposition between East and West remained a struggle that still burdened him. If he could, he would have kept us all safely and forever within the Arab fold, shielded us from the intrusive and constantly changing American way of life that now seemed so different to him from the brilliant beacon it was when he'd first arrived on these shores, right out of high school.

I believe he was proud of my writing. It was he, after all, who had planted the seed in me on that afternoon when I was twelve. But I had become a novelist rather than a journalist, as he'd hoped. To him, fiction was not quite as noble or effective as truth-telling. Yet in writing fiction, I had, in a way, become my mother—something he'd also seemed to want. She had studied journalism. But her passion, like mine, lay in writing fiction, although, as far as I knew, she'd only published her one short story.

I was surprised that my father never understood my life-long obsession with dance—neither the major role he'd played in it nor the saving grace music and dance had been for me in those years fraught with loss. When, as an adult, I began to take intensive ballroom dance classes, to perform, and later to teach dancing, he thought it was silly. I was a writer, he reminded me. I should "act like a lady," he'd say, a phrase he hadn't used since I was a child, to impress on me what he considered to be proper female behavior.

What he didn't know was how much I longed to move the way he and I used to, to dance with a partner who held me with the same casual grace he once had, who moved to the drums the same way he had. I couldn't explain to him how each time I happened upon such a partner, I would devour the moment, dreading its end. Rediscovering dance brought back those moments of carefree delight of my childhood. My father, though, inexplicably, no longer felt the urge to dance. Perhaps it revived too many youthful, painful memories. Dancing was, unfortunately, a passion I could no longer share with him, my first dance partner.

IS THERE EVER enough time or even a right time or way to say goodbye? To cram a lifetime of feelings and love into a few heart-wrenching and confusing moments?

I felt an unbearable numbness invade me at my father's hospital bedside. The fullness of grief brought with it the coating of detachment I'd felt more than fifty years earlier in my mother's hospital room in Bethesda. It had prevented me from asking her what was churning in my mind. Not whether she'd live—for that answer I already suspected—but whether she loved me, whether she was proud of me. Most of all, I wanted her to reassure me I would manage once she was gone. I hadn't been able to ask her any of that as I faced the terrifying inevitability of her death. Those unasked questions dogged me for years.

Days earlier, when my father had been conscious enough to still be speaking, albeit with his eyes closed, I'd pushed myself to ask him what I wished I'd asked my mother in her final days.

"Daddy," I whispered, "do you love me?"

Without hesitating, as he had on so many occasions, he had a ready answer for me. "A lot," he said, clearly.

A lot. My heart ripped. Although I knew he had summoned every ounce of energy in his frail body to give me that short answer, I pushed on, desperate to keep hearing his voice.

"This much?" I asked, blinking back tears as I smiled, opening my arms wide in an effort to get him to look at me.

Too weak to open his eyes, but perhaps sensing my gesture, he'd replied, "*Shwai* more."

Shwai, the Arabic word for "a little." His use of the word coupled with the English word "more" reassured me he knew exactly who he was speaking to, even with his eyes closed. I was his half-American, half-Arab daughter, Kathryn Elizabeth Fatima, who had a foot planted in both the East and the West.

I had lived this conflict of not being entirely Arab or entirely American, of being tugged mercilessly by both sides of me. My path was always poised on the precipice of a cataclysmic collision of cultures. And yet, I *was* half American and half Arab, and I could vacillate between the two worlds, holding onto what I cherished from one, while accepting I could also belong to the other. My father, fully Arab, had been unable to do this. But he had finally understood and accepted this about me.

"Shwai more." A little more. I sensed a faint smile cross his lips.

I smiled through my tears. Despite his ailing heart having been broken so many times, my father was still capable of loving me—loving all of us—more than all the air I could gather within my arms.

"Shwai more." They were the last words he'd ever speak to me.

PERHAPS THIS IS what my father was also telling me. It was time to move beyond the sadness of our pasts. For him, the losses of his homeland and of his early loves. For me, the loss of my American link, of my mother. Each of my halves will always live within me, simultaneously loved and valued. Each time I dance, taking those joyful times with both of them into my heart, is a chance to move forward. To find peace. To dance the journey of life is to dance through the pain and darkness, into the light.

My father and mother at their wedding reception in Old Hickory, Tennessee, 1951

My mother and I Tehran, 1956

My father explaining the working of the English language
school to the Shah of Iran 1957

My father, mother, and I Jerusalem, 1957

My brother Munib and I in Honolulu, 1962

acknowledgments

The journey of writing this memoir, which describes a short and often painful but impactful early period of my life, was made less daunting by the help of several talented editors who, in the early drafts of the manuscript, helped me see the elements that would make this a story. A big thanks to them for their input and encouragement: Beth Bruno, Mike McIrvin, Carrie Cantor, and Suzanne Sherman. A special thanks to the gifted Michelle Orwin, who helped me hone the final draft and distill what to leave in and what to leave for another time and project. She is a generous, kind, and meticulous editor and a sheer delight to work with. Lorraine Fico-White did an excellent job with the first copy edit.

As always, every member of my amazing writing group encouraged me in the process. A particular thanks to Ginnie Hartman for her valuable input, and to Tom Milani and Barbara Esstman for their careful reading of the manuscript and for their comments.

A special thanks to the inspiring Brooke Warner of She Writes Press for taking on the project and for believing so passionately in her authors; thanks to Lauren Wise for her tireless guidance and following up with the production of the book, and for the talented SWP editorial and design team who further polished it and created the evocative cover.

I wish to thank all members of my wonderful Arab and American extended families for their love and support throughout my childhood and beyond. I thank my husband,

Ahmad, who never lets me lose faith in my vision; my children, Shereen, Omar, and Yasmeen who fill my life with such joy; my step-mother, Gamila, and my sisters, Rana and Lina, for their love and for recreating my family after much early loss; and finally I thank my parents, Jean and Khalil, for showing me how two disparate worlds can become one.

about the author

Kathryn K. Abdul-Baki was born in Washington DC to an Arab father and an American mother. She grew up in Iran, Kuwait, Beirut, and Jerusalem, where she attended Arabic, British, and American schools. She attended the American University of Beirut, Lebanon, has a BA in journalism from George Washington University in Washington DC, and an MA in creative writing from George Mason University, Virginia. She has published five books of fiction, some of which have been taught at universities in multicultural literature, women's studies, and Arab studies departments. She is recipient of the Mary Roberts Rinehart award for short fiction. Abdul-baki has three grown children and currently resides with her husband in McLean, Virginia.

SELECTED TITLES FROM SHE WRITES PRESS

She Writes Press is an independent publishing company founded to serve women writers everywhere. Visit us at www.shewritespress.com.

Blue Apple Switchback: A Memoir by Carrie Highley. $16.95, 978-1-63152-037-2. At age forty, Carrie Highley finally decided to take on the biggest switchback of her life: upon her bicycle, and with the help of her mentor's wisdom, she shed everything she was taught to believe as a young lady growing up in the South—and made a choice to be true to herself and everyone else around her.

Last Trip Home: Story of an Arkansas Farm Girl by Wanda Maureen Miller. $16.95, 978-1-63152-339-7. After growing up on a small Arkansas farm in the 1940s and 1950s and struggling with poverty, her father's lecherous grip, and a husband in the Klan, Grace Marie Hall escaped to a life in California—but now her father has died, and she returns to Arkansas for what she hopes will be her last trip home.

At the Narrow Waist of the World: A Memoir by Marlena Maduro Baraf. $16.95, 978-1-63152-588-9. In this lush and vivid coming-of-age memoir about a mother's mental illness and the healing power of a loving Jewish and Hispanic extended family, young Marlena must pull away from her mother, leave her Panama home, and navigate the transition to an American world.

Life's Accessories: A Memoir (And Fashion Guide) by Rachel Levy Lesser. $16.95, 978-1-63152-622-0. Rachel Levy Lesser tells the story of her life in this collection—fourteen coming-of-age essays, each one tied to a unique fashion accessory, laced with humor and introspection about a girl-turned-woman trying to figure out friendship, love, a career path, parenthood, and, most poignantly, losing her mother to cancer at a young age.

Her Name Is Kaur: Sikh American Women Write About Love, Courage, and Faith edited by Meeta Kaur. $17.95, 978-1-93831-470-4. An eye-opening, multifaceted collection of essays by Sikh American women exploring the concept of love in the context of the modern landscape and influences that shape their lives.

Change Maker: How My Brother's Death Woke Up My Life by Rebecca Austill-Clausen. $16.95, 978-1-63152-130-0. Rebecca Austill-Clausen was workaholic businesswoman with no prior psychic experience when she discovered that she could talk with her dead brother, not to mention multiple other spirits—and a whole new world opened up to her.